Expository Preaching in Africa

Expository Preaching in Africa

Expository Preaching in Africa

Engaging Orality for Effective Proclamation

Ezekiel A. Ajibade

© 2021 Ezekiel A. Ajibade

Published 2021 by HippoBooks, an imprint of ACTS and Langham Publishing.
Africa Christian Textbooks (ACTS), TCNN, PMB 2020, Bukuru 930008, Plateau State, Nigeria
www.actsnigeria.org

Langham Publishing, PO Box 296, Carlisle, Cumbria CA3 9WZ, UK
www.langham.org

ISBNs:
978-1-83973-214-0 Print
978-1-83973-498-4 ePub
978-1-83973-499-1 Mobi
978-1-83973-500-4 PDF

Ezekiel A. Ajibade has asserted his right under the Copyright, Designs and Patents Act, 1988 to be identified as the Author of this work.

All rights reserved. No part of this publication may be reproduced, stored in a retrieval system or transmitted, in any form or by any means, electronic, mechanical, photocopying, recording or otherwise, without the prior written permission of the publisher or the Copyright Licensing Agency.

Requests to reuse content from Langham Publishing are processed through PLSclear. Please visit www.plsclear.com to complete your request.

All Scripture quotations, unless otherwise indicated, are taken from the Holy Bible, New International Version®, NIV®. Copyright ©1973, 1978, 1984, 2011 by Biblica, Inc.™ Used by permission of Zondervan.

British Library Cataloguing-in-Publication Data
A catalogue record for this book is available from the British Library

ISBN: 978-1-83973-214-0

Cover & Book Design: projectluz.com

The publishers of this book actively support theological dialogue and an author's right to publish but do not necessarily endorse the views and opinions set forth here or in works referenced within this publication, nor guarantee technical and grammatical correctness. The publishers do not accept any responsibility or liability to persons or property as a consequence of the reading, use or interpretation of its published content.

Contents

Acknowledgements xi

Introduction 1

1 Homiletic Theories and the Concept of Expository Preaching 7

2 Form and Content in Expository Preaching. 23

3 Africa in the History of Christian Preaching 49

4 Orality and Gospel Communication 71

5 Using African Orality to Contextualize Expository Preaching 125

6 Antecedents from Korean, African-American, and
    Ghanaian Experience 157

7 Sample Expository Sermons Based on African Orality. 171

8 Dangers of Contextualization. 189

9 Conclusion. 195

  Appendixes 201

  Bibliography 221

Acknowledgements

This book evolved from my PhD dissertation in Christian preaching, so my appreciation will go to those involved in the three phases. The first are those who supervised the dissertation to such a level that it could be published in this form. They are Dr. Solomon Ademola Ishola, Dr. David Allen, and Dr. David Olford. Dr. Grant Lovejoy was a great inspiration, and I am forever grateful for his encouragement and the resources he provided.

I appreciate the faculty members and staff of the Nigerian Baptist Theological Seminary, Ogbomoso; the Southwestern Baptist Theological Seminary, Fort Worth, Texas; Calvin Theological Seminary, Grand Rapids, Michigan; and the team at Stephen Olford Center, Memphis, Tennessee. Several of my friends were so helpful while I was carrying out my research in the United States between 2016 and 2017; they include Dr. Bernard Ayoola and his wife, Joke; Prof. Abiodun Akinwuntan; and Revs. Simon Olatunji, Wisdom Asita, Seun Aremu, and Paul Oluleye. Thanks to Kayode Alawonde, Emmanuel and Bola Oshiokhale, Jide and Funmi Ologuntoye, and many more.

In the course of my research, my students in MDiv and degree classes of 2016/2017 session at the Nigerian Baptist Theological Seminary (NBTS), Ogbomoso, were very helpful in the field work. At the practical stage, the Acting Dove of the seminary did well in the homiletical drama production and presentation, and the media team led by Pastor Yemi Akande is greatly appreciated.

The second phase is when the dissertation first became a book as a maiden edition of the NBTS Advanced Theological Education Studies Series. My heartfelt appreciation goes to the president of the seminary, Rev. Prof. Emiola Nihinlola, a great mentor who felt this work is worth selecting for that purpose.

The third phase is when Prof. Emiola Nihinlola showed a copy of the book to Dr. Elizabeth Mburu on one of their accreditation visits. She read it and recommended it to Langham for a fresh publishing that would reach to the wider world. I am grateful to Liz for such a memorable gesture. Thanks to Vivian Doub and all who worked hard to see this book published in this form.

Finally, I appreciate my wife, Olajoke, and my children, Sharon and Victor, who have been pillars of support and encouragement in life's journey. Once again, to God alone be all the glory.

Introduction

Preaching the written word of God stands out among the elements of worship in the church of Christ from age to age. The communicating of the word has often been considered sacred, though the methods of doing so have varied. However, preaching the Word of God is powerful and has never lost the inherent capability to change lives from generation to generation, culture to culture, and one phase of Christian history to another.

Since I had the opportunity to spend ten weeks at the Stephen Olford Center for Biblical Preaching, Memphis, Tennessee, in the United States in 2013, my attraction to the art of expository preaching has grown daily. The center was opened in 1988 for the purpose of restoring expository preaching to the pulpit and was the vision of Stephen Olford (1918–2004), a great expositor who had a great impact upon the sacred art of preaching in his over fifty years of pulpit ministry. He was regarded by Billy Graham as "the greatest combination of pastor, teacher, evangelist," and by John MacArthur as one who "championed the necessity of strong, passionate, expositional preaching."[1] This center is part of Olford's legacy and has encouraged and equipped pastors and lay leaders from around the world to pursue and fulfil the Great Commission.

My attraction to expository preaching is not a mere emotional affinity, but arose from a deep discovery and understanding of the art over time as well as constant and regular practice of this style of preaching, observing its deep impact in transforming lives, and seeing the spiritual excitement it generates in listeners. This affinity also arose from the training of over four hundred pastors and lay leaders using the Stephen Olford Ministry Legacy materials around Nigeria in the past few years.[2] Further, my affinity had to do with the experiences I gained from studying Christian preaching at the doctoral level and from teaching the same to seminary students as a faculty member of the Nigerian Baptist Theological Seminary, Ogbomoso.

---

1. Billy Graham quoted in David L. Olford, ed. *A Passion for Preaching: Reflections on the Art of Preaching; Essays in Honor of Stephen F. Olford* (Nashville: Thomas Nelson, 1989), 21–23. John MacArthur wrote this as part of his endorsement in John Phillips, *The Life and Legacy of Stephen Olford* (Memphis: Olford Ministries International, 2006), inner back cover.

2. The Stephen Olford Ministry Legacy materials consist of the titles "Anointed Biblical Preaching and Teaching," "The Essentials of Expository Preaching," and "The Essentials of Evangelistic Preaching."

In the midst of this excitement came the burden: expository preaching is yet to take root in the soils of Africa. It is not difficult to gain access to what is being preached in many churches in Africa in a globalized world powered by media. A simple survey will reveal a dearth of sound biblical exposition. Much of what would be found is topical preaching, or any other category besides expository. Moreover, a survey of literature is an exercise in futility because of the paucity of materials on African preaching. This burden was also compounded by the nature and beauty of expository preaching. If expository preaching is concerned with communicating God's word with due consideration of its historical, grammatical, and literary essence, how can it be sold to a continent with a relatively low level of literacy, and to a large number of preachers who are also in this category? How can these preachers discover and transmit this historical, grammatical, and literary content as well as the context and richness of a passage to the people they minister to? Some preachers have expressed their reservations by saying, "This is a great method of preaching, but it is cumbersome and time consuming. And how do you want me to do this in my village where the majority are uneducated?" This response illustrates the need to propose contextualization of expository preaching for Africa through the effective use of orality.[3]

Contextualization is planting, watering, and nurturing the gospel message within the culture so much that people feel a sense of ownership of it and are ready to run with it without tampering with the biblical roots and essence of the message. In the context of expository preaching, contextualization is making the message first of all biblical, then African, so that it is faithful to the inspired word but incarnated in the culture of Africans. Orality describes the African practice and worldview of interpreting and communicating thoughts in oral rather than written forms. African orality makes use of such literary devices as stories, proverbs, idioms, drama, poetry, dance, myths, fables, folklore, or combinations of these to not only deliver messages but also to assimilate them, to use them to interpret the world and process wisdom with or without the technology of literacy.

Contextualization is a very important concept especially in the fields of theology and missiology. Such terms as incarnation, inculturation, local theology, indigenization, and intercultural theology were used before the term "contextualization" "broke upon the slumbering world" in 1972 when a

---

3. These are responses gleaned from my personal communication with local church pastors and leaders as I visit both urban and rural areas to preach, teach or disciple.

Theological Education Fund report titled *Ministry in Context* was published.[4] Several models of contextualization have been proposed over the years. Stephen Bevans in *Models of Contextual Theology* articulates the translation, anthropological, praxis, synthetic, transcendental, and countercultural models.[5] These models are not exclusive or exhaustive, but in the words of S. Ademola Ishola, "the synthetic model best describes the concept of contextualization as it treats biblical text as basic, while taking the sociocultural context seriously."[6] Though Ishola's work is a missiological study and not necessarily homiletical, the synthetic model is assumed. The synthetic model serves as middle ground between the translational and anthropological models. In this model, the gospel, culture, tradition and cultural change – they "are held in creative tension as culture and the gospel are balanced against each other, and church tradition is balanced against the concerns of the local situation."[7]

It is important, however, to get a proper perspective of and background to the problems associated with expository preaching in Africa. Preaching is not new to Africa; the continent is going into its third century of the firm rooting of Christianity, not considering the Christian activities in North Africa in the first centuries that died prematurely.[8] However, most preaching is not yielding the results of life transformation that it ought to. Flooding the pulpits with topical sermons has not been sufficient to make people well-rooted in the word of God, nor is the quality of Christianity witnessed in the continent capable of bringing much needed societal transformation.

A recent attempt to revitalize preaching is the new emphasis on expository preaching. Some homileticians promote the inductive method, and some insist on the deductive. Nevertheless the question has been, which of the methods will meet the specific need of Africans? Some preachers and students of preaching are coming to appreciate expository sermons, especially in the deductive sense. But there are fears that the method will meet some brick walls such as illiteracy, lack of exegetical materials, and possible boredom associated

---

4. Krikor Haleblian, "The Problem of Contextualization," *Missiology: An International Review* 11, no. 1 (January, 1983): 96.

5. Stephen B. Bevans, *Models of Contextual Theology* (Maryknoll, NY: Orbis, 2004).

6. S. Ademola Ishola, "Towards a Contextualized Missiological Approach to the Yoruba Religio-Cultural Milieu," abstract (PhD diss., Southwestern Baptist Theological Seminary, 1992), n.p.

7. Neville Bartle, "A Model for Contextualizing Theology for Melanesia," *The Mediator* 3, no. 1 (2001): 87.

8. Peter Falk, *The Growth of the Church in Africa* (Bukuru: African Christian Textbooks, 1997), 23.

with the technique in some quarters due to the technicalities and intricacies involved. How then can this proven-effective means of communicating God's word become exciting to African preachers and their hearers? Not much work has been done to answer these questions.

This book, therefore, explores the use of orality as a resource for developing an expository preaching method that is both biblical and African. The contents include explaining the dynamic composition and essence of expository preaching; evaluating the elements of expository preaching both in preparation and delivery that promote contextualization; and identifying how such elements of African orality as myths, proverbs, folklore, dance, drama, poetry, and storytelling can be useful resources for the entire process of expository preaching. We will also discuss culturally relevant ways in which expository sermons can be presented to both the literate and non-literate people in the African society and explain how a contextualized form of biblical exposition can bring about effective discipleship, spiritual revival, and socio-political and economic transformation. This book's position is that understand and utilizing oral elements from African tradition and culture will enrich expository preaching by making it more meaningful, generating more interest, and impacting more extensively those who listen. The concentration will be mainly on expository preaching and sermons and uphold the fact that expository preaching is synonymous with biblical preaching and not in a contest with the other types or methods.

"Africa" will be broadly used as a location because of the term's ability to be used in a generic sense, though not without some contentions. Not everyone agrees that Africa can be treated as one single entity, for the geographical region is vast and inhabited by people of great diversities in social systems, customs, and community life and who speak over an estimated one thousand different languages.[9] But several factors can allow for generic treatment. Wilbur O' Donovan suggests seven commonalities including emphasis on community life in an extended family and clan, relationships between the living and the dead, and a viewpoint toward the spirit world and relationships between the spiritual and physical worlds. Other commonalities are placing a higher priority on people and human relationships than on technology and material things; histories of colonial rule and experiences of independence; and a holistic view of life with an emphasis on events rather than schedules and time as in

---

9. Viola Nzira, *Social Care with African Families in the UK* (Abingdon: Routledge, 2011), 12.

Europe and America.[10] These commonalities are why such areas of study as African traditional religion, African Christian theology, African Christian ethics, and African philosophy exist and why this work is on preaching that can be contextualized in an African experience. While references are made to other nations around the continent, most of the research work was carried out in the context of Nigeria, and the results weighed alongside what happens in other countries.

It is hoped that this work will contribute to the ongoing debate on the dichotomy in biblical methods of communicating God's word through preaching, especially the scholarly research on whether inductive or deductive methods of preaching are most effective in communicating the gospel today. But the most significant contribution is the adaptation of preaching to culture. This material is intended to unveil a considerably appropriate method of preaching that is rooted in African oral culture and yet faithful to the historical, grammatical, and literary content of Scripture. Here, readers will find an abridgment of the inductive and deductive or propositional methods of sermon preparation and delivery. The proposed method considers expository preaching to be sacrosanct yet capable of communicating to Africans in their sociocultural and political milieus – a crucial role of expository preaching. It is also hoped that this book will serve as a resource for African gospel preachers who will imbibe the expositional method over the topical and one that can aid in the quest for an African Christian preaching, which is still a great area of need in academic research.

---

10. Wilbur O'Donovan, *Biblical Christianity in African Perspective* (Carlisle, UK: Paternoster, 1996), 3–4.

1

Homiletic Theories and the Concept of Expository Preaching

Every discipline is based on certain underlying theories, and preaching is not excluded. In "My Theory of Homiletics,"[1] Haddon Robinson proposes a theory when he defines expository preaching as "the communication of a biblical concept, derived from and transmitted through a historical, grammatical, and literary study of a passage in its context, which the Holy Spirit first applies to the personality and experience of the preacher, then through the preacher applies to the hearer."[2] Robinson then outlines three approaches to homiletics that reflect the presuppositions in his definition. The first is that "preachers communicate ideas." Sermons are developed and communicated as ideas, and the "most effective way to structure a speech is to build it around a single concept."[3]

The second assertion in Robinson's theory is that "the idea of a passage should govern the idea of the sermon." The authority of a sermon resides in the text, and not preachers, because preachers must bend their thoughts to Scripture and not use Scripture to support their thoughts.[4] Robinson's third assertion is that "biblical preaching must be applied." The duty of preachers is not just to interpret a scriptural text; they must go further to discern what the Holy Spirit would want to say to their own generation.[5]

---

1. Haddon Robinson, "My Theory of Homiletics," in *The Art and Craft of Biblical Preaching: A Comprehensive Resource for Today's Communicators*, ed. Haddon Robinson and Craig Brian Larson (Grand Rapids: Christianity Today International, 2005), 58.
2. Robinson, "My Theory," 58.
3. Robinson, 58.
4. Robinson, 58.
5. Robinson, 58.

Robinson wrote in the context of expository preaching, which homileticians over the centuries have classified as one among other types of preaching, such as topical and textual preaching. While arguments and variations abound over such classification, for Robinson expository preaching is a philosophy of biblical preaching rather than a type or method, and he clearly indicates that his approach to homiletics, notwithstanding any classification, is reflected in the presuppositions of his definition.[6]

However, what Robinson presents in these three simple assertions may be more complex than it first appears and has produced a world of homiletical approaches over which volumes have been written. Robinson opens up this possibility when he concludes that "a biblical sermon can take many forms. Just as the biblical writers used many different genres of literature to communicate their ideas, preachers are free to use any form that will adequately represent what Scripture teaches."[7] But most homiletic theories are built around these three presuppositions.[8]

Before we go further, it is important to define some terms and sort out the place of expository preaching among other preaching classifications, and to see that it is more a philosophy than method, as Robinson and several modern homileticians have come to posit. The first term is "biblical." Paul Scott Wilson states that preaching is biblical when it is based on the Bible and uses biblical words, stories, and images to communicate, thereby recognizing the authority of the Bible over the life and conduct of the church and bringing the Bible to bear upon the preaching event.[9] This principle has been understood and applied in a variety of ways in the history of preaching.

Second, what Robinson refers to as the sermon idea is also variously known as the thesis or theme sentence, a major concern of the text, a focus statement, or a controlling idea.[10] Scott describes a double-barreled approach which builds into a theme sentence a "hermeneutical transition between then and now" and is concerned with "both saying and doing what the biblical text says and

---

6. Robinson, 58. See also John A. Broadus, *On the Preparation and Delivery of Sermons* (New York: Armstrong and Son, 1870), 306–8; Donald L. Hamilton, *Homiletical Handbook* (Nashville: Broadman, 1992), 25–26; and David L. Larsen, *The Anatomy of Preaching: Identifying Issues in Preaching Today* (Ibadan: Christ and We, 2000), 32.

7. Robinson, "My Theory," 59.

8. Robinson's theory and position are pivotal to this work because in a way, they bring together a blend of the divergent theories under the banner of biblical exposition, leaving the style and form to the discretion of the preacher and the communication need of the audience.

9. Paul Scott Wilson, *Preaching and Homiletical Theory* (St. Louis: Chalice, 2004), 7.

10. Wilson, *Preaching and Homiletical Theory*, 15.

does, or with what God in the biblical text says and does."[11] Some, like David Buttrick, oppose the theme sentence and advocate a series of "moves"; Richard L. Eslinger argues for image and narrative as a postmodern cultural-linguistic model. Eugene Lowry proposes a five-stage homiletical plot, while Lucy Rose and John McClure propose the collaborative roundtable model. The arguments go forth and back as the homiletical theories keep evolving.[12]

Some authors have tried to bring together this array of theories and the types of sermons they produce. Ronald J. Allen, for instance, identifies four patterns of preaching – namely traditional, contemporary, subjects, and theology – and provides full-text examples of sermons that follow each pattern.[13] Richard L. Eslinger did a similar job, but he concentrates on the work of his colleagues in the school of the New Homiletic and on inductive preaching to design a "web" based on the inductive and narrative homiletic of Fred Craddock and Eugene Lowry, narrative preaching in the African-American tradition, David Buttrick's homiletic moves and structures, and Paul Scott Wilson's sermon in four pages.[14]

Sticking to the importance of a theme sentence, and not necessarily condemning whichever old or new approaches are used in determining it, Wilson concludes that,

> The sermon should invite Christians to think in significant ways about significant matters of faith and life. Avoiding a thesis statement can be a form of tyranny, for the preacher demands that the listeners discover the preacher's meaning without offering what is needed. Once the congregation knows with confidence what is being said, they have genuine freedom to react. Preachers who use thesis statements often do so out of respect for their congregation as listeners. They may also use such statements to form consciousness or to invite participation in a metaphor or story, as opposed to presenting something objective for consciousness merely to receive. Preachers use thesis statements to witness to God as clearly as possible in order to equip the saints for ministry.[15]

---

11. Wilson, 16.
12. Wilson, 16–19.
13. Ronald J. Allen, ed., *Patterns of Preaching: A Sermon Sampler* (St. Louis: Chalice, 1998).
14. Richard L. Eslinger, *The Web of Preaching: New Options in Homiletic Method* (Nashville: Abingdon, 2002).
15. Wilson, *Preaching and Homiletical Theory*, 23.

In his attempt to discuss the place of the thesis statement as the hub of homiletical communication, Wilson has touched on a critical issue in preaching that will linger for a long time to come. This is the dichotomy between deductive and inductive sermons, and this dichotomy has so much to do with expository preaching and contextualization. But first, the concept of expository preaching will be discussed.

The Concept of Expository Preaching

Bryan Chapell defines an expository sermon as "a message whose structure and thought are derived from a biblical text, that covers the scope of the text, and that explains the features and context of the text in order to disclose the enduring principles for faithful thinking, living, and worship intended by the Spirit who inspired the text."[16] Deriving the structure and thought from a biblical text inspired by the Spirit are the key points in Chapell's definition. It is the structure that ensures no part of the text is left behind and that the study of the text leads to an articulation of principles which enhance the worship of believers. Structure and articulating principles are strong points in the art of expository preaching. They are, however, the subject of much criticism by the New Homiletic school which will be considered in the next chapter.[17]

Central Propositions

The principles derived from the text are also called "propositions." Ramesh Richard affirms that expository preaching is "the contemporization of the central proposition of a biblical text that is derived from proper methods of interpretation and declared through effective means of communication to

---

16. Bryan Chapell, *Christ-Centered Preaching: Redeeming the Expository Sermon* (Grand Rapids: Baker Academic, 2005), 31.
17. The New Homiletic has been promoted by theorists like Fred Craddock, David Buttrick, Henry Mitchell, Charles Rice, Edmund Steimle, Morris Niedenthal, Richard Jensen, Lucy Rose, Thomas Troeger and Eugene Lowry. While there are similarities and differences in their shades of advocacy, the New Homiletic as presented by these theorists emphasizes creating an experience where the speaker and audience participate together in the process of understanding. See Eugene Lowry, *The Sermon: Dancing the Edge of Mystery* (Nashville: Abingdon, 1997), 20; Scott M. Gibson, "Critique of the New Homiletic: Examining the Link between the New Homiletic and the New Hermeneutic," in *The Art and Craft of Biblical Preaching: A Comprehensive Resource for Today's Communicators*, ed. Haddon Robinson and Craig Brian Larson (Grand Rapids: Christianity Today International, 2005), 477; and Paul Scott Wilson, *Preaching and Homiletical Theory* (St. Louis: Chalice, 2004), 136–37.

inform minds, instruct hearts, and influence behavior toward godliness."[18] A proposition is defined as "the point to be discussed or maintained in argument usually stated in sentence form near the outset" or "an expression in language or signs of something that can be believed, doubted, or denied or is either true or false."[19] In expository preaching, propositions are most likely stated at the outset of a sermon, but are not necessarily ideas to be believed, doubted, denied or argued as true or false. Rather they assume a position of divine statements, inspired opinions, or statements of truth based on the authority of the word of God. Augustine is usually quoted as saying, "When the Bible speaks, God speaks."[20] This position is seriously challenged by supporters of radical relativism who oppose any authority and believe no one has the right to tell another person what to do.[21]

The central proposition of a biblical text referred to by Richard, and that "a single proposition must permeate the entire sermon,"[22] is a position purportedly held by homileticians throughout the history of expository preaching and communication theory. However, differences exist over how this central proposition is derived – whether it should be supplied by the preacher or the text. This derivation also has to do with the type of exposition the preacher is engaged in.[23] While some homileticians have attempted to categorize preaching into various types, making expository preaching one type, others have attempted to classify expository preaching itself into various types. For example, Joel C. Gregory itemizes atomistic exposition, synthetic exposition, and literate exposition.[24] Regardless of the type, the structure of the expository sermon is then built around the central proposition, and the outline is produced based on the flow of the text.

---

18. Ramesh Richard, *Preparing Expository Sermons: A Seven-Step Method for Biblical Preaching* (Grand Rapids: Baker Books, 2001), 19.

19. "Proposition," *Merriam-Webster Dictionary,* https://www.merriam-webster.com/dictionary/proposition.

20. Augustine of Hippo cited in Chapell, *Christ-Centered Preaching*, 31.

21. Chapell, 31.

22. Richard, *Preparing Expository Sermons*, 20.

23. Richard, 20.

24. Joel C. Gregory, "Expository," in *The New Interpreters Handbook of Preaching* (Nashville: Abingdon, 2008), 381–82.

Textual/Biblical Exposition

Textual or biblical exposition as described by Chapell is equally vital to the definition of expository preaching held by many other authors. David Lim defines expository preaching as "the oral communication of applied propositional ideas which are derived from exegetical and theological examination of the text."[25] Expository preaching presupposes a careful study of all the nuances of a given text before applying the text to particular situations in life. The word "exposition" is from the Latin root *expositio* which means "a setting forth." Biblical exposition, therefore, "expounds, expresses, and exposes the Bible to an audience and the audience to the Bible."[26] Expository preachers must be good exegetes of the Bible, and as an interpreter, they are given the responsibility of studying a text, discovering the original intention of the author and the original understanding of the audience, and then communicating their findings.[27] This biblical exposition is why Lim frames expository preaching as "a homiletical art, which takes into account authorial intent in delivering God's Word to the contemporary listeners."[28]

Lim also insists that despite the disinterest of the postmodern generation in biblical preaching, which they consider old fashioned or outmoded, the philosophy behind expository preaching is still sound, so the method must be used. All that is needed is enrichment that, according to Lim, comes through relevant and powerful communication methods that will give meaning to contemporary hearers of the Word.[29] Communication in this sense is the ability to form a connection between the text, the preacher, and the audience. Richard asserts that "for our communication to be effective, we must understand the worldview, reasoning process, and culture of the audience. And then using analogies and illustrations, appropriate style and delivery, and relevant application we will claim their obedience."[30] Not considering this communication demand is why a gap often exists between text, preacher, and audience, and why some have regarded expository preaching as boring and ineffective and are seeking new ways to capture the hearts of modern people.

---

25. David Lim, "Expository Preaching and Generation X: Honoring 2 Timothy 4:5," in *Preaching to Postmodern-Minded Listeners* (Oradea, Bihor: Emmanuel University Press, 2007), 21.

26. Richard, *Preparing Expository Sermons*, 21.

27. Richard, 21.

28. Lim, "Expository Preaching and Generation X," 9.

29. Lim, 21.

30. Richard, *Preparing Expository Sermons*, 24.

Text-Driven Sermons

The central role the text plays informed the derivation of "text-driven sermon" which David L. Allen describes as essentially synonymous with expository preaching: "authentic biblical preaching must by definition be text driven and hence expository in nature."[31] The choice of the term "text-driven" by Allen and his colleagues is quite significant. He is wary of several absurdities that have been placed under the umbrella of "exposition" today and therefore opt for this more descriptive term that represents the theological foundation that "God has spoken. God is not silent. He has revealed himself in Jesus, who is the living Word."[32] Allen is also quick to clarify that text-driven preaching has nothing to do with enslavement "to artificial outlining techniques such as a three-point structure and alliteration."[33] What is permitted under the umbrella of expository preaching is a "wide variety of styles and structures to communicate the meaning of the text."[34] This clarification is important to the discussion in chapter 2 on sermon form and content. The preacher's motto should indeed be "*Textus Rex* – 'the text is king.'"[35] The English word "text" is from a Latin word that means "to weave," so the structure of a text is a network of relationships between the elements of the text.[36]

The Holy Spirit and Word of God

When a biblical text is studied with the proper tools,[37] proper structure is derived with an appropriate central proposition. Then appropriate communication can be constructed to bridge the ancient Scripture with modern minds and needs,

---

31. David L. Allen, "Preparing a Text-Driven Sermon," in *Text-Driven Preaching: God's Word at the Heart of Every Sermon*, ed. David L. Allen, Daniel L. Akin, and Ned L. Matthews (Nashville: B&H Academic, 2010), 105.

32. David L. Allen, "Introduction," in *Text-Driven Preaching: God's Word at the Heart of Every Sermon*, ed. David L. Allen, Daniel L. Akin, and Ned L. Matthews (Nashville: B&H Academic, 2010), 3.

33. Allen, "Introduction," 3.

34. Allen, 7.

35. Allen, 7.

36. Allen, "Preparing a Text-Driven Sermon," 106.

37. Haddon Robinson mentions such hermeneutical tools as lexicons, concordances, grammars, word study books, Bible dictionaries and encyclopedias, commentaries, bibliographies, and computer study aids. Haddon W. Robinson, *Biblical Preaching: The Development and Delivery of Expository Messages* (Wheaton, IL: Oasis International, 2012), 62–64. Nihinlola also discusses these and a few other tools. Emiola Nihinlola, *The Task of Bible Interpretation* (Ogbomoso: Nigerian Baptist Theological Seminary, 2014), 27–35. See also Wayne McDill, *The 12 Essential Skills for Great Preaching* (Nashville: B&H, 1994), 54–66.

for expository preaching is geared toward life transformation. This goal is summed up in Stephen Olford's definition that expository preaching is "the Spirit-empowered explanation and proclamation of the text of God's Word with due regard to the historical, contextual, grammatical and doctrinal significance of the given passage, with the specific object of invoking a Christ-transforming response."[38] The place of the Holy Spirit is very significant Olford's definition, and he states unequivocally that God's word and his Spirit are never opposed to each other. One of the greatest displeasures the Holy Spirit can be made to feel occurs when a preacher consciously or continuously contradicts the word of God. To be an effective biblical expositor, therefore, Olford states,

> There must be submission and dependence upon God's Spirit in every aspect of preaching. This includes being sensitive to His leading and working in the study, as well as in the pulpit. Planning and preparation are recommended, but they must be submitted to God and entrusted to Him for His sovereign guidance, working, and overruling if He should so choose.[39]

Bryan Chapell corroborates Olford's position by adding that each time the word of God is proclaimed, the work of the Spirit is brought to bear on people's lives. The word of God remains the sword of the Spirit, and the duty of the preacher is actually the "second sermon" because the Holy Spirit is the one who gave the message, inspired the word, and is the only one who can convict and convert the heart of the hearers.[40]

Types of Expository Preaching

Not all authors agree on the need for a definition of expository preaching or that expository preaching can be defined. Joel C. Gregory objects to "expository preaching" being used to define any single mode of preaching, asserting that it is rather more of "an attitude toward biblical authority than a definition of homiletic form."[41] This attitude of biblical authority has been held by evangelicals as late as the twentieth century. But many who practiced the art of expository preaching seldom used the term, so there is little agreement on

---

38. Stephen F. Olford and David Olford, *Anointed Expository Preaching* (Nashville: B&H Academic, 1998), 69.
39. Olford and Olford, *Anointed Expository Preaching*, 99.
40. Chapell, *Christ-Centered Preaching*, 33.
41. Gregory, "Expository," 381.

its definition. Gregory gives two ways in which expository preaching may be described – by morphology and by historical examples.[42] Under morphology he lists the following types of preaching:

- Expository preaching – This form uses a biblical unit of thought which may be a single word, phrase, verse, paragraph, chapter, or biblical book.
- Atomistic exposition – A painstaking approach which examines individual words. Martin Lloyd Jones (1899–1981) is well known for using this type.
- Synthetic exposition – Deals with large texts and looks for "catalytic verses" in the passage to explain the whole. The preaching of Campbell Morgan (1863–1945) represents this approach.
- Literate exposition – This form examines a biblical paragraph treating five to ten verses. The preaching of Alexander Maclaren (1826–1910) is identified with this form.[43]

The significance of Gregory's assertions may be evident when the preaching of those he lists are considered. However, it is difficult to use their styles to articulate a proper description of expository preaching. For example, as much as Alexander Maclaren is known as "the prince of expositors," he often preached from just a verse or two. According to James A. Keith, a look at Maclaren's *Expositions of the Holy Scripture* reveals that out of 1,536 text-supported sermons in this collection, 1,420 are based on only one verse (54 percent) or a few consecutive verses (46 percent). Some argue whether Alexander Maclaren and others who preach from one or a few verses can be regarded as expository preachers. However overwhelming opinion still places Maclaren as an expositor in the positive light.[44]

Examples from Church History

A description or definition of expository preaching based on agreed examples from the course of church history provides a catalog of preachers who used the approach. John Chrysostom (347–407), who expounded several biblical books, is regarded as the first patristic expositor. John Calvin is regarded as the

---

42. Gregory, 381–82.
43. Gregory, 381–82.
44. James A. Keith, "The Concept of Expository Preaching as Represented by Alexander Maclaren, George Campbell Morgan, and David Martyn Lloyd Jones" (PhD diss., Southwestern Baptist Theological Seminary, 2003), 142.

"flower of Reformation exposition." Reformers Martin Luther, John Knox, and Huldrych Zwingli were also good at it. Then came the Puritans who inherited the emphasis on the expository form from these Reformers, as exemplified by Richard Baxter (1615–1691). The Puritans, however, went into too many details.[45] The nineteenth century was the golden era of expository preaching in the English language, and the succession of preachers included Frederick Brotherton Meyer (1847–1929), Joseph Parker (1830–1902), and Alexander Whyte (1836–1921). The flower of nineteenth-century American exposition was John Albert Broadus (1827–1895).[46]

In the twentieth century rose academic expositors like Haddon Robinson, pastoral expositors like Martyn Lloyd Jones and James Ogilvie, and media expositors like Charles R. Swindoll, John MacArthur Jr., and Warren Wiersbe. Included in this list is the "London Pastor," Stephen Olford (1918–2004) who later occupied the Calvary Baptist Church pulpit in New York City. He exemplified an expository preaching technique rooted in the homiletic of William Graham Scroggie (1877–1958), but is now vanishing. Stephen Olford regarded Graham Scroggie as his homiletical mentor and revered him as a scholar and an expositor of God's word who made the deepest impression on him as he trained to become a preacher. Among several things that Olford learned from Scroggie was his "Golden Hammer" of three questions that open up any text of God's word: What is the dominating theme? What are the unifying thoughts? And what is the motivating thrust? The first question deals with selecting one theme, proposition, or subject from a passage. The second deals with breaking down the theme or proposition from the context into the headings and subheadings. The third question deals with the doctrines or challenges of the passage.[47]

Gregory's observation that the expository method is vanishing is valid, especially in the face of the New Homiletic and strong positioning of narrative preaching in a postmodern world. It is however likely that just as Stephen Olford and E. A. Johnston attempted to exhume the work of Scroggie,[48] there may be the need to exhume his style and adapt it in whatever way necessary since this sermon form remains dynamic. For now, Scroggie's method is still popular among several biblical expositors but with variation in styles. Perhaps

---

45. Keith, "Concept of Expository Preaching," 382.
46. Keith, 382.
47. Keith, 382.
48. Stephen Olford and E. A. Johnston, *Olford on Scroggie: Stephen Olford's Notes on the Sermon Outlines of Graham Scroggie* (Port Colborne: Gospel Folio, 2008), 21–24.

Eslinger was thinking of this popularity when he comments that in spite of the "Copernican revolution in preaching" of the New Homiletic, especially from the mid 1980s, now two generations beyond this the "old rationalist homiletic" still persist and actually "dies hard."[49]

Gregory's perspective is not in agreement with others who have written on the history of expository preaching. But his purpose here is to prove that expository preaching has been practiced throughout history, and that several preachers who engaged in it were not even conscious they were doing "expository preaching." The goal of other homiletic historians was to establish that preaching has always been expository. This focus can be seen in the work of James F. Stitzinger.[50] He traces the history of expository preaching from the biblical period to the early church (100–476), the medieval period (476–1500), the Reformation period (1500–1648), and the modern period (1649–present). His conclusion is that

> a study of the history of expository preaching makes it clear that such preaching is deeply rooted in the soil of Scripture. Thus, it is the only kind that perpetuates biblical preaching in the church. Throughout history, a few well known men in each generation representative of a larger body of faithful expositors have committed themselves to this ministry of biblical exposition. Their voices from the past should both encourage the contemporary expositor and challenge him to align his preaching with the biblical standard. Scripture demands nothing less than God-enabled exposition as demonstrated by those worthy saints who have dedicated their lives to this noble task.[51]

David Allen briefly traces the history of expository preaching in the introduction of *Text-Driven Preaching* and acknowledges that "the best preaching throughout church history has always been expository preaching."[52]

---

49. Richard L. Eslinger, *The Web of Preaching: New Options in Homiletic Method* (Nashville: Abingdon, 2002), 12.

50. James F. Stitzinger, "The History of Expository Preaching," *Masters Seminary Journal* 3, no. 1 (Spring 1992): 6–32.

51. Stitzinger, "History of Expository Preaching," 32.

52. Allen, "Introduction," 3.

Bible-Centered Preaching

Expository preaching, as a synonym with biblical preaching or text-driven preaching, has always been the task of anyone who would be a spokesperson for God. When Paul commanded Timothy to preach the word, he was not telling him to mount the pulpit and speak but to "base his spoken word on the written Word" (1 Tim 4:13; 2 Tim 2:2). The call to preach, therefore, is constantly a call to preach biblically.[53] Stephen Olford corroborates this assertion when he states that "in the strictest sense of the term, authentic preaching is expository preaching."[54]

Sidney Greidanus accuses some homileticians of causing confusion about the term "expository preaching" when they attempted to compare it as a category with other categories such as topical preaching or textual preaching. The traditional distinctions as explained by Leonard Sweet are topical preaching, which elaborates on a specific topic or theme and seeks to relate it to life; textual preaching, in which preachers choose a passage from the Bible and use it as a springboard to discuss their own theme or thrust; and expository preaching, where a Scripture passage is chosen and allowed to determine its own point and speak for itself authoritatively.[55] Greidanus argues that this comparison has led to so many misleading representations that the term "expository preaching" is practically meaningless and is losing its original meaning which is to "exposit the Word of God."[56]

Expository preaching remains Bible-centered preaching, and does not matter whether the text is short or long.[57] David L. Allen argues that any volume of text can suffice for effective expository preaching because linguists now assert that the structure of meaning goes beyond the sentence level, but the paragraph unit provides the best opportunity for deriving meaning when expounding a Scripture text. According to Allen, "expository preaching should at minimum deal with a paragraph (as in Epistles), whereas, in the narrative portions of Scripture, several paragraphs that combine to form the story should be treated in a single sermon since the meaning and purpose of the story itself cannot be derived when it is broken up and presented piecemeal."[58]

---

53. Sidney Greidanus, *The Modern Preacher and the Ancient Text: Interpreting and Preaching Biblical Literature* (Grand Rapids: Eerdmans, 2003), 10.

54. Olford and Olford, *Anointed Expository Preaching*, 4.

55. Leonard Sweet, *Giving Blood: A Fresh Paradigm for Preaching* (Grand Rapids: Zondervan, 2014), 70.

56. Greidanus, *Modern Preacher*, 11.

57. Greidanus, 11.

58. Allen, "Preparing a Text-Driven Sermon," 107.

All that is required is to open up the text and let it speak its message "clearly, plainly, accurately, relevantly, without addition, subtraction, or falsification."[59] Donald R. Sunukjian submits that true biblical preaching is simple faithfulness to the meaning and flow of the original author and the ability to make the text relevant to a contemporary audience. If biblical material is treated in this manner, it does not matter whether the sermon is textual, topical, or expository; they can all be biblical messages.[60] Sunukjian's position has much merit, but not many conservative expositors would agree. Many would appreciate expunging any term besides "expository preaching" from the homiletical discourse, if at all possible. For example, after Ray C. Stedman praises Martyn Lloyd Jones, John R. W. Stott, and Stephen Olford for representing the British evangelical tradition of expository preaching, he states that in his judgment, expository is "the only true form of preaching."[61] According to Stedman, while expository sermons derive their content from Scripture, other modes of preaching often lack biblical content, "causing those in the pews to drown in words while thirsting for knowledge."[62]

Life Transformation

In all the definitions presented here, the ultimate goal of expository preaching is life transformation, what Bryan Chapell identifies as "faithful thinking, living, and worship."[63] Ramesh Richard states the goals of expository preaching as to "inform minds, instruct hearts, and influence behavior toward godliness."[64] Sunukjian buttresses this by affirming that "the purpose of the sermon is not to impart knowledge but to influence behavior – not to inform but to transform. The goal is not to make listeners more educated but more Christ

---

59. John R. W. Stott, *Between Two Worlds: The Art of Preaching in the Twentieth Century* (Grand Rapids: Eerdmans, 1982), 126.

60. Donald R. Sunukjian, *Invitation to Biblical Preaching: Proclaiming Truth with Clarity and Relevance* (Grand Rapids: Kregel, 2007), 13. Topical sermon is the most attacked among other forms of sermons besides expository. But scholars are proving that topical sermons can be expository. In *Art and Craft of Biblical Preaching*, see Steven D. Matthewson, "What Makes Textual Preaching Unique," 412–17; Timothy S. Warren, "Can Topical Preaching also be Expository?" 418–20; Don Sunukjian, "The Biblical Topical Sermons," 421–23; Timothy S. Warren, "Topical Preaching on Bible Characters," 424–26; Warren, "Topical Preaching on Contemporary Issues," 427–30, and Warren, "Topical Preaching on Theological Themes," 431–33.

61. Ray Stedman, "The Primacy of Preaching," in *A Passion for Preaching: Reflections on the Art of Preaching, Essays in Honour of Stephen F. Olford* (Nashville: Thomas Nelson, 1989), 61.

62. Stedman, "Primacy of Preaching," 61.

63. Chapell, *Christ-Centered Preaching*, 31.

64. Richard, *Preparing Expository Sermons*, 19.

like."[65] This transformation, however, begins in the life of the preacher who has internalized the word before delivering it. The expositor is perhaps the most important actor after the Holy Spirit in the task of expository preaching since it is impossible to offer what one does not possess. This is why Haddon Robinson defines expository preaching as "the communication of a biblical concept, derived from and transmitted through a historical, grammatical, and literary study of a passage in its context, which the Holy Spirit first applies to the personality and experience of the preacher, then through the preacher, applies to the hearers."[66] Therefore the working definition for expository preaching in this book is the following: the incarnational communication of the text of God's word considering its historical, grammatical, and literary intention in a form that is faithful to the text and meaningful to the hearers in their sociocultural context, with the ultimate aim of enhancing total transformation into Christ-likeness.

Advantages and Disadvantages

Expository preaching has several advantages that make it the only expression of biblical preaching in its full essence. First, it presents the word of God which remains the only agency of spiritual transformation in human life and situations. Second, expository preaching shows the authority of God's word. It is still the best medium of presenting the claims of the Scriptures, and any preacher who stands to declare the mind of God through his word carries and manifests delegated authority. Third, the work of the Spirit is allowed to manifest in expository preaching. Whenever God's word is proclaimed, the work of the Spirit is brought to bear on people's lives.[67] Fourth, expository preaching addresses all life situations because the Bible reflects every human predicament and shows the way out of them. Expository preaching also protects preachers from using their own paradigms to analyze the predicaments of others. Fifth, expository preaching gives preachers a secure and repeatable approach. They do not need to invent sermon ideas because they are always there in the text.[68]

Not everyone agrees with the positive statements made above about expository preaching. Some have significantly criticized the method as dry

---

65. Sunukjian, *Invitation to Biblical Preaching*, 12.
66. Robinson, *Biblical Preaching*, 21.
67. Chapell, *Christ-Centered Preaching*, 30–33.
68. Gregory, "Expository," 383.

and dull and lacking the substance to reach a postmodern world. This is true when preachers engage in "mere historicizing of the text," and all they do is to bore the people with verb parsing and archeological facts and data, or when preachers are not willing to do the "tough, exhausting exegesis" required.[69] Expository preaching is also ineffective when expositors lack the skill for contextualizing the message of the Bible to their contemporary audience.

Another criticism of expository preaching is that preachers may not connect with culture and human experience from the pulpit once they see daily human life as a mere arena in which to apply the scriptural message. Such a view can end in a utilitarian approach to Scripture.[70] John S. McClure also fears that expository preaching may lead to some form of authoritarianism when preachers unconsciously identify biblical authority as their own authority. Preachers can only be helped in this situation when they recognize the need for personal doctrinal understanding when approaching Scripture and expounding it.[71] Yet in the conclusion of Robinson, "The type of preaching that best carries the force of divine authority is expository preaching" because behind it is the "power of the living God."[72]

Discussion Questions

1. Identify and discuss some of the common denominators among the definitions of expository preaching shared in this chapter.

2. Thinking about the sermons you have preached and those you have listened, what amount of exposition is reflected in those sermons.

3. Reflect over the disadvantages and criticisms levelled against expository preaching and enumerate how you would like to avoid those pitfalls as a biblical preacher.

---

69. Gregory, 383.
70. John S. McClure, "Expository Preaching," in *Concise Encyclopedia of Preaching*, ed. William H. Willimon and Richard Lischer (Louisville, KY: Westminster John Knox, 1995), 132.
71. McClure, "Expository Preaching."
72. Robinson, *Biblical Preaching*, 20, 21.

2

Form and Content in Expository Preaching

Identifying expository preaching as one among other categories of preaching has produced much discussion on the form and content of preaching. As Greidanus observed, contrasting expository preaching with other categories such as topical preaching and textual preaching by some homileticians has created confusion and misunderstandings that have caused expository preaching to be considered useless and its original meaning to be lost.[1] This categorizing also presents expository preaching as a form of preaching rather than a substantive method. Expository forms have been ridiculously described by some critics as "three points and a poem," and a "form of Aristotelian logic," and as "finding sensible, orderly things to say about scriptural texts rather than letting those text say things their own way," and as dissecting and rearranging the word into a "lawyer's brief."[2] These indirect indictments of expository preaching are based on the erroneous ways some people engage in it and on its assumed form.

Greg R. Scharf also asserts creating a taxonomy of preaching has created more problems than solutions. For him, expository preaching remains the way to preach, assuming the sermon is not just verse-by-verse exegesis, simply running commentaries, or a captioned survey of a passage.[3] Scharf concludes that, "Success in preaching is defined by the extent to which the message gets through to the intended listeners in a form they can recognize as a word from

---

1. Greidanus, *Modern Preacher*, 11.

2. Greidanus, 18. Greidanus compiled these opinions from homileticians such as Fred Craddock and Don Wardlaw.

3. Greg R. Scharf, *Let the Earth Hear His Voice: Strategies for Overcoming Bottlenecks in Preaching God's Word* (Phillipsburg: P&R, 2015), 82.

God himself."[4] The first thing to establish is that expository preaching is biblical preaching and does not need to compete with any other category. Then the point of discussion can move to the form and content of expository preaching, though scholars have divergent opinions on these. Some argue that we should see a difference between form and content, and others argue that form and content cannot be separated.

Jeffrey D. Arthurs is in the first school of thought. In the task of standing between the world of Scripture and a contemporary audience, Arthurs holds that a preacher is free to make use of testimonies, music, parables, questions and answers, story, objects, lesson techniques, and any variety of form that brings glory to God.[5] This school could be regarded as part of contemporary development in homiletical theories, even when they are presented with scriptural back-up. J. I. Packer does not subscribe to the efficacy or necessity of using anything outside conventional preaching. While commenting on the condemnation of monologue as an ineffective means of communication and the quest for books, films, TV, tapes, group study, and discussion as acceptable substitutes, Packer describes preaching as communication but something more than what is currently thought of as communication. The concern of communication in preaching is not the same as the concerns of modern communication theory. Packer was not against books, films, tapes, and study groups because they all have their roles in communicating God's word, but "the place where God sets the preacher is not their place."[6]

For Arthurs, "the defining essence of an expository sermon lies primarily in its content, not its form."[7] Sermons may have three points, follow a text verse by verse, end with an invitation, be delivered within a narrow range of decibels, be a certain amount of minutes, use a conversational or oratorical voice, and be delivered from a wood or Plexiglas pulpit. What is important is to understand the difference between biblical doctrine and communication procedure. The Bible is replete with diverse forms and genres, and Jesus was a master user of variety. Dialogues, debates, doxologies, letters, lists, laws, parables, proverbs, prayers, hymns, taunts, baptismal formulas, analogies, symbols, visions, mnemonic devices and several other rhetorical forms can

---

4. Scharf, *Let the Earth Hear*, xx.

5. Jeffrey D. Arthurs, *Preaching with Variety: How to Re-create the Dynamics of Biblical Genre* (Grand Rapids: Kregel, 2007), 16.

6. J. I. Packer, "Why Preach?," in *The Preacher and Preaching: Reviving the Art*, ed. Samuel T. Lorgan Jr. (Phillipsburg, NJ: P&R, 1986), 15.

7. Arthurs, *Preaching with Variety*, 15.

be used to communicate the text of God's word and to demonstrate faithful stewardship of the divine task.[8]

Robert A. Allen also defends the separation of form and content. In his article "The Expository Sermon – Cultural or Biblical?" he states his thesis that "the expository method, as biblical, should continue to provide the basis for sermon preparation while the expository form, as cultural, should be recognized as only one of many forms an exegetically developed sermon can take."[9] Allen associates the expository method with the concept of hermeneutics and the expository form with homiletics. Accordingly, Allen upholds expository preaching as normative when it is "grounded in a high view of Scripture and founded on a historical-grammatical exegesis... because that is the only method by which we can be sure we will indeed 'preach the word.'"[10] The content of an expository sermon is therefore the Scriptures. But Allen argued that the method commonly called expository preaching in which biblical texts are organized into a propositional, linear, or didactic outline should be opened for discussion as only one among several other methods of organizing a sermon and remaining faithful to the scriptural text.[11] In other words, expository preaching is only one of the forms an expository message can take.

Allen's position is informed by his survey of the Scriptures where he deduced that preaching assumed a variety of methods such as the use of visuals by Jeremiah, the poetic device called "taunt" by Isaiah, drama by Ezekiel, and exegetical prayer by Daniel.[12] Sermons in the New Testament also reflect such forms as parables, stories, and vocal dialogue, all indicating both inductive and deductive methods of communication.[13] Allen argues that the method of sermon preparation which produced the "three-point" sermon heard from many pulpits had its origins in the nineteenth century and is more cultural than biblical. It is derived from the age of writing,[14] and he identifies it as the

---

8. Arthurs, *Preaching with Variety*, 17.
9. Robert A. Allen, "The Expository Sermon – Cultural or Biblical?" *Journal of Ministry and Theology* 2, no. 2 (Fall 1998): 213.
10. Allen, "Expository Sermon," 221.
11. Allen, 221.
12. Allen, 215.
13. Allen, 217–18.
14. Allen, 220.

"linear western-style logic of the expository preaching . . . which has indeed served the western church well for many years."[15]

Allen's conclusion and challenge is that a sermon can only be called expository when the text is faithfully explained and applied and the audience understands God's word and will. It does not matter if the sermon fits the conventional structure of expository preaching. Preaching then can be done cross-culturally through the use of "story-telling, inductive argument, debate, drama, generalization, specific examples, narrative preaching, or any number of other styles while at the same time maintaining absolute fidelity to the exposition of the text."[16] What should not be compromised is dealing with one passage of Scripture at a time and maintaining hermeneutical integrity, cohesion, movement and direction, and life application.[17]

The other school of thought holds that form and content cannot be separated. Fred Craddock, who strongly upheld this position, states that

> The separation of form from content is fatal for preaching, for it fails to recognize the theology implicit in the method of communication. When a man preaches, his method of communication, the movement of his sermon, reflects his hermeneutical principles, his view of the authority of Scripture, church and clergy, and especially his doctrine of man. This is revealed verbally and non verbally in the point of contact made with the listeners and the freedom of response permitted them. It is a fact that much preaching contradicts by its method the content of its message.[18]

Here Craddock is building a foundation for a homiletic method that will shake the foundation of preaching as it used to be. The concept of form and method may be quite confusing because several homileticians use the terms without clear definition. Craddock explains that he is proposing a method and not "the method." He states that "forms of preaching should be as varied as the forms of rhetoric in the New Testament, or as the purposes of preaching or as the

---

15. Allen, 222. Fred Craddock disowns this "traditional method" as not being native to America but ascribed to Aristotle. He posits that it prevailed in Europe and was from there mediated to American seminaries and pulpits. Fred B. Craddock, *As One without Authority* (1983, reprint St. Louis: Chalice, 2011), 45.

16. Allen, "Expository Sermon," 225.

17. Allen, 226.

18. Craddock, *As One without Authority*, 5.

situations of those who listen." But his celebration of the inductive method appears to relegate every other sermon form that is not narrative.[19]

Craddock and his book *As One without Authority* have become references, for good or bad, for evaluating contemporary preaching and the philosophy that should guide it. Craddock's proposal of the inductive method which is aimed at reaching the postmodern world brought the harshest criticism of the deductive form of expository preaching and raised many disciples in that school of homiletics who are still developing diverse ways of enhancing it. Craddock opposes a separation between the method of preaching and the theology of preaching. He believes that the content of preaching and its method are fundamentally theological. He holds that "the method is the message. So it is with preaching: how one preaches is to a large extent what one preaches."[20]

Ronald J. Allen, aligning with Craddock's philosophy of the inseparability of form and content and its contemporary implication, avers that

> An exciting development in recent preaching is to let the form (genre), movement, and function of a biblical passage inform the form, movement, and function of a sermon. Genre and meaning work together. The meaning of a text and its form do not exist in the same relationship as a candy bar and its wrapper, in which you can unwrap the candy bar and throw away the wrapper. The phenomenon of hearing a passage from the Bible is a part of the meaning of the passage.[21]

Allen introduces more dynamics into the concepts of contents and forms when he categorizes sermons into expository-deductive, expository-inductive, topical-deductive and topical-inductive.[22] His reason for doing so is that a sermon can be understood either from its content or its movement. From the content dimension, a sermon is either an expositon of a biblical text or an intepretation of a topic. From the movement dimension, a sermon is either deductive or inductive.

The nuances of form that Allen introduces as "genre" in parenthesis brings out the various dynamic (unrelated) intentions of homileticians when they refer to form and content. They do not always intend the same definitions

---

19. Craddock, 45.
20. Craddock, 44.
21. Ronald J. Allen, ed., *Patterns of Preaching: A Sermon Sampler* (St. Louis: Chalice, 1998), 73.
22. Allen, *Patterns of Preaching*, xi.

when they refer to the terms even when they do not define them.²³ Greidanus actually observes that the word "form" is ambiguous. It could stand for forms of literature at all levels and could at the most elementary level indicate such technical terms introduced by form criticism and preliterary or literary units. His use of forms could be at the level of the Bible as a whole, major literary types or "genres," and smaller literary units.

But an evaluation of the positions discussed so far reveals that content of Scripture and its interpretation is static. Form is its dynamic dimension. From the positions of Arthurs and Allen, form is extrinsic as it deals with how the message is presented to the audience, bearing in mind their overall social-cultural context. Scripture does not limit any preacher to any straight-jacket method of sermon presentation, nor is expository preaching a stereotyped form in its essence. Craddock's school also has this fact in mind, but they see the form of sermon as more of a "movement" of the passage to be preached. Movement is a primary a methodological concern, and the question is whether the sermon moves and in what direction. This movement and its direction are what the community of listeners experience as the word of God is being shared.²⁴

Finally, form can be seen in terms of genre. While affirming that expository preaching is distinguished by being biblical both in form and content, Greidanus holds that genre is critical both to classifying literary styles and as an "epistemological tool for unlocking meaning in individual texts."²⁵ It is therefore important that the form of the text be reflected in sermons since it provides the clue for shaping the sermon and ensures that justice is done to the original form and content that the first hearers experienced.²⁶ But Greidanus warns that the goal of shaping the sermon after the form of the text must not be enslaving. It is possible to run into trouble when handling some epistles and Psalms and for the form of a sermon to weaken the message of a text and ultimately distort it. For example, a text may carry the potential of evoking amazement while its form may jeopardize this if the sermon follows that form.²⁷

Jeffrey D. Arthurs also notes the importance of form as one of the factors that tell how much participation a preacher receives from the listeners. For example, he observes that riddles and parables induce thoughts and that their

---

23. Greidanus, *Modern Preacher*, 20.
24. Craddock, *As One without Authority*, 45.
25. Greidanus, *Modern Preacher*, 16–17.
26. Greidanus, 19–20.
27. Greidanus, 19.

brevity, metaphorical quality, and conciseness make listeners consider issues more deeply than the words or phrases spoken. Such participation influenced by form generates a tendency in listeners to buy into the idea introduced by that form.[28] But Arthurs warns that it is dangerous to become a fundamentalist to forms or enslaved to the exact genre of a text because "no single sermon can replicate all the dynamics of a text," and preachers must always be conscious that they are standing between the two worlds of the text and their listeners.[29]

Dennis M. Cahill attempts to strike a balance between the emphasis on form aside from content and on form as inseparable from content. He criticized the notion that form, another way to look at a sermon design, is not necessary, and that all a preacher needs to do is repeat what the text says.[30] This view follows the opinion of Karl Bath, who did not subscribe to introduction, conclusion, or sermon divisions and who believed that sermon forms only obscure God's word.[31] Cahill argues that biblical writers had a concern for and were intentional in their rhetorical design. Paul's sermon in Acts 13:14-46, addressed to a predominantly Jewish audience, does not follow the same form or design as the sermon he preached in Athens to a gentile Greek audience in Acts 17:17-30.[32] Forms can never be done away with because many times they are embedded in the text. The concern should be the attitude of some preachers who allow design and structure to overshadow the content of the message because of their desire for eloquence or aesthetics. The balance should thus be as follows:

> Sermons must always be designed and thus must be concerned with issues of form. The preacher must always wrestle with questions of structure. And yet such matters must never be allowed to take precedence over the content of the gospel we preach. Indeed, form must always flow from content. Sermon form must be the servant of the text, not its master. It is right, then, once the preacher has done the work of exegeses and study and has a message to speak, to carefully consider the form of the sermon.[33]

---

28. Arthurs, *Preaching with Variety*, 26.
29. Arthurs, 27.
30. Dennis M. Cahill, *The Shape of Preaching: Theory and Practice in Sermon Design* (Grand Rapids: Baker Books, 2007), 46.
31. Cahill, *Shape of Preaching*, 47. However, Cahill argues that even Barth's sermons had an introduction, conclusion, and internal structure.
32. Cahill, 17.
33. Cahill, 47-48.

Many involved in the discussion of forms and content are simply concerned about the integrity of the text and effective communication. Their goal is to make the ancient word of God meaningful to contemporary listeners. That is not an easy task, though. So much variety and diverse theories have been brought to the task of preaching that it takes extra diligence to track the various methods being promoted by homileticians around the world. What is most important is that preaching be expository and that the preacher recognizes the primal place of the audience in the preaching assignment. Therefore, it is the task of preachers to discover the best form by which they can communicate to people in their various sociocultural backgrounds and realities. Even when forms are considered in terms of scriptural genres, preachers must still be ready to penetrate the culture as those not enslaved to forms. Timothy Keller suggests that "we are to compare and contrast the message of the text with the beliefs of the culture so they can understand themselves more fully."[34] He further states,

> To reach people gospel preachers must challenge the culture's story at points of confrontation and finally retell the culture's story, as it were, revealing how its deepest aspirations for good can be fulfilled in Christ. Like Paul, we must invite and attract people through their culture's aspirations – call them to come to Christ, the true wisdom and the true righteousness, the true power, the true beauty.[35]

Expository preaching should, therefore, be principally a biblical exposition communicated in a form that will be meaningful and impactful to the hearers.

The Deductive-Inductive Dichotomy

The various forms and shapes that expository sermons could take have been identified. Among the most discussed are the deductive and inductive. We will take a careful look at these two and see what are their advantages and disadvantages when engaging them.

---

34. Timothy Keller, *Preaching: Communicating Faith in an Age of Skepticism* (New York: Viking, 2015), 20.

35. Keller, *Preaching*, 20.

The Deductive Sermon

The deductive sermon starts on the platform of an accepted truth or proposition and involves explicating its significance to the hearers. The main idea is stated at the beginning of the sermon and is developed logically in a linear form as the sermon progresses. The sermon could be built around logical reasoning which transits from an acceptable major premise to joint discovery of minor premises. Preachers can handle these major premises by freely using a variety of exploratory methods whereby they investigate the implications of the premise and such activities as "explore its application, examine its limits, consider exceptions, or probe its effect."[36]

Dave L. Bland traces the history of deductive sermons to the medieval period and the creation of manuals called the *artes praedicandi* or *Arts of Preaching*. These manuals promoted preaching in a thematic form called university or thematic sermons. The preachers "began with a theme statement and developed it into three divisions. After dividing the theme into three parts, preachers employed the nine or more standard modes of amplification available to aid in the expansion of the sermon."[37] Thus the sermon was viewed organically and developed like a tree symbolizing that was alive and carried an aesthetic value. This process became more rigid with the arrival of Peter Ramus (1515–72), the French humanist who in trying to make sermons simpler and clearer "took the deductive reasoning and developed it into a fixed, mechanized system of logic separated from rhetoric."[38] This simple and direct approach became a feature of the Puritan plain style sermon[39] which began with a statement of doctrinal belief followed by an outline explaining the text on which the doctrine is based and a conclusion that includes application for daily living. The Puritan plain style is based on William Perkin's method of exposition. Its steps can be summarized as follows:

1. Read the text clearly from canonical Scripture.
2. Explain the meaning of this Scripture reading.
3. Gather a few profitable points of doctrine from the passage.

---

36. Dave L. Bland, "Deductive," in *The New Interpreter's Handbook of Preaching*, ed. Paul Scott Wilson (Nashville: Abingdon, 2008), 375.

37. Bland, "Deductive," 376.

38. Bland, 376.

39. Michael F. Ross, *Preaching for Revitalization* (Ross-Shire, Scotland: Christian Focus, 2006), 187.

4. Apply the doctrines to the life and practice of the congregation in straightforward and plain speech.

But gathering a "few" profitable points of doctrine may not be as few as Perkin suggests. On some occasions, more time is spent on the doctrine supported by several passages rather than on the exposition of Scripture.[40]

The attacks on expository preaching began when it was identified with the deductive method. One of the criticisms leveled against expository preaching by Joel C. Gregory is its rhetorical structure. The rhetoric principles or canons as outlined by Cicero included intention – the speaker discovers what is to be said; arrangement – the speaker arranges the speech in a particular order based on purposeful intention; style – the speaker clothes his or her thoughts with the right language; memory – the speaker fixes the speech in memory; and delivery – the speaker delivers the speech. John Chrysostom and Augustine promoted these principles as they adapted them to preaching and rightly used them to argue the case of Christianity against the attacks of pagans in their days. These principles greatly influenced nineteenth-century preaching as seen in the work of John A. Broadus who wrote *A Treatise in the Preparation and Delivery of Sermons*, which Craig Loscalzo describes as a "training manual in rhetorical skill applied to preaching."[41] The truth, however, is that rhetoric in its variety of meanings never dies. Even Loscalzo made reference to David Buttrick, a well-known New Homiletician, who affirmed that since rhetoric tells how a speaker can speak and people can hear in any generation, century after century, preachers have learned from rhetoricians.[42]

In his criticism of the rhetorical structure of expository preaching, Gregory observes that

> American evangelical exposition has sometimes been hijacked by alliteration, euphony, or overly clever outlines. God forgive the preacher who outlined an "expository" sermon on the prodigal son "His Madness, His Badness, and His Gladness." Far too often such homiletic circus tricks and shell games substitute for the tedious discipline of exegesis that gives substance to exposition.[43]

---

40. Bland, "Deductive," 376.

41. Craig A. Loscalzo, "Rhetoric," in *Concise Encyclopedia of Preaching*, ed. William H. Willimon and Richard Lischer (Louisville, KY: Westminster John Knox, 1995), 410.

42. Loscalzo, "Rhetoric," 414.

43. Joel C. Gregory, "Expository," in *The New Interpreter's Handbook of Preaching*, ed. Paul Scott Wilson (Nashville: Abingdon, 2008), 383.

Gregory's comment is lightweight compared to the barrage of condemnations that the deductive method in an assumed association with expository preaching has received. One of the most celebrated is Craddock's *As One without Authority*. Here Craddock observes the public disfavor and ridicule which the pulpit has suffered.[44] With preaching seen as "crosses to be borne," some preachers have backed out of preaching or gone into other forms of ministry that do not involve formal preaching.[45] Craddock goes on to argue that seminaries offered little or negligible work in homiletics which was handled by what he termed a retired "reactivated" pastor, while others just kept following Greek rhetoric.[46] Some attempted solutions include more seminary training in homiletics, Bible, and theology and a revival of topical preaching so there would be relevance and contact in preaching. Another solution is venturing into dialogical preaching which shares sessions before preaching and solicits feedback after it. Dialogical preaching may include a press conference sermon or planned interruption from the congregation.[47]

Craddock's most significant contribution, however, is his emphasis on "movement" as a primary methodological concern in preaching that will ever make an impact on the changing generation of listeners he had in mind. After stating movement as the most important question, he explains two directions in which a sermon moves – the deductive and the inductive. As explained earlier, the deductive moves from general truth to particular application or experience, which Craddock regarded as the traditional method or movement where conclusion precedes the development, representing in his words "the most unnatural mode of communication."[48] Craddock sees the deductive method as the authoritarian foundation of traditional preaching. He derides that for deductive preachers "to have placed more responsibility on the listener, to have left alternatives open to him, to have permitted his response to being the conclusion, would have been to create panic, insecurity, and thus totally frustrate the flock."[49] In deductive preaching there is no democracy, no dialogue, no listening by the speaker, and no contributing by the hearers.[50] Later in this work when the responses of other homileticians are considered

---

44. Craddock, *As One without Authority*, 3.
45. Craddock, 4.
46. Craddock, 5.
47. Craddock, 16–18.
48. Craddock, 46.
49. Craddock, 46.
50. Craddock, 46.

in the light of Craddock's position, it will be obvious that while his claim has some merits, there are several demerits to his methodology. Craddock went on to propose another method which is the inductive.

The Inductive Sermon

The inductive method is the homiletic antonym of the deductive and is the method of movement advocated by Fred Craddock. In an inductive sermon, thoughts move "from the particular of experiences that have a familiar ring in the listener's hear to general truth or conclusion."[51] This method involves identifying with the listeners and using analogy creatively, whereby preachers resist the temptation to impose their ideas on the listeners but let the conclusion be theirs. It is a "democratic sharing" where the listeners complete the sermon.[52]

Admitting that it was popularized by Craddock, Charles L. Campbell notes that since the 1970s the inductive method has had a significant influence on the theory and practice of homiletics. He describes the inductive method as a process in which the preacher "does not simply deposit conclusions in the hearer's mind but enables the congregation to participate actively in the movement and meaning of the sermon. The inductive movement encourages the listeners to think their own thoughts, feel their own feelings, draw their own conclusions, and make their own decisions."[53] Michael A. Brothers describes the inductive sermon as "engagement between text, preacher, and hearer, in which hunches are tested and played out through experiences in a quest for the discovery of a biblical truth. Often this discovery is a surprise!"[54]

While inductive and narrative preaching may not be regarded as synonyms, there are strong similarities between the two, especially since inductive preaching has had a strong influence on the development of narrative preaching. First, stories specialize in the particular and are central to inductive preaching. Second, inductive preaching "even without the presence of specific stories, tends to move like a good story, inviting the congregation to travel along with the preacher."[55]

---

51. Craddock, 47.

52. Craddock, 52–53.

53. Charles L. Campbell, "Inductive Preaching," in *Concise Encyclopedia of Preaching*, ed. William H. Willimon and Richard Lischer (Louisville, KY: Westminster John Knox, 1995), 270.

54. Michael A. Brothers, "Inductive," in *The New Interpreter's Handbook of Preaching*, ed. Paul Scott Wilson (Nashville: Abingdon, 2008), 390.

55. Campbell, "Inductive Preaching," 270.

Campbell admits that inductive preaching began a new era in contemporary homiletics, but he opines that the method is not new in rhetorical and homiletical practice. He traces the foundation of inductive preaching to modern science and affirms that Craddock's method was a product of his own scientific practice, historical-critical exegesis which he attempts to recapture in his sermon movements. Furthermore, something similar to the inductive method can be traced to the first modern rhetoric, the *Dialogues des Morts* of François Fénelon, which took on the nature of seventeenth-century experimental science.[56] In terms of rhetorical connection, Fénelon's proposals are very similar to these new homiletical methods. Campbell also suggests that two thousand years earlier, Aristotle in his *Rhetoric* developed a form of inductive rhetorical movement in which rhetorical argument begins with an *endoxa*, which is the listeners' "common sense" or common belief, and moves inductively to a new conclusion by probable arguments rather than rigid syllogisms. Campbell concludes by stating that "although Aristotle's emphasis on rational argument and persuasion is very different from the more experiential emphasis of inductive preaching, the seeds of inductive preaching can be found in Aristotle's own rhetorical theory."[57]

This background on inductive preaching is crucial to the discussion of the deductive-inductive dichotomy and especially the bastardization of expository preaching as three-point Aristotelian logic. Therefore, a more extensive critique of the inductive method is necessary.

Merits and Demerits of the Inductive Method

The inductive method is praised for directly engaging the hearers from the beginning of the sermon to the end. Since the hearers are fully participating, no effort is need to get their attention at the beginning or to introduce some final steps of application. The hearers not only discover biblical truth, they claim it for themselves by the end of the sermon. The tension produced by the inductive process also leads to the discovery of new meaning in familiar passages.[58] Another advantage is the placement of authority, which shifts from the preacher's conclusion to that reached by the interaction between the listeners and the biblical text. Brothers states,

---

56. François Fénelon, *Dialogues des Morts* (Paris, 1683), cited in Campbell, 271.
57. Campbell, 272.
58. Brothers, "Inductive," 391.

Because of this shift of authority, some homileticians have stated that the inductive form is best for addressing controversial issues when the preacher is at odds with the congregation; whereas others support it as a fitting response to the changing role of authority in the culture at large, thereby providing best opportunity for the sermon to be heard.[59]

The question of authority is never one to brush aside in biblical theology or homiletics, and this is where the inductive method has often failed to stand up to criticism. Craddock himself brought up this criticism while laying the foundation for his dispensation of the New Homiletic manifested in the inductive method or movement. While itemizing some of the reasons why preaching should be rejected, he opines that the disenchantment against preaching is "not because of its peculiar fault" but because it is part of a traditional and entrenched institution, and all such institutions – religious, political, or others – are being called into question.[60] Adding to this Craddock argues that the power of words to effect anything has been minimized in preaching because speakers of traditional religious language have refused to retire old words and to recognize that now scientific language demands clarity, precision, and freedom from ambiguity.[61]

Craddock further lists the arrival of television which replaces the oral with the visual and of individualism in which the socializing effect of voice and sound is minimized. According to Craddock, "the universe grew silent with the development of a literal culture. The spoken word came to be regarded as a modification of the written rather than vice versa."[62] Other factors include an increase of tentativeness in preachers; the transformation art, architecture, and music; and most importantly, the completely new relationship between the speaker and the hearer. According to Craddock, many believe that Christendom is no more, that the authority of the clergy, institutions, and even Scripture is no more, and that democracy has undermined high places including the pulpit.[63] In this parlance, Craddock describes what he sees as the reality of postmodern attitudes and the end of preaching with spiritual authority.

However, something that seems to evade some analysts of Craddock's position is the fact that he is speaking in a context. He is specific in his appraisal

---

59. Brothers, 391.
60. Craddock, *As One without Authority*, 5.
61. Craddock, 7.
62. Craddock, 10.
63. Craddock, 11–15.

of the American society before coming up with some of his conclusions, and he describes a problem with American Christianity. He starts by stating that the American church is characterized by activism, "as distinguished from the church elsewhere in the world."[64] His condemnation of the deductive method is based on the fact that it was not native to American soil, but rather imported from Europe to American seminaries and pulpits.[65] In his judgment, "the inductive process is fundamental to the American way of life."[66] He states succinctly that

> There are now at least two generations who have been educated in this way through college. Experience figures prominently in the process, not just at the point of receiving lessons and truth to be implemented, but in the process of arriving at these truths. Because the particulars of life provide the place of beginning, there is the necessity of a ground of shared experience. Anyone who preaches deductively from an authoritative stance probably finds that shared experiences in the course of service as pastor, counselor, teacher, and friend tends to erode the image of authority.[67]

These fundamental statements question universalizing the inductive method as the better or best way to preach. Even in the face of globalization, it is not socially accurate to think that the problems in Christianity in America or Europe are the problems in Christianity in Asia or Africa.

The question of authority is critical to biblical Christianity and preaching the word of God. John Stott attests to the fact that "seldom if ever in its long history has the world witnessed such a self-conscious revolt against authority."[68] In an age in which traditionally accepted authorities like family, school and university, state, church, Bible, pope, and even God are being challenged, "anything which savors of 'establishment,' that is, of entrenched privilege or unassailable power, is being scrutinized and opposed."[69] The era of immunity to criticism is over. It is obvious that rational human beings made in God's image must on occasion question authority such as in cases of social injustice, authoritarian regimes, minority discrimination, and exploitation of the poor.

---

64. Craddock, 6.
65. Craddock, 5.
66. Craddock, 49.
67. Craddock, 49.
68. John R. W. Stott, *Between Two Worlds: The Challenge of Preaching Today* (Grand Rapids: Eerdmans, 1994), 51.
69. Stott, *Between Two Worlds*, 51.

But when change is advocated to such an extent that there is no longer any objective standard of truth or goodness, something is definitely wrong.[70]

Criticism might have been milder if inductive preachers had just challenged the authority of the preacher, which in itself is a faulty premise for sound biblical teaching, though this challenging of the authority of preachers in America should not be universalized.[71] Scripture assumes that preachers do not have any authority of their own. They stand in the pulpit as representatives of God to present the word of God, which is the reason for the qualifications for anyone who takes on the pulpit ministry. If something is wrong with the ways preachers preach or live that invites a challenge to their authority to stand and speak God's word, then their personal authority to preach should be challenged, but not the inalienable right of God's servants to represent their Master on the pulpit like the prophets, apostles, and teachers who are the forebears of the word. Until today, Africans recognize the authority of a spiritual leader to deliver the message of God as one standing in for God, a view they inherited from traditional religion where priests are accorded the awe of one representing the Supreme God to deliver his message to his people.[72]

But to challenge the authority of Scripture or even to accept the questioning of its authority by postmodern listeners is as good as removing the foundation upon which the entire Christian faith is based because "every sermon preached presupposes a certain theology and a concept of authority."[73] This is why Allen presents a strong critique of the New Homiletic and postmodern preaching represented by the inductive method. In his article "A Tale of Two Roads: Homiletics and Biblical Authority," he traces challenging the authority of Scripture to the Enlightenment when the old road marked with the sign "Authority of Revelation" was juxtaposed with a new sign, "Authority of Reason," and a fork was formed. Many travelers just passed by without noticing the fork, some confused the two signs as similar, and many more simply assumed that

---

70. Stott, 52.

71. Packer, "Why Preach?" 11–12.

72. See Elizabeth Onyedinma Ezenweke and Loius Kanayo Nwadialor, "Understanding Human Relations in African Traditional Religious Context in the Face of Globalization: Nigerian Perspectives," *American International Journal of Contemporary Research* 3, no. 2 (2013): 61–70.

Margaret Doll citing O'Donnell also affirms the authority of African preachers whether their teaching is theologically sound or not. See Margaret Doll, "Literacy and Orality Working Together: The Intersection of Heart and Mind," *Orality Journal* 4, no. 1 (2015): 72, citing Katherine O'Donnell, "Umuhimu wa Biblia: An investigation into how Tanzanian Christians perceive and engage with God's Word" (MA dissertation, Redcliffe College, 2013).

73. David L. Allen, "A Tale of Two Roads: Homiletics and Biblical Authority," *Journal of the Evangelical Theological Society* 43, no. 3 (Sept 2000): 491.

the two routes would lead to the same ultimate destination.[74] Barth created the dichotomy between the word of God and the word of Scripture.[75] Scripture only becomes the word of God "when it is taken and used by God to speak to us and when it is heard by us as the witness to divine revelation." Scripture is more of a presentational rather than authorial speech. Revelation is what could be considered the word of God, not the Bible or preaching which are only derivatively and indirectly Word of God.[76] The implication of this view is that "if the written words of Scripture are not to be considered as God's revelatory speech, then the preaching of the Bible in an expositional manner becomes less important – which is exactly what we see in the so-called "New Homiletic."[77]

Considered since 1965, the New Homiletic is now being seen as identical with the postmodern form of preaching described in recent essays by Reid and Lucy Lind Hogan, Eugene Lowry, Alyce McKenzie, Jeffrey Bullock, and James W. Thompson. Paul Scott Wilson considers contemporary homiletics, the New Homiletic, and postmodern homiletics as synonyms and gives the following characteristic features of their sermons: they engage the experience of the hearers, seek to confirm rather than prove, value experience over abstraction, and conceive of forms as an extension and expression of content. These sermons are also often inductive, and they employ narrative and allow for participation and disagreement.[78]

In his critique, Allen criticizes Jacques Derrida who popularized deconstruction which insists that there is no "center" for philosophy or theology or anything[79] and Paul Ricoeur who rejected the propositional revelation of Scripture and whose thought "undergirds much of the narrative theology movement as well as the New Homiletics with its emphasis on narrative preaching and its weakened Biblical authority."[80] Hans Frei, following Barth, represents the post-liberal approach, and his contribution is his critique of the historical-critical approach to scriptural text while advocating a literary-critical approach.[81]

---

74. Allen, "Tale of Two Roads," 490.
75. Allen, 490.
76. Allen, 493.
77. Allen, 497.
78. Paul Scott Wilson, *Preaching and Homiletical Theory* (St. Louis: Chalice, 2004), 136–37.
79. Allen, "Tale of Two Roads," 500.
80. Allen, 506.
81. Allen, 508.

The importance of tracing the work of these hermeneutists is that hermeneutics ultimately informs homiletics, however short or long it takes to form a connection. By 1971, Allen posited that the New Homiletic was born when Craddock published *As One without Authority*.[82] In 1978, Craddock published *Overhearing the Gospel* which built on Kierkegaard's concept of communication by indirection. In this work, Craddock "placed the audience instead of the text in the driver's seat regarding sermon purpose."[83] He believes that the church has been saturated with the content of the gospel; therefore traditional expository preaching became absolutely ineffective.[84] Buttrick and many of his co-travelers further the thoughts of Craddock in their writings and posit that the idea of Scripture being the word of God is not grounds for biblical authority. Such incredible words as "sexist" and "anti-Semitic" are used for the Scriptures: "There is no pure gospel; no, not even in the Bible! To be blunt, the Christian Scriptures are both sexist and anti-Semitic. Faith is ever an admixture with cultural notion. Perhaps all we can do is to preach at the point of our conversion from the mind of the age, and leave the rest to the working of God's Spirit. But then, that's what preachers have done for centuries."[85] These authors present a highly sceptical view of the Scripure, and in the minds of hearers, the view they promote erodes the authority upon which preachers stand when they preach the word of God.

In an emotional response to Edward Farley's negative assessment of the text of Scripture, Allen asks,

> Think of it! A "postbiblicist paradigm of preaching" . . . the "tyranny" of the text of Scripture must be overthrown so as not to "turn the preacher away from the world of the gospel." Something about that statement takes my breath away! Must we be postbiblicist in our homiletic to be postmodern? Is this to be the road upon which homiletics travels in the new millennium? Is there no sure word from God in the text anymore? Is there no "thus saith the Lord"? Is the idea that the words of the Bible are the very speech of God no longer tenable? Cannot the "sense" of

---

82. Allen, 509.
83. Allen, 509.
84. Allen, 510.
85. David Buttrick, *A Captive Voice: The Liberation of Preaching* (Louisville, KY: Westminster John Knox, 1994), 75.

the text connect with its reference in a way that is both historical and yet leaves room for the multi-dimensionality of language?[86]

Allen's conclusions are that others from ancient past forward have travelled the road of Scriptural authority in their preaching endeavor, and Scripture remains the word of God. For Allen, "God's revelation to us is personal, propositional, and inclusive of several other categories (such as metaphor) as well. God's words are inseparable from his self-revelation." Preaching can be done because there is a word from God, and in agreement with Peter Adam, Allen states, "the first theological foundation for preaching, then, is that God has spoken."[87]

Thus Allen rejects the anti-authority stance of the New Homileticians and their celebration of the inductive method as sacrosanct. While Allen praises the revelation of God's word as personal and propositional, he posits that preaching must follow certain linear or alliterated arrangements for it to be expository. He indeed agrees that God's revelation is equally inclusive of categories such as metaphor. In another article titled "Preaching and Postmodernism: An Evangelical Comes to Dance," Allen observes that many of the insights of the New Homiletic are valuable, and evangelical preachers need to learn from such ideas as Buttrick's sermon movement, proper treatment of Scripture narrative, placing listeners in the sermon event, and the importance of imagination in preaching. However, Allen adamantly disagrees with the New Homileticians on the following points:

> Reality and truth are not socially constructed, objectivity when balanced with subjectivity is possible, narrative is not everything and some metanarratives are true, there are valid as well as invalid interpretations, pluralism and relativism have not won the day philosophically or theologically, and as long as there is a God in heaven, there is a final authority.[88]

According to Allen, recognizing God as the final authority means that whenever he speaks, listening and obedience are imperative.[89] In the same vein, Campbell commends inductive preaching as helping to revive the theory and practice of preaching since the 1970s until today because of its ability to highlight "the communicative significance of sermonic movement, the centrality

---

86. Allen, "Tale of Two Roads," 514.

87. Allen, 515.

88. David L. Allen, "Preaching and Postmodernism: An Evangelical Comes to the Dance," *Southern Baptist Journal of Theology* 5, no. 2 (Summer 2001): 75.

89. Allen, "Preaching and Postmodernism," 75.

of particularity and concreteness, and the importance of congregational participation in sermon."⁹⁰ However Campbell warns that scientific thinking in recent years no longer emphasizes "communal paradigms or frameworks within which purportedly inductive inquiry takes place"; therefore, there is a need to rethink inductive preaching.⁹¹

Merits and Demerits of the Deductive Method

Dave L. Bland identifies the ability to manage cognitive principles and concepts as one of the merits of deductive preaching. While the inductive method focuses more on the particulars of human experience, Bland insists that "sermons should not dwell exclusively on the particulars."⁹² Rather there is the need for sermons to identify ideas and concepts that are universal and transferable into any context or culture, and this is exactly what deductive preaching does – serving as a "helpful vehicle in transferring a concept of the gospel from one particular setting to another."⁹³

Craddock and the New Homiletic school have done more than enough in providing negative criticism of the deductive method. Bland itemizes the "pejorative" labels the method has received including pedantic, lacking in new insights, three points and a poem, wooden and mundane, authoritarian, reducing the text to nothing more than a proposition, tending to misuse Scripture, tending toward moralistic preaching, and rendering the listeners passive. Deductive reasoning and preaching are indeed pronounced terminal.⁹⁴

Little would Bland agree to this relegating deductive preaching to oblivion. While he would not ask preachers to return to the method as a primary means of sermon preparation and delivery, deductive preaching should not be excised. Bland states that

> Though each of the above accusations can be true of deductive preaching, none of the faults is inherent in its nature. When it falls victim to one of these abuses, the problem lies less in the form itself and more in the artless application of it. In other words, the main problem with deductive preaching is the lack of creativity and imagination on the part of the one who employs it. In terms

---

90. Campbell, "Inductive Preaching," 272.
91. Campbell, 271.
92. Bland, "Deductive," 376.
93. Bland, 376.
94. Bland, 375.

of form itself, then, the accusations leveled against it have little justification.[95]

Given this incisive statement, the big question is what should be the way forward for Christian preaching? Where should a good preacher lean – toward deductive or toward inductive? With so much to imbibe from the inductive method in spite of its anti-authority and postmodern stance, and with the good advice to not jettison the deductive method but rather be creative and avoid abusing it, is there a meeting point between the deductive and inductive positions? The literature suggests a positive answer.

The Inductive-Deductive Bridge

Expository preaching is right at the center of the deductive-inductive controversy as has been observed in the discussion so far. Yet it remains sacrosanct as the preaching model that is biblical and nonnegotiable. The inductive preacher seeks to practice biblical preaching that jettisons propositions, and the deductive preacher holds that God's word is propositional and conceptual. The irresolvable difference is authority, but the authority of Scripture cannot be negotiated. Other differences can be taken care of in the following ways.

First, the deductive-inductive dichotomy is not always as excellently distinct as the New Homileticians portray it. For example, Scott M. Gibson observes that all good sermons have sermon points. These are sub-ideas that support the greater idea that the preacher is trying to communicate. All good sermons have the elements of unity, order, and progress. While unity communicates a sense of completeness, order, "whether deductive, inductive, or a combination of both," creates a sense of flow for the listeners, and progress indicates that the preacher has a destination in mind.[96] Gibson identifies point form in the rhetorical moves of David Buttrick, in the induction of Fred Craddock and Ralph Lewis, in the narrative of Edmund Steimle, in the homiletical "plots" of Eugene Lowry, and in the scenes and "pages" of Paul Scott Wilson. These elements all suggested some form of organization.[97] For example, Eugene Lowry's plot for a sermon suggests the following: I. Upsetting the equilibrium ("oops") II. Analyzing the discrepancy ("ugh") III. Disclosing the

---

95. Bland, 375.
96. Scott M. Gibson, "Point Form," in *The New Interpreter's Handbook of Preaching*, ed. Paul Scott Wilson (Nashville: Abingdon, 2008), 401.
97. Gibson, "Point Form," 403.

clue to resolution ("aha"). IV. Experiencing the gospel ("whee"). V. Anticipating the consequence ("yeah").⁹⁸ Bland also observes a deductive strain of reasoning in David Buttrick's homiletic moves:

> A series of five or six moves make up the development of Buttrick's sermon. Within each move are a series of stages one must follow beginning by stating the single meaning or idea of that module, followed by imaging the idea, and then closing out the move by restating the single meaning. Thus, Buttrick's moves are a creative way for preachers to integrate deductive movement into the body of a sermon.⁹⁹

The difference between the deductive and inductive is that while the former introduces the sermon idea at the beginning and then builds on it, the latter leads listeners to the idea.¹⁰⁰ Therefore, if the sermon is based on point form and logical sequencing of thought, the dichotomy becomes irrelevant.

Second, both approaches can work together in some situations, which is the situation Donald Sunukjian attempts to explain in his article "Preaching Inductively and Deductively."¹⁰¹ He explains that induction and deduction can be in an overall sermon pattern: in a preview, in the body of the message, and in reading the text. He gives an illustration using a sermon preview. In a preview, preachers often make statements or raise the questions they intend to answer. Right away they are dealing with induction or deduction. By making a statement like, "Today we're going to see that with God the shortest distance between two points is often a zigzag," the preacher is stating a deductive main idea. But when this statement is followed by a preview like – "I want us to see first of all that God deliberately takes us on a zigzag path. We're going to turn to a time in Israel's history when God did that very thing. Then I want to answer the question why. Why does God do that? What's his purpose? And finally, I want to see how God keeps us encouraged when we don't seem to be heading toward point B" – the preacher has mapped out the sermon. The first preview element is deductive: "We're going to see *that* God does it deliberately." The second preview element is inductive: "We're going to see *why* he does it." A question to be answered in the message have been asked. The third preview element is also inductive: "We're going to see *how* he keeps us encouraged."

---

98. Lowry, *Sermon: Dancing the Edge of Mystery*, 25.
99. Bland, "Deductive," 377.
100. Gibson, 403.
101. Donald Sunukjian, "Preaching Inductively and Deductively," *Preaching Today* (n.d.).

So the preacher has used a combination of induction and deduction which has absolutely nothing to do with whether this sermon pattern is deductive or inductive.[102]

It can be inferred from Sunukjian's illustration that many times, preachers approach their sermon both deductively and inductively without being conscious of doing so. He simply suggests that when listeners hear upfront a point that a preacher is going to make, the sermon is deductive, and when they hear the questions a preacher raises and answers through a progression, the sermon is inductive.[103] Many sermons contain these elements.

Hugh Litchfield also believes that a sermon can be organized both deductively and inductively. All that is required for an outline to qualify is unity, balance, and movement.[104] Since an outline can use the deductive or inductive approach or both, it is left for the preacher to decide which to use, but this must be done with some level of creativity.[105] Haddon Robinson also upholds that induction and deduction can be combined in a sermon. One way is by identifying a personal or ethical problem, mentioning it between the introduction and the first point, exploring its root, and possibly discussing an inadequate solution. The sermon can then move on with the proposal of a biblical principle or approach to the problem in the second point, and for the rest of the sermon, the biblical principle can be explained, defended, and applied.[106]

Third, the Scripture genre should determine what method to use. Jeffrey D. Arthurs discusses the need to preach with variety because God laid down in the Scriptures an example of a great Communicator by his freshness and creativity. He notes that the Bible is a rich collection of literary forms such as poetry, law, parable, and story to mention a few. If God would communicate in such a variety of genres, his example should be mirrored in sermons.[107] John M. Rottman lists further variety in literary forms such as history, praise, lament, letters, apocalyptic, prophecy, and proverbs. But he sees such classifications as arbitrary because of other minor forms such as genealogy and diatribe, and some New Testament speeches that may not be considered worthy of extended

---

102. Sunukjian, "Preaching Inductively and Deductively."
103. Sunukjian.
104. Hugh Litchfield, "Outlining the Sermon," in *Handbook of Contemporary Preaching*, ed. Michael Duduit (Nashville: Broadman & Holman, 1992), 165–66.
105. Litchfield, "Outlining the Sermon," 165–66.
106. Robinson, *Biblical Preaching*, 126.
107. Arthurs, *Preaching with Variety*, 22.

treatment. Whatever the genre, respecting the form of the text is the beginning of good exegesis and preaching.[108]

Rottman identifies the value of historical criticism in helping a preacher see the importance of the form of biblical texts and form criticism in helping to identify oral and literary forms which preceded the final form of the biblical text. The problem arises when, due to rhetorical considerations, minimal connection exists between the text form and the sermon form. This is part of the reason why the New Homiletic emerged and insisted that narrative sermons ought to take a narrative form.

Simply put, when a Scripture genre lends itself naturally to a deductive form, there is no point forcing an inductive outline on it. This is obvious with most didactic passages of the Bible like the laws, epistles, and the teaching passages in the Gospels that are not parabolic. And when a genre lends itself to an inductive treatment, the sermon should naturally follow that method.

Fourth, culture should determine the method. The culture of a people, their speaking, listening, and comprehension style, should determine whether a sermon should be inductive or deductive or a combination of the two in communicating the gospel. Scripture from which every good sermon emanates is a product of the culture of the day. This is the view of Thomas Long when he observed that "the Bible itself demonstrates how quite diverse literary forms are borrowed from the culture to serve as vehicles for proclamation."[109] Citing the nature of the Gospels and the variety of forms reflected in them as an example, Long states that

> In this passage, a logical argument is being developed; in that text, a straightforward narrative is being told; over here, an enigmatic parable is being unfolded; over there, a hymn is being sung. All these forms – story and syllogism, poem and pronouncement, epistle and apocalypse – are found in the culture, but in every case the borrowed form is employed to serve the proclamation of the gospel.[110]

Those who strongly advocate for the inductive method or the deductive have not been able to prove adequately that one of them is more "spiritual" or biblical than the other. Effectiveness has rather been measured based on the demands

---

108. John M. Rottman, "Literary Forms," in *The New Interpreter's Handbook of Preaching*, ed. Paul Scott Wilson (Nashville: Abingdon, 2008), 65.

109. Thomas G. Long, *The Witness of Preaching* (Louisville, KY: Westminster John Knox, 2005), 135.

110. Long, *Witness of Preaching*, 135.

of the time of their use and the skill of the preacher in executing them. Times change, and culture is dynamic. Even the advent of postmodernism that has brought much advocacy for inductive preaching cannot be overgeneralized in spite of globalization. In the history of Christian preaching, the church has transited from one form to another, and none has proved to be normative. It is often the rhetorical situation that determines which is better.

Discussion Questions

1. Discuss your understanding of the relationship between form and content in expository preaching.
2. With your understanding of the inductive and deductive forms, how would you categorize the sermons you have preached in the past twelve months and why would you categorize them as such?
3. From a study of the culture in which you live and carry out your preaching ministry, which form of biblical exposition would you consider best and why would you consider it so?

3

Africa in the History of Christian Preaching

Many authors have traced the history of preaching from the Old Testament to the New Testament and into the apostolic era and early church, the medieval period, the Reformation, and through to the twentieth century. Most focus on the historical situation in each period and the preaching and preachers that characterized it. Their efforts to cover the history of Christian preaching are obviously based on their scope and objectives for the book. Something that is often missing, however, is the specific place of Africa in the history of preaching. The authors either assume that nothing really took place in Christianity in Africa until the arrival of the Western missionaries in the nineteenth century, or some preaching events had occurred but were not popularly acknowledged.

Most books on the history of preaching with general titles, those that are not dedicated to a specific country like France or Britain, do not give Africa consideration. For example, John Broadus in his *A Treatise in the Preparation and Delivery of Sermons* traces preaching history from biblical sermons to the early Christian centuries, the medieval period and Reformation, and the great French and English preachers. Yngve Brilioth in his *A Brief History of Christian Preaching* alludes to the synagogue as a foundation for his discourse, but spreads his history only from Jesus to Anglicanism, and his work was more thematic than biographical. Clyde E. Fant and William M. Pinson Jr. in *20 Centuries of Great Preaching: An Encyclopedia of Preaching* simply begin with Jesus and end with Martin Luther King Jr. Edwin Charles Dargan in *The Art of Preaching in the Light of Its History* follows the Old Testament to Reformation patterns and adds modern homiletic in Europe and America. In his two volumes, *The Anatomy of Preaching: Identifying Issues in Preaching*

Today and *The Company of Preachers: A History of Biblical Preaching from Old Testament to the Modern Era*, David L. Larsen did quite extensive work tracing the history of preaching from Genesis to A. W. Tozer. Hughes Oliphant Old in *The Reading and Preaching of the Scriptures in the Worship of the Christian Church* is among the few authors who cared to add a section on the history of preaching in Africa.[1]

Sundkler and Steed lamented the lack of a source book on the history of preaching in Africa. According to these authors, "preaching in Africa is a theme only very occasionally treated in the literature. The African sermon is the result of the instant, proclaimed with great conviction and then left to the listeners' memories, easily forgotten. Only an infinitesimal part of these African sermons have survived by way of the printed word."[2] But piecing together some information is still possible. Even while not describing the place of African Christians in the history of preaching, some books give evidence that great precursors of preaching can be traced to Africa. When the names of such North Africans as Origen of Alexandria, Egypt; Tertullian and Cyprian of Carthage in what is now Tunisia; or Augustine of Hippo in what is now Algeria are mentioned, the history of Christian preaching in Africa is being traced, consciously or unconsciously.

Some argue whether North Africa in the days of these early church fathers was culturally part of Africa as claimed by some writers like Thomas C. Oden. Oden holds that "Africa" in ancient texts referred to the "massive continent that stretches far to the south of the Mediterranean" having diverse cultures and languages. It included historic cultures in ancient North Africa known as the "Nilotic, Berber, Libyan, Numidian, Nubian, Ghanaian and others dating back to prehistoric times."[3] However while reviewing Oden's book, Steven Byran argues that during the early centuries of the Common Era, North Africa was in

---

1. John A. Broadus, *Lectures on the History of Preaching* (New York: A. C. Armstrong, 1907; reprint Birmingham: Solid Ground Christian Books, 2004); Yngve Brilioth, *A Brief History of Christian Preaching*, trans. Karl E. Mattson (Philadelphia: Fortress, 1965); Clyde E. Fant and William M. Pinson Jr., eds. *20 Centuries of Great Preaching; An Encyclopedia of Preaching*, 13 vols. (Waco, TX: Word, 1971); Edwin Charles Dargan, *The Art of Preaching in the Light of Its History* (New York: Doran, 1992); David Larsen, *The Company of Preachers: A History of Biblical Preaching from Old Testament to the Modern Era* (Grand Rapids: Kregel, 1998); Hughes Oliphant Old, *The Reading and Preaching of the Scriptures in the Worship of the Christian Church*, vol 5. (Grand Rapids: Eerdmans, 1997–2004).

2. Bengt Sundkler and Christopher Steed, *A History of the Church in Africa* (Cambridge, UK: Cambridge University Press, 2000), 672–3.

3. Thomas C. Oden, *How Africa Shaped the Christian Mind: Rediscovering the African Seedbed of Western Christianity* (Downers Grove, IL: InterVarsity, 2007), 16.

no way connected with sub-Saharan Africa as it is known today.[4] "Africa" was the name given to a Roman province that was roughly made up of the modern countries stretching from Algeria and Tunisia to western Libya. The region south of the Nile was not called "Africa"; rather, the Romans knew it as "Nubia," the Greek speakers as "Ethiopia," and the Egyptians and Hebrews as "Cush."

However, North Africa is part of the African continent, and these church fathers are an essential part of the global history of Christianity. As Shorter notes, "Africa provided a shelter and a help to Jesus Christ in the first and last days of his life. It was in Africa that he found shelter when persecuted by Herod, and on his way to Calvary he found a helper in the African Simon of Cyrene. Thus, Africa has been involved in the salvation story of humanity, and it may be that Africa now has a special message to give to the rest of the world."[5] Thus the preaching of these North African church fathers is important in the history of preaching.

Early Periods

Fant and Pinson narrate the story of Origen (185–254) who was born in Alexandria, Egypt. Origen became the foremost expositor of Scripture in the early church and was known for his allegorical method. But in his commentaries before he went into his figurative, allegorical interpretation, he first did complete and careful exegesis of the literal meaning of a text. Origen's allegorical interpretations were wild, and two reasons are given to explain why. First, allegory was a common method in his day. Origen agreed with his contemporaries that Scripture has a higher and lower meaning and that just as a human being is made up of body, soul, and spirit, so Scripture possesses a threefold sense: grammatical, moral and spiritual.[6] It should be noted that one of the connecting points some have made between the early church fathers and African preaching is the use of symbolism and allegory. However, Shorter advises that such comparisons should not be used as a point of distraction from the specific genus of African preaching.[7]

---

4. Steve Bryan, "Review of *How Africa Shaped the Christian Mind: Rediscovering the African Seedbed of Western Christianity* by Thomas C. Oden," *Africa Journal of Evangelical Theology* 27, no. 1 (2008): 79–80.

5. Aylward Shorter, "Homiletic and Preaching in Africa," in *Concise Encyclopedia of Preaching*, ed. William H. Willimon and Richard Lischer (Louisville, KY: Westminster John Knox, 1995), 230.

6. Fant and Pinson, *20 Centuries of Great Preaching*, 35.

7. Shorter, "Homiletic and Preaching in Africa," 231.

Second, Origen faced the difficult task of reconciling the laws and regulations of the Old Testament with the faith and ethics of the gospel. He thought that when the literal meaning of the text does not give enough nourishment for an edifying meditation, the allegorical has to take over.[8] However, Origen made three great contributions to the history of Christian preaching which should not be overshadowed by the defects of his fanciful allegorizing. First, he was the first preacher to establish the form of sermon as discourse on a specific biblical text. Second, he was the first to lay great emphasis on the value of careful exegesis of the historical and grammatical significance of any given text. Third, he was the first preacher to compose a series of homilies on entire books of the Bible. In his early career, preaching was informal, looking simply like a Christian testimony rather than a formal address. Allegory has almost gone into extinction as a method, but Origen will be remembered for the form of the sermon as biblical exposition.[9]

Aylward Shorter wrote about Augustine of Hippo who also was from North Africa, and over five hundred sermons which he preached to his congregation at Hippo in Tunisia have survived. These include thematic sermons and continuous expositions of biblical books including Psalms and the Fourth Gospel. Augustine's sermons were brief, simple, and apparent artlessness, but this form concealed "the consummate artistry of one of the greatest orators who ever lived."[10] Augustine was not just a great preacher; he was one of the first theoreticians in the field of homiletics. His book *De doctrina christiana* (*On Christian Doctrine*) is one of the earliest textbooks on homiletics. The content of this book indicates that Augustine did see Christian rhetoric as a stumbling block to gospel communication, as is now being assumed in some homiletical circles. According to Shorter,

> He does not bother with the principles of secular rhetoric on the assumption that they have been acquired earlier at school. The aim of specifically Christian eloquence is not to impress the Christian audience but to make it possible for the audience to understand and accept what is taught. That is done by fulfilling all three of the duties of a speaker listed by Cicero: teaching, delighting, and moving. Each has its role in the strategy of Christian persuasion, and each of these duties is related to one of the three levels of style.

---

8. Fant and Pinson, *20 Centuries of Great Preaching*, 36.
9. Fant and Pinson, 37.
10. Aylward Shorter, "History of Preaching," in *Concise Encyclopedia of Preaching*, ed. William H. Willimon and Richard Lischer (Louisville, KY: Westminster John Knox, 1995), 192.

> The plain style is used for teaching, the middle for delighting, and the grand for moving. The Christian teacher cannot be persuasive, however, unless his life proclaims what his preaching does. Unlike Aristotle's ethos, this trust in the speaker is not created by the speech but outside of it in daily life.[11]

This is a summary of Augustine's theory of homiletics. It has survived for several centuries and is still making its mark on modern rhetoric.

One of the struggles of the New Homiletic is with the concept or act of persuasion, something ancient rhetoric is instrumental in achieving. In the New Homiletic, experience is the cherished goal and persuasion does not have a place. Yet the concept of persuasion permeates the writings, ministry, and preaching of Paul and has been fundamental to the task of preaching for several centuries. He uses the Greek word *peitho* which means "to convince," and "to persuade." In the active voice, it signifies "to apply persuasion, to prevail upon or win over, to persuade," in order to bring about a change of mind influenced by reason or moral consideration.[12]

These contributions of just two of the African early church fathers indicate that Africa had a place in the beginning of Christian preaching both in theory and practice. The historical contributions of Africa to world Christianity is still a subject that calls for wider research and publicity so that the impression does not continue to be that all Christianity is today is due only to the contributions of the West or the East. This is the main thrust of Thomas Oden's argument in his book *How Africa Shaped the Christian Mind*, which includes an outline of Christian activities in the first millennium which he titles "Literary Chronology of Christianity in Africa in the First Millennium."[13]

The Period of Silence

The momentum of African contributions was not sustained beyond the first few centuries of the church because of doctrinal controversies, the dangerous importation of Greek philosophy into Christian thinking, and the erosion of

---

11. Shorter, "History of Preaching," 192.

12. W. E. Vine, Merrill F. Unger and William White Jr., "Persuade," *Vine's Complete Expository Dictionary of Old and New Testament Words* (Nashville, TN: Thomas Nelson, 1996), 469.

13. Oden, *How Africa Shaped the Christian Mind*, 157–97. Another helpful resource is Frederick Quinn, *African Saints: Saints, Martyrs and Holy People from the Continent of Africa* (New York: Crossroad, 2002).

biblical theology in the thinking of many church fathers.¹⁴ Here is Stitzinger's summary of the first four hundred years of postapostolic preaching:

> The first four hundred years of the church produced many preachers but few true expositors. The Apostolic Fathers (ca. 96–125) followed a typological method of interpretation in their works. Second-century Fathers (ca. 125–190) such as Justin Martyr and Tertullian composed apologies in defense of Christianity. Third century Fathers (ca. 190–250) such as Cyprian and Origen were polemicists, arguing against false doctrine. Origen's utilization of an allegorical method of interpretation stimulated an increased interest in exposition of the text. Unfortunately, his allegorizing was detrimental to true biblical exegesis and reduced interest in exposition among his followers in the Alexandrian School. In the fourth century (ca. 325–460), a significant group engaged in serious Bible study. Six notable preachers in this period were Basil, Gregory of Nazianzen, Gregory of Nyssa, Augustine, John Chrysostom, and Ambrose.¹⁵

Stitzinger's observation is significant because it describes the apparent demise of Christianity (and ultimately preaching) in Africa. John Wesley Zwomunondiita Kurewa follows up by drawing attention to the need for sub-Saharan Africans to learn from what he terms the errors of Roman North African Christianity. He observes that Christianity was so strong in Africa that it produced such great fathers as Tertullian, Cyprian, and Augustine, as earlier mentioned. But the church did not survive the onslaught of the Vandals, Arian Christians and barbarians who invaded North Africa between 430 and 534. Kurewa argues that one of the reasons was because "the church in North Africa did not identify with the common people – the church was not indigenized; it was a Latin Church."¹⁶ Corroborating this assertion, Peter Falk observes that "the church experienced one of the most disastrous calamities of its history in the invasion of North Africa during the seventh and eight centuries."¹⁷ Another reason was that Christianity did not penetrate North Africa beyond the Roman

---

14. James F. Stitzinger, "The History of Expository Preaching," *Masters Seminary Journal* 3, no. 1 (Spring 1992): 13.

15. Stitzinger, "History of Expository Preaching," 13–14.

16. John Wesley Zwomunondiita Kurewa, *Preaching and Cultural Identity: Proclaiming the Gospel in Africa* (Nashville: Abingdon, 2000), 19. See also Peter Falk, *The Growth of the Church in Africa* (Bukuru: African Christian Textbooks, 1997), 50.

17. Falk, *Growth of the Church in Africa*, 23.

frontier or the Romanized population which was a small and wealthy segment. As Kurewa observes, the use of Latin was a source of undoing for the church. Instead of using the indigenous Punic and Berber languages, Latin was used in services, literature, and Bible translation. When the Muslims struck North Africa after the Vandals, nothing much was left of the church.[18] All through the Middle Ages and Reformation, there was a blackout of any significant Christian activity in Africa.

The Resurgence of Christianity

Christian activities were few in the fifteenth, sixteenth, and seventeenth centuries on the borders of Africa and south of the Sahara. The only time anything meaningful can be said about Christianity in Africa is from the nineteenth century when new Christian life sprang up and gave rise to Christian mission and preaching.[19] From a missiological perspective, Taiye Adamolekun broke down the growth periods of Christianity in Africa between the nineteenth and twentieth centuries into five, and each of these periods produced different kinds of preaching and preachers in their own classes and for their generation.[20] Much insight into preaching in Africa can be gleaned from what took place in these periods.

Period of Denominationalism and Missionary Activities

The first period of denominationalism and missionary activities was when missionary bodies were set up in Europe and America, and their missionaries came and opened permanent mission stations among the Africans. This was shortly after the abolition of the slave trade, an event that in itself stimulated a fresh zeal for mission among the Europeans and Americans.[21] For example reaching out to the freed slaves in Sierra Leone created a combined mass of Euro-Americans and Africans who would reach out to their own people with the gospel.[22] Some of the denominations and organizations that were involved in this work include the Anglicans, the Church Missionary Society

---

18. Falk, 50.
19. Falk, 23.
20. Taiye Adamolekun, "Main Trends in the Church Growth in Nigeria," *European Scientific Journal* 8, no. 23 (October 2012): 4.
21. Adamolekun, "Main Trends," 4.
22. Falk, *Growth of the Church in Africa*, 105.

(CMS), the Wesleyan Methodists, the Presbyterians, and the American Baptist Mission. Others were the Roman Catholics, the Qua Iboe Mission, and the Sudan Interior Mission.[23]

At this time, trained missionaries broke language barriers through the use of interpreters and learning indigenous languages. They trained African ministers; built churches, schools, and hospitals; and baptized many converts.[24] Some of the Africans involved were freed slaves. African agents were mainly trained at Fourah Bay College and other mission training centers around the world. Locally recruited agents were also at the forefront of missions.[25] Francis and Gibson observe that "beyond North America, preaching among colonists receives little or no attention in recent major surveys of English-language preaching in modern period though Old discusses some African preachers like Bishop Samuel Ajayi Crowther, who preached to colonists.... Similarly, a focus on sermons remains rare among colonial historians and literary scholars as a whole."[26]

Period of Independent Churches

The second period of the evolution of independent churches began from the late nineteenth century. These churches were part of the protest movements of indigenous people who were being marginalized by foreign missions. A nationalistic spirit also gradually awakened because of the activities of European colonial powers after the partition of Africa in 1885. The discriminatory practices of white church leaders led to some protests which brought about the establishment of African-led churches. These were formed in Southern Africa in the 1870s and the Niger Delta area in the 1890s, and the movement spread across the continent.[27] Some indigenous African preachers who emerged at this time include Samuel Ajayi Crowther, Moses Ladejo Stone, and D. B. Vincent, later known as Mojola Agbebi.[28]

---

23. Adamolekun, "Main Trends," 4.

24. Adamolekun, 4.

25. David Killingray, "Passing on the Gospel: Indigenous Mission in Africa," *Transformation* 28, no. 2 (April 2011): 95.

26. Keith A. Francis and William Gibson, *The Oxford Handbook of the British Sermon 1689–1901* (Oxford: Oxford University Press, 2012). Samuel Ajayi Crowther is more properly located in the second period.

27. Francis and Gibson, *The Oxford Handbook*.

28. S. Ademola Ajayi, *Baptist Work in Nigeria 1850–2005: A Comprehensive History* (Bodija, Ibadan: Book Wright, 2010), 170–83.

The contributions of some of these preachers is necessary here, and others will be mentioned later. Samuel Ajayi Crowther (1807–1891) was the first Anglican bishop in black Africa, and he is renowned for being the first to translate the Bible into Yoruba. There is not much record of his preaching except that Hughes Oliphant Old wrote that he was the "first black African preacher."[29] Some insights may be gleaned from Cowther's communication style and the content of his sermons may be studied in his letters and memoirs.[30]

Representatives of the Baptist genre among these early preachers are Moses Ladejo Stone (1842–1913) and Mojola Agbebi. Stone was discipled by W. J. David from whom he must have learned preaching as Stone interpreted for David, accompanied him on visitation, and occasionally assisted him in preaching. Though Stone had little education and could not speak English fluently, his extensive reading, sense of humor, knowledge of Scripture, and eloquent speech endeared him to the congregation and caused his native Ebenezer Baptist Church in Lagos to grow. So much was he gifted that Rev S. G. Pinnock compared him to Spurgeon.[31]

One of the most outstanding sermonic contributions of Mojola Agbebi (1860–1917) was his inaugural sermon delivered at the celebration of the first anniversary of the "African Church" in Lagos on 21 December 1902. His sermon reflected not just nationalism and perhaps good speaking; he was out to be celebrated as an apostle of African mission and a prophetic preacher to his generation when there was confusion between the tenets of Christianity and the lording of colonialism. However as good as the sermon was, the text and the content struggled in congruence. Agbebi also demonstrated his inadequate knowledge of biblical revelation by placing Islam almost above Christianity in dating and value. Also biblical exposition was not reflected in the glimpses of the sermons of these men at this time.[32]

---

29. Old, *Reading and Preaching of the Scriptures*, 204–6.

30. See Jesse Page, *The Black Bishop Samuel Adjai Crowther* (New York: Fleming H. Revell, 1908).

31. Femi Adelegan, *Nigeria's Leading Lights of the Gospel Revolutionaries in Worldwide Christianity* (Bloomington, IN: WestBrow, 2013), 374–76; see also D. F. Oroniran, *The Baptist Heritage: A Nigerian Perspective* (Ibadan: Titles, 2013), 423.

32. Akinsola Akinwowo, "The Place of Mojola Agbebi in the African Nationalist Movements: 1890–1917," *Phylon* 26, no. 2 (2nd Qtr. 1965): 131; Klaus Koschorke, Frieder Ludwig, Mariano Delgado, eds., *A History of Christianity in Asia, Africa and Latin America, 1450–1990: A Documentary Source Book* (Grand Rapids: Eerdmans, 2007), 219.

Period of Indigenous African Churches

The third period of indigenous African churches was between the 1920s and 1940s. This twentieth-century phenomenon was a reaction against the "European complexion of the Western-Oriented Churches" and one which sought through "direct communication with the Holy Spirit and their own official etiology to evangelize Africa by their own methods."[33] These churches are also called the *Aladura*, or the African instituted churches. But they can be classified as the Ethiopian, those which emphasized independence while still retaining an essential part of their parent church doctrines and practices, and the Zionists, those which emphasized the work of the Holy Spirit and entertained various forms of revelation and healing.[34]

Some of the factors that contributed to the rise of African Independent churches include the motivation of Henry Venn, the rise of nationalistic feelings, mass movements led by charismatic figures, and circumstances like the worldwide influenza epidemic and economic depression which followed. Others are the desire to evangelize, the passion for a purer form of Christianity, and the freedom to exercise gifts of leadership.[35] Some of the preachers that emerged in this period are Moses Orimolade and Christianah Abiodun Akinsowo (Cherubim and Seraphim); Sophia Odunlami and J. B. Shadare (Faith Tabernacle); David Odubanjo, I. B. Akinyele, and Joseph Ayo Babalola (Christ Apostolic Church); Joseph Osintelu (Church of the Lord, Aladura); and Major Lawrence (Holy Flock of Christ).[36] All of these including Garrick Braid from the Niger Delta were from Nigeria. Preachers from other regions of Africa that could be located include William Wade Harris (Liberia), Walter Matiffa (Lesotho), Simeon Kimbangu (Belgian Congo), and Samson Oppong (Ghana). These were evangelists with special charisma.[37]

Among those mentioned above, Simon Kimbangu (1887–1951) was a great healer but was also known to be a preacher of God's word during the colonial era in Congo. He opposed the cults of fetishes and instructed that they be destroyed. He preached faith in one God, taught against polygamy, and condemned all forms of immorality. Kimbangu's sermons raged against non-Christian dance which often encouraged debauchery and lewdness. There

---

33. Adamolekun, "Main Trends," 6.

34. Deji Isaac Ayegboyin and S. Ademola Ishola, *African Indigenous Churches: An Historical Perspective* (Bukuru: Africa Christian Textbooks, 2013), 9–10.

35. Ayegboyin and Ishola, *African Indigenous Churches*, 12–16.

36. Adamolekun, "Main Trends," 7–8.

37. Ayegboyin and Ishola, *African Indigenous Churches*, 13.

was such awe and power in his preaching that it spread all over the country like a flood sweeping away all strange gods. Young men would be so motivated by his sermons that they would go from house to house collecting and destroying *minkisi* images. Kimbangu's sermons can be regarded as moralistic preaching, and they have their disadvantages. But as far as his people were concerned, "the salvation which Jesus Christ brought to humanity had now come to them through Simon Kimbangu, and his preaching was to alleviate their plight and suffering by delivering them from the domination of white as Moses did for the people of Israel when they were being oppressed by the Pharaoh." This activity did not go down well with the Belgian colonial administration who investigated, arrested, tried, and condemned Kimbangu to one hundred and twenty lashes and death. This sentence was later changed to life imprisonment.[38] The African Independent churches in the history of Christianity in Africa have been highly lauded by several authors, scholars, and observers of the growth of Christianity in the continent for representing the true face of Christianity that reflects African cultural identity.[39] The form and content of their sermons will be mentioned later, but it must be noted that while there is much to appreciate in the sermons of this movement, much more needs to be done to increase the richness of the theological content and ability to effect transformation that is truly Christ-like and produces such a testimony in the society that people are genuinely regenerated.

It is difficult to lay hold of the sermons of several of the preachers mentioned in these eras because quite a number of them were not literate or were rather oral preachers, but God used them in tremendous ways. Recently in Nigeria, Moses Oludele Idowu has worked to piece together the life and ministry of such men as Ayo Babalola, Moses Orimolade, Daniel Orekoya and other pioneers of African Independent churches. He has produced a six-volume "African God's General Series," and he is planning to add more. What he cannot do (as is usually the case) is to discuss their preaching life or sermons.

Period of Charismatic and Pentecostal Movements

The fourth period is the rise of charismatic evangelical and Pentecostal churches. This was from the 1970s. During this period liberation theology

---

38. Emmanuel Martey, "Prophetic Movements in the Congo: The Life and Work of Simon Kimbangu and How His Followers Saw Him," *Journal of African Instituted Church Theology* 2, no. 1 (2006): 2.

39. See Kurewa, *Preaching and Cultural Identity*, 20.

also arose, especially as Africa languished under the pang of colonial rule and a clamor for independence began to rend the air. One typical example of a preacher in this period is Timothy Njoya, whom Old describes as a prominent example of liberation theology "transported into Africa."[40]

The population of Christians increased as a result of the revivals of the 1930s. But a time came when some Christians began to regroup into evangelical groups or churches in revolt against idolatrous traditional values that were being considered antithetic to Christianity. Especially from the 1970s onward, the relationship between the youth and established churches became strained as the youth were exposed to university education, foreign education in Europe and America, and American evangelists and literature coming into the continent. This tension led to the proliferation of churches and ministries, and a new set of preachers emerged.[41] These preachers included Benson Idahosa, Enoch Adejare Adeboye, W. F. Kumuyi, David Oyedepo, Francis Wale Oke, Mike Okonkwo, Ayo Oritsejafor, Nicholas Duncan-Williams, Charles Agyin-Asare, James Saah, Christanah Doe Telter, and several others around the continent.

Period of "Reverse Mission"

It is to be noted that the present, fifth period has gone beyond just charismatic, evangelical, and Pentecostal. First, this period has become a mix of them all. Second, the world is experiencing what is termed a "reverse mission" in which Africans are not only reaching Africans in the diaspora but also evangelizing Europeans and Americans who have lost their early position in Christianity and its propagation.

Other terms used for reverse mission are "mission in reverse" or "mission in return." They all mean that nations which once sent missionaries are now receiving missionaries. But Harvey C. Kwiyani sees the term as a misnomer. According to him, mission remains mission, and it does not matter wherever it originates. Wherever the church is, God's commission to take the gospel to all nations remains an imperative. What makes the concept of reverse mission more questionable is the fact that though migration has largely provided the opportunity for this kind of effort, the mission done is not like what the early missionaries did for example when they came to Africa. Many Africans who migrate to the West to start churches mainly reach out to people of their own background and not Westerners who are purportedly in need of the real

---

40. Old, *Reading and Preaching of the Scriptures*, 182.
41. Adamolekun, "Main Trends," 8.

gospel.⁴² Some of the largest churches in Europe are now led by Africans. Examples of preachers in this category are Matthew Ashimolowo and Sunday Adelaja.⁴³

Adelaja does not only represent the reverse mission; he adequately paints the picture of Pentecostal preaching in Africa today. He is the founder and senior pastor of the Embassy of the Blessed Kingdom of God For All Nations Church which is touted to be the largest in Europe with twenty-five thousand members and daughter and satellite churches in over fifty countries worldwide. Adelaja is recognized as a universally gifted teacher of the word of God with an extraordinary operation of the gifts of the Spirit. He has authored almost forty books and has recorded over one thousand sermons. His sermons are more topical than expository in nature. In spite of the impact he has made in Europe and all around the world as a preacher of the word, Adelaja has been criticized, like many of his Pentecostal colleagues, for emphasizing prosperity, and has been outrightly accused of sexual immorality. He has denied all allegations. Presently he is facing trouble in his host country, the Ukraine, and among the evangelical body there. Ashimolowo's story is also similar. Very gifted, though more of a motivational speaker, he is also under investigation by the British government for financial impropriety.⁴⁴

Protestant Africa between 1920 and 1960

Bengt Sundkler and Christopher Steed give insight into some of the homiletical activities that took place in Protestant Africa between 1920 and 1960, which is a large portion of Adamolekun's periods highlighted above. They classified their discussion into what characterizes the village homily, the seminary trained pastor, and revival messages.

The village homily or sermon is characterized by the preacher's weekly choice of text, either in line with a lectionary or from personal freedom of choice. The preacher is more concerned with the text verse by verse and not in paragraphs. The "Ovambo sermon" in Namibia may just choose the first verse

---

42. Harvey C. Kwiyani, *Sent Forth: African Missionary Work in the West* (Maryknoll, NY: Orbis, 2014), Kindle edition.

43. Killingray, "Passing on the Gospel," 97.

44. "Will Europe's Third-Largest Church Punish Pastor for Multiple Affairs?" christianitytoday.com/news/2016/may/will-embassy-of-god-punish-sunday-adelaja-multiple-affairs.html, accessed on 22 February 2021; "KICC, Ashimolowo's church under alleged fraud investigation," https://www.vanguardngr.com/2017/02/kicc-ashimolowos-church-alleged-fraud-investigation/, accessed on 22 February 2021.

or first few verses of the text and neglect the content of the text as a whole. Local proverbs are brought in to connect with the congregation as they help complete the proverb when the preacher begins it.[45] It is common for the elders to come and discuss the sermon with the preacher after the service. Moralistic preaching that attacks drinking, dance, and polygamy but veils out much of the gospel message is well tolerated.

Moralistic preaching is defined as drawing morals from a biblical text even when the author of the text does not intend such meaning. When preaching from genres including the Decalogue, proverbs, and prophets, or such passages as the Sermon on the Mount and other teachings of Jesus on right behavior and Paul's moral exhortation in his letters, it is proper to naturally follow the text movement. But moralizing occurs when the biblical author does not intend to teach morals, but the preacher still seeks to draw a moral from the text.

Moralizing remains a critical part of African preaching today, perhaps because community culture seeks to rebuke misconduct. And moralizing seems to be the immediate goal of many preachers as soon as they get to the text or the pulpit. Preaching involves drawing lessons for application, correcting, rebuking, and encouraging (2 Tim 4:2), but each and all must be done in faithfulness to the text. The danger of moralistic preaching is that

> it distorts the message of the text, it weighs down the congregation with tiresome dos and don'ts, and it conceals the gospel. Preachers would serve their congregations better if they would inquire first about the Bible's good news that, "in Christ God was reconciling the world to himself" (2 Cor 5:19), and next about the text's original relevance: What was the author's message (theme), and why did the author write this at that time (goal)? This lays the biblical foundation for preaching relevantly to the church today.[46]

Village sermons are also characterized by rhetorical interrogations like "Am I wrong here?" or "Do I tell a lie now?" and an empathic positive response from the congregation. In the words of Sundkler and Steed, "In that milieu the sermon was never just an isolated solo performance but a giving, receiving and responding in an electrifying fellowship where those concerned, preacher and listener, were bound together by an overwhelming experience of challenge and renewal." It is indeed an opportunity to bring the power of the gospel to save,

---

45. Sundkler and Steed, *History of the Church in Africa*, 666.

46. Sidney Greidanus, "Moralism," in *The New Interpreters Handbook of Preaching*, ed. Paul Scott Wilson (Nashville: Abingdon, 2008), 127–28.

heal, and deliver to bear on the African village. This type of sermon represents the exploits of the first generation of preachers in the continent who had limited training but were "carried by the enchantment of a new discovery of the Word and its transforming power."[47]

The seminary-trained pastors in the mainline churches started as teachers in mission schools and transferred their pedagogical skills into their preaching. Indeed, their continuous sermon preparation week by week for decades became their personal contribution to what is now known as African theology. The form of their sermon is the combination of a theme, two or three points developed from the text, and a final appeal. The content is a "typological parallel between the Gospel message and the Old Testament with its People of God." But this homiletical form is an encumbrance, a kind of imprisonment as a Tanzanian theological student who later became a bishop regarded it. Yet these sermons are delivered with "characteristic African eloquence, fluency and conviction."[48]

From the twentieth century began the introduction of preaching aids and "model sermons" as seen among the Luba Presbyterians in southern Kasai. The model sermon was preached by a missionary and later one of the ordained African pastors. This sermon was supposed to be faithfully reproduced the following Sunday by over fifty catechists in a hundred chapels. More prepared homiletic materials surfaced by the middle of the twentieth century in South Africa, Zambia, and Ghana, and these simply encouraged some laziness in the gospel preachers who would not even care to prepare one new sermon in a month.[49] This practice has continued in modern times in some Pentecostal churches. In Nigeria, the most popular practice of this tradition is in the Deeper Life Bible Church. I have learned from observation and personal interaction with some of the pastors and members that on several occasions the sermons preached on Sundays and the Bible studies administered during the week are direct replicas of what the general overseer prepared. With the arrival of satellite communication, his messages, especially during their annual Christmas and Easter retreats, are now simply aired via satellite to all the congregations across the nation. While some members enjoy this tradition and feel a sense of connection with the powerful overseer, some see it as lacking in appropriate contextualization, stifling the personal growth of the local pastors, and showing some signs of imperialism by the leadership of the church.

---

47. Sundkler and Steed, *History of the Church in Africa*, 666.
48. Sundkler and Steed, 668.
49. Sundkler and Steed, 669.

The last part of Sundkler and Steed's discussion is on revivals in various regions of Africa. Notable is that of southern Cameroun in 1937 and East Africa in the 1920s.[50] These revivals created their own kinds of sermons, especially the personal "testimony" of a revivalist, or any other person chosen to speak, emphasizing sin and victory over sin. Testimony preaching has become a common phenomenon in Africa and is a component of orality in the continent. Many who were former Muslims, idol worshippers, or notorious criminals have been converted and move around sharing their testimony. Many people gather to hear such testimonies, and they can be great tools in the conversion of souls. However some limitations to this method of witnessing are that some of these "testimony preachers" are not grounded in God's word, nor are they discipled or receive ministry training before they are invited to mount pulpits. Some survive the ministry, but many leave after they have nothing more to say than their testimony.[51]

Theologically trained pastors who were influenced by this movement used this approach for several decades, and it worked in two ways. First, they received enthusiastic responses from the people they ministered to, and they received international invitations from churches in the West and Asia. Among such preachers were William Nagenda of Buganda (1912–1973), Bishop Festo Kivengere (1919–1988) of southern Buganda, and Zulu revivalists like Nicholas Bengu (1909–1985) of South Africa and Job Chiliza (1886–1962).[52] Old gives some light on Festo Kivengere's life. He was a great evangelist in Uganda who succeeded Janani Luwum (1922–1977) who was martyred in the days of Idi Amin. There is a record of a sermon Kivengere preached at the Intervarsity conference in Urbana in 1961 which showed him as someone who typically and vividly contextualized Bible stories as a basis for an evangelistic appeal. As good as the sermon was, the outline demonstrated structural defects including a lack of congruence between the text and sermon and the use of multiple passages. It was not too expository in nature.[53] Stephen Olford also acknowledges Kivengere as "one of the best-known products" of a spiritual movement that is the "longest and most remarkable of any spiritual awakening" on the African continent.[54]

---

50. Sundkler and Steed, 671.

51. Ezekiel Adewale Ajibade, *Common Pulpit Errors and Solutions* (Ibadan: Baptist Press Nigeria, 2016), 41–43.

52. Sundkler and Steed, 671.

53. Old, *Reading and Preaching of the Scriptures*, 200–202.

54. Stephen Olford, *Heart Cry for Revival* (Ross-shire, Scotland: Christian Focus, 2005), 152.

Nicholas Bhengu was discipled by evangelist Job Chiliza. Ministering under the auspices of the Full Gospel Church, Bhengu's preaching was described as thunderous. He preached with all his heart and pleaded with the sinner to respond to the gospel message. Blacks and whites listened to him as he travelled from one town to another pitching tents and preaching for at least one hour. People came in their thousands to hear Bhengu preach, for spiritual enlightening, and for healing and deliverance. After his sermons, people returned stolen goods, and thieves handed over their knives, guns, and other weapons. Wherever he preached, the rate of crime and violence reduced.[55]

These preachers had a tendency to load their sermons with several Bible quotations which gave an impression of their Bible knowledge. But the revival produced a massive and lasting turning of men and women to the kingdom, which is evidenced by the return of over 79 percent of converts the following year for more Bible study and instruction.[56]

Contemporary and Future Preaching

The work of Ronald J. Allen becomes very relevant at this point as a connector between the contents and form of sermons discussed so far, what came up later, and what is likely to be the future of preaching in Africa. In June 1990, Allen visited the Mindolo Ecumenical Foundation in Kitwe, Zambia, for a research leave. In two months, he had the opportunity to listen to forty-eight sermons in chapels, Sunday worship services, and other meetings. He was also able to look through books of sermon outlines used in some churches and prepared by Africans.[57] Allen's audience was fairly representative – made up of preachers from all the English-speaking corners of the continent, men and women, from small and large congregations, fresh and long-ordained, clergy and laity, serving in such churches as Anglican, Roman Catholic, various Reformed, Methodists, Baptists, Pentecostals, Assemblies of God, and Salvation Army. Only independent African churches were missing in this sample.[58]

Allen observed that all of the sermons were based on a biblical text, and they followed a form where the preacher first gave an exposition of the text and then applied the lesson from the exposition to the hearers, employing a

---

55. ThabisoAflame, "Africa God's General series: Nicholas Bhengu – The African Apostle," ThabisoAflame Blog (6 November 2010).
56. ThabisoAflame, "Africa God's General series."
57. Ronald J. Allen, "African Christianity: A Soft Report," *Homiletic* 16, no. 1 (1991): 5.
58. Allen, "African Christianity," 6.

few illustrations and stories. Something that struck Allen was the character of moral exhortations in the sermons – a stress on listeners behaving in certain prescribed ways. This "imperative mode of preaching" which was a style these preachers professed to have learned from their missionary tutors appeared to be the standard for many African preachers, but Allen opines that it is not the best for an African church that is now filled with second- and third-generation Christians. In his words,

> If this is a representative sample, there is cause for concern in Africa. At the simplest level, moralism is the death of the church. To be sure, the Gospel does contain moral elements. For the Gospel is the dipolar news that God unconditionally loves each and all, and that God calls for justice for each and all. But the imperative preacher loses sight of the pole of Gospel promise and concentrates almost exclusively on the pole of Gospel demand. This leaves hearers with the impression that the dominant role of religion is to regulate moral activity. The step is very short from moralism to works-righteousness. Those under the influence of it think that they must exhibit proper moral behavior in order to be worthy of God's love.[59]

Allen warns that this kind of preaching is one of the reasons for the exodus of many from American churches in the past decades, and he hopes that Africa, which is experiencing an overflow, will not go the way of America. The function of religion is beyond moralism; people seek an interpretation of the meaning of life. Identifying Christianity with their African roots is another yearning of the people, and from insights gained from the rise of African Independent churches, Africans desire to develop "patterns of Christian faith and life which integrate Christianity and the traditional African religious heritage."[60]

Allen concludes that with the current success of the definition of the Africanization of Christian theology, African preaching should begin to take a contextualized nature which will impact the form of sermons. His reason for this is that

> African religious life contains practically no propositional exposition similar to Euro-American style systematic theology. Instead, the world view, beliefs, and moral expectations of native African religion are expressed in myth, story, song, and drama. I

---

59. Allen, 7.
60. Allen, 8.

am told that education in the villages even today makes extensive use of stories which help the learners relate the myth and morality of the community to the everyday world of the village. Critical interpretation of Christianity and traditional African religion will likely mean a more narrative approach to preaching than is typical of the sermons we heard.[61]

Allen's position, therefore, is that preaching was gratefully handed over by the missionaries to African preachers, and they have tried to be faithful to it because according to them, "we were taught to preach this way at theological college."[62] But Christianity in Africa has gone beyond leaning on what the missionaries taught. If preaching will make the impact it ought to in the present and future generations of Christians in the continent, the shape and form of sermons must effectively communicate through the culture of the people to transform their lives. The languages of myths, stories, song, and drama that they understand must be used to communicate the gospel with them.

Aylward Shorter also made a survey of contemporary preaching in Africa in Reformation churches, Catholic churches, churches with Orthodox traditions, and African Independent churches. He discovered that African preaching possesses many common characteristics, and its important theological works are deducible from "the living voice of sermons and in the act of preaching itself."[63] He notes the following characteristics, some of which are a confirmation of the observations of Bengt Sundkler and Ronald J. Allen.

First, African preaching in contemporary times is characterized by a hermeneutical method that fixes a typological function to biblical events and traditions and reinterprets them in a way that meets contemporary needs. Symbolic and allegoric explanation is placed above historicity because according to Shorter, African thinking is traditionally mythical.[64] This opinion may be typical of Africa, but Shorter's apparent approval of typological function and allegorical explanation as a hermeneutical method favored by the New Testament may not be absolutely acceptable. Also, such a method would not be a strong contribution to the best relationship that hermeneutics and homiletics should possess if Africans long to know the truth, apply it, defend it, and preserve it for future generations.

---

61. Allen, 8.
62. Allen, 8.
63. Shorter, "Homiletics and Preaching in Africa," 229.
64. Shorter, 229.

The second characteristic mentioned before is the use of folktales, proverbs, and other materials from oral tradition and rural life to illustrate and illuminate biblical truths in a sermon.[65] The third is the use of events in politics, current affairs, and technology in the sermon. These elements should be employed to form a nexus between the biblical story and the modern community. The fourth characteristic is the introduction of monologic preaching, though Shorter quickly observes it is far from the way African congregations want to see preaching done. As earlier observed by Allen, this attitude may be more predominant among mainline congregations. But Shorter states that the ideal African preacher

> uses direct address to hearers, so that they become participants in the sermon and actors in the biblical story. Congregational participation is achieved in a variety of ways, sometimes through poetry, sometimes through a direct invitation to the congregation to answer a question or complete a phrase, and sometimes through the singing of hymns during the sermon.[66]

Preaching in African Independent churches and Pentecostal gatherings gives more room to this characteristic celebration and communal involvement. Lasting for several hours, these sermons can involve the preacher running up and down between the lines of worshippers, shouting as a sign of forceful preaching in the power of the Holy Spirit, and intermittent singing, dancing, ecstatic experiences, prophecies, and communal prayers. They can also involve pastoral conversations between sermons and liturgical acts, prophetic messages, and faith healings.[67]

For African Independent churches and sometimes African Pentecostal churches to represent the face of African preaching as has been touted by several authors, some characteristics of their preaching should be retained. But many more should be discarded. On the positive side, Tiwatola Abidemi Falaye observes that African Independent churches have championed the cause of preaching the total gospel to the total African person in ways it was not presented or taught by the white missionaries who proclaimed some biblical truth but left out such things as "faith healing, loud prayer and others." By loud prayer she means corporate prayers where a spiritual leader dictates what to

---

65. Shorter, 230.
66. Shorter, 230.
67. Shorter, 230–31.

pray about and everyone raises their voice in supplication. This prayer is a part of normal African worship.[68]

Kasomo Daniel also corroborates Shorter's description of preaching in a typical African Independent church stating that,

> Proclamation is lived, danced, acted out with constant interaction between the Bible reader, preacher and congregational response.... Sermons are interspersed with prophecy, confessions, testimonies to joy or grief, laying on of the hands, faith healing and exorcism. Thus the need of the individuals is shared and carried by the church. Demons are addressed, cursed and expelled by means of numerous symbolic acts. If something is funny, people laugh without in any way marring the seriousness of the matter.[69]

The problem with the African Independent churches, however contextualized their worship and ultimately their preaching are, is their hermeneutics. A sound hermeneutic produces a sound theology and in turn informs a sound homiletic. Many of these congregations hold a high view of the Old Testament and its rituals and sacrifices, but they neglect the completed work of Christ. While they still syncretize with some African traditional practices that tend toward magic and charms, image, and human veneration, they will not be able to model the kind of sound doctrine in which Paul instructed Timothy (see 1 Tim 6:3–5).[70]

As for the Pentecostals, Enyinnaya succinctly observes that "Pentecostal hermeneutics due to its literal approach tends to make normative what was simply intended to be descriptive. Lack of familiarity with important hermeneutical principles makes Pentecostal hermeneutics weak and flawed."[71]

The fifth characteristic that Shorter mentions and that has a close affinity with those mentioned above is the use of choric story form, using African folktales and etiological stories "in which the audience is made to participate in the telling of the story and by singing a refrain at specified intervals." The sermon may be formed as a choric story using themes from oral literature

---

68. Tiwatola Abidemi Falaye, "The Relevance of African Independent Churches to the Yoruba of South Western Part of Nigeria," *Journal of Philosophy, Culture and Religion* 13 (2015): 10.

69. Kasomo Daniel, "An Assessment of the Connectedness of Mainstream and Independent Churches in Africa," *International Journal of Applied Sociology* 2, no. 2 (2012): 6–7.

70. Emiola Nihinlola and Mojisola Olaniyan, eds., *Discovering the Other Side: Challenges of Other Religions* (Ibadan: Flourish Books, 2008).

71. John O. Enyinnaya, "Pentecostal Hermeneutics and Preaching: An Appraisal," *Ogbomoso Journal of Theology* 13, no. 1 (2008): 148.

and "amplifying them in light of biblical teaching and Christian doctrine."[72] Shorter's last characteristic is reading the Bible in a dramatized form, acting out Bible stories with a rich use of humor and local flavor. The sermon may even be a commentary on the drama.[73]

Shorter concludes that "Preaching in Africa is popular and can be said to possess considerable entertainment value. . . . It remains to be seen whether preaching can withstand competition from the increasing influence of the mass electronic media in the growing towns and cities of Africa."[74] There is an element of truth in his closing assertion, but this is where the task of fairly balancing biblical preaching with culture will have to be done. While there is the need to contextualize using several oral elements present in African culture, preaching cannot afford to go the way of mere entertainment. Recognizing this issue is the only way that Shorter's fear for the survival of African Christianity in the face of competition with mass electronic media will be allayed.

Africans have the Bible and a basis for good exposition, but they also have a heritage of orality as their medium of communication and assimilation. The task ahead is discovering how to effectively blend these oral elements into sound teaching and preaching of God's word so that Africans remain African but also richly biblical in their Christianity. Therefore the next chapter will take a more detailed look at the concept of orality.

Discussion Questions

1. Why is Africa not often well reflected in the history of Christian preaching, and how can this be avoided for future generations?
2. How much do you agree with Aylward Shorter's characterization of African preaching and how much of these characteristics are reflected in the preaching done in your environment?
3. Would you consider that preaching in Africa needs to break away from the forms the missionaries handed over to us and an indigenous form be developed, yet without compromising the sanctity of Scripture? How can this be pursued?

---

72. Shorter, "Homiletics and Preaching in Africa," 230.
73. Shorter, 231.
74. Shorter, 231.

4

Orality and Gospel Communication

In this chapter we will examine orality as a phenomenon in communication in an attempt to establish that Africans are predominantly oral in their nature and culture and that they enjoy communication best in an oral atmosphere. This examination will encompass gospel communication which includes preaching and its relationship with orality, along with some of the strong criticisms that have been levelled against the orality movement despite its fast-moving influence and acceptance around the world and the results it is yielding. Implications will then be drawn for expository preaching in Africa based on the conclusion that literacy and orality are not mutually exclusive, and that a preaching method that appreciates the oral nature of Africa but does not jettison the literate components of the society can be developed and used to further the ministry of the word.

Orality as a Communication Phenomenon

A common definition of orality is "the thought and verbal expression in societies where the technologies of literacy (especially writing and print) are unfamiliar to most of the population."[1] Orality characterizes a society that relies on spoken communication rather than written. Speech communication preceded the invention of writing, and under normal circumstances, human

---

1. Bauta D. Motty, "Contextualizing Theological Education in Africa: A Case of ECWA Theological Seminary, Jos, Nigeria (JETS)," in *Beyond Literate Western Model: Contextualizing Theological Education in Oral Contexts*, ed. Samuel E. Chiang and Grant Lovejoy (Hong Kong: International Orality Network, 2013), 153.

beings raised in a community of others are first exposed to and grow up to communicate by speech before they learn reading and writing, if they do at all.[2]

Walter Ong, a celebrated scholar in the field of orality, has classified oral cultures into primary, residual, and secondary.[3] Primary orality refers to cultures which have not been touched by any knowledge of writing.[4] It is difficult to find such cultures today because most of the world's people-groups are exposed to the existence and technology of reading and writing, even when they cannot read or write.[5] Residual orality describes people who know how to read and write but do not utilize their reading skills after leaving school, and they may not derive pleasure from reading.[6] Secondary orality relates to those "sustained by telephone, radio, television, and other electronic devices that depend for their existence and functioning on writing and print."[7] This group of contemporary learners is also referred to as "digitorial" because while they access information through digital means, they are actually exhibiting the traits of oral learners.[8] An understanding of where people fit in these three categories is important for effectively communicating with them. Ultimately as Lovejoy avers, few people are purely oral or purely literate. Most people are a combination of both.[9]

However orality is not so easily defined, especially given the several dimensions of meaning it has acquired over the years. This term has been claimed at the linguistic level by Bible translators and used as "Bible storying" which targets non-literate people. Business ventures and non-government

---

2. Grant Lovejoy, "That All May Hear," Lausanne Content Library, Lausanne Movement (3 June 2010).

3. Walter J. Ong was a Jesuit priest and scholar of language and its evolution as a means of communication. He taught and wrote at the Jesuit institution St. Louis University. In describing his work, Wolfgang Saxon wrote that "He studied communication in its various forms, from oral traditions to print culture, from manuscripts to cyberspace. Father Ong wove his theological, psychological and philosophical insights to show the contrasts he saw between orality and literacy. He was considered an outstanding postmodern theorist, whose ideas spawned college courses and were used to analyze anything from the Rev. Dr. Martin Luther King Jr.'s soaring oratory to subway graffiti." Ong's most celebrated work remains *Orality and Literacy: The Technologizing of the Word* (London; New York: Routledge, 1983). See Wolfgang Saxon, "Walter J. Ong, 90, Jesuit, Teacher and Scholar of Language," *New York Times* (25 August 2003).

4. Ong, *Orality and Literacy*, 10.

5. Ong, 11.

6. Lovejoy, "That All May Hear," 2.

7. Ong, *Orality and Literacy*, 10–11.

8. W. Jay Moon, "I Love to Learn but I Don't Like to Read: The Rise of Secondary Oral Learning," *Orality Journal* 2, no. 2 (2013): 55.

9. Grant Lovejoy, "But I Did Such a Good Exposition": Literate Preachers Confront Orality, IMB (accessed 6 November 2016).

organizations (NGOs) use the term orality for media, and Sigmund Freud used it to classify in his theories of psychosexual development behaviors.[10] These various uses are why Charles Madinger defines orality as "a complex of how oral cultures receive, remember and replicate (pass on) news, important information and truths."[11] Orality is a complex because it is a composition of complicated but unrelated parts, and because it can be used in multiple applications, it can be a model in various situations. Therefore, no single discipline can lay claim to a particular definition of orality.[12]

For example, storytelling, or storying, cannot be a synonym for orality as many who are involved in orality have assumed. Storytelling is only an application of orality principles. According to Charles Madinger,

> storytelling or "storying" uses the principles of orality but is more precisely an application of its principles. Thus, orality is not equivalent to storytelling. Saying it is equivalent is like a coffee lover defining the culinary arts as making a good cup of coffee. The coffee results from successful application of culinary arts but is not exhaustive of those arts. In the same way, storying is a product of orality. To use a more comprehensive description, orality consists of the principles and processes that make many products real to those receiving them.[13]

However, storytelling is a large segment of oral communication today. Harriet Hill states that

> while orality is not limited to story-telling, and story-telling isn't limited to orality, they go together well, and are especially memorable when song, dance, and drama are included. Familiar stories with unfamiliar, Kingdom-of-God endings grab our attention. We find ourselves in the story and are challenged. We repeat the story and it becomes one of our stories. Everyone loves a story—even people who are able to read.[14]

---

10. Charles Madinger, "Coming to Terms with Orality: A Holistic Model," *Missiology: An International Review* 38, no. 2 (April 2010): 201.
11. Madinger, "Coming to Terms with Orality," 204.
12. Madinger, 204.
13. Madinger, 204.
14. Harriet Hill, "Conversations about Orality," *Missiology: An International Review* 38, no. 2 (April 2010): 216.

To avoid conflating orality with storytelling, Madinger suggests a holistic or comprehensive model of orality which employs seven converging disciplines, and he asks essential questions preceding, in the core of, and after any attempt to deliver news, information, or training in oral societies. These seven disciplines are culture, language, literacy, social networks, memory, the arts, and the media. Madinger claims that "any message to oral cultures can multiply the probability of transformation when enhanced by a communication strategy built on a holistic model of orality" and that these disciplines are part of God's natural design.[15]

In another work, Madinger argues that according to Ong's definition, orality can only be regarded as primary. In that sense, orality is "the use of the spoken word to formulate, send, receive, and understand message."[16] In another sense and at a deeper level, orality is a "significant learned framework for interpreting the world around us."[17] While the first sense considers the external perception of people in oral cultures and garners the tools to communicate with them, the second delves into their worldview. In determining the boundaries of orality, a syllogistic test like the following can be considered:

1. A country or culture of origin determines the framework for understanding the world.
2. Orality is a significant factor in the framework of how people understand the world.
3. Orality is a function of one's country or culture of origin.[18]

The implication of this syllogism is that "if the framework of orality is established through context produced by one's culture of origin, all other possibilities of holding an orality preference must be related in some way to that culture of origin."[19]

There is a developmental explanation for this process. If people's life and growth are rooted in orality, this orality affects how they think, and it builds a framework through which they process information and "order the world"

---

15. Madinger, "Coming to Terms with Orality," 205–11.
16. Charles Madinger, "Will Our Message 'Stick'?: Assessing a Dominant Preference for Orality for Education and Training," in *Beyond Literate Western Contexts: Honor and Shame and Assessment of Orality Preference*, ed. Samuel E. Chiang and Grant Lovejoy (Hong Kong: International Orality Network, 2015), 127.
17. Madinger, "Will Our Message 'Stick'?" 127.
18. Madinger, 127.
19. Madinger, 127.

with the help of those around them as they grow in language learning. For example, a mother who tells her child stories (without the use of books) and sings songs provides a framework through which the child will interact with the world both intellectually and socially. The child can learn new skills, and a new frame of reference like textuality can be added to their life, but the child's basic framework into which other frameworks must be fixed is that of orality.[20] This explains why orality is entrenched in cultures and why it becomes an almost permanent feature of communities which develop in an orality context, notwithstanding their level of exposure to literacy. Certain characteristics of oral cultures affect the way people learn and communicate. The following characteristics are typical.

Use of Mnemonics and Formulas

Since primary oral cultures have no texts, they have to package complex ideas in memorable ways so they can easily retain and retrieve them. Therefore, thoughts are packaged in "heavily rhythmic, balanced patterns, in repetitions or antitheses, in alliterations and assonances, in epithetic and other formulary expressions, in standard thematic settings . . . in proverbs which are constantly heard by everyone so that they come to mind readily."[21] Mnemonic patterns help people shape their words for less stressful oral repetition. In a teaching-learning process, mental pictures in stories, dramatic enactment, and songs help people in primary oral cultures gain deeper meaning and remember lessons for future use.[22]

The Speaker's Convenience

Oral structures give great consideration to pragmatics, that is, the speaker's convenience rather than syntax as in written discourses. A typical example is the Douay version of Genesis 1:1–5 which uses the conjunction "and" nine times because the version was produced in a predominantly residual oral culture and was translated close to the original Hebrew, which largely uses additives rather than subordinate clauses. The Douay version reads,

---

20. Madinger, 127–28.
21. Ong, *Orality and Literacy*, 34.
22. W. Jay Moon, "Teaching Oral Learners in Institutional Settings," in *Beyond Literate Western Contexts: Contextualizing Theological Education in Oral Contexts*, ed. Samuel E. Chiang and Grant Lovejoy (Hong Kong: International Orality Network, 2013), 150.

> In the beginning God created heaven and earth. And the earth was void and empty, and darkness was upon the face of the deep; and the spirit of God moved over the waters. And God said: Be light made. And light was made. And God saw the light that it was good; and he divided the light from the darkness. And he called the light Day, and the darkness Night; and there was evening and morning one day.[23]

Ong compares the Douay Version with the New American version which translates the Hebrew "ands" as "and," "when," "then," "thus," and "while" for narrative flow and to reflect the analytic, reasoned subordination which is a characteristic of writing and print orientation.[24]

Holistic in View and Expression

Since they rely on mnemonics and formulas to put memory to use, oral thoughts and expressions employ pithy phrases and prefer epithets rather than clusters of integers. They speak of the "brave soldier" rather than "the soldier," the "beautiful princess" rather than the "princess," or the "sturdy oak tree" rather than the "oak tree."[25] The reason adduced is that pithy statements are products of hard work over several generations and must not be dismantled because they are received wisdom. Oral cultures do not savor analysis and breaking up thoughts, which is considered "high risk procedure."[26] Print cultures prefer to analyze, dissect, and compartmentalize abstract principles, but oral cultures view matters from the context as a whole and with everyone involved. They prefer to navigate from the whole to the parts.[27]

Repetition of Word and Statements

Words require some kind of continuity, or repetition of what has just been said, in order to keep the speaker and the hearers on track. For example, some of the hearers may not understand every word of a speaker says due to acoustical problems, but as the speaker restates the words in the same or similar ways, they get what they missed. Another reason for redundancy is the need for the

---

23. Ong, *Orality and Literacy*, 36.
24. Ong, 36–37.
25. Ong, 38.
26. Ong, 39.
27. Moon, "Teaching Oral Learners," 149.

speaker to keep speaking while processing what next to say. Stopping in the middle of the speech is not a creative alternative.[28]

Conservative and Traditional

Oral societies are saddled with the responsibility of painstakingly repeating again and again the conceptualized knowledge that has been handed down to them through the ages if they will not be lost. Since this knowledge is not written, people need to dutifully adhere to preserving it. But according to Ong, a problem with this traditionalism and conservatism is that, though with good reasons, they inhibit intellectual experimentation. According to him, "knowledge is precious and hard to come by, and society regards highly those wise old men and women who specialize in conserving it, who know and can tell the stories of the days of old."[29]

While the problem of conservativism is true to a certain extent, recent research by scholars of African philosophy, emanating from predominantly oral cultures, have determined that the idea of conservatism is not an absolute assessment. For example in H. Odera Oruka's *Sage Philosophy*, he is able from his research to distinguish between popular wisdom and didactic wisdom. Popular wisdom has to do with well known "communal maxims, aphorisms and general common sense truths," and didactic wisdom has to do with "an expounded wisdom and deeply rational thought emanating from certain individuals in the community." According to Oruka, "while the popular wisdom is often conformist, the didactic wisdom is at times critical of the communal set-up and the popular wisdom." The sages he interviewed in Kenya demonstrated these two dimensions of wisdom.[30]

But Ong is quick to point out that the tendencies toward traditionalism and conservativism do not mean that oral cultures do not have their own kind of originality. In fact, they demonstrate originality when they tell the same old story in a unique way to fit a unique situation or generate audience response. Myths have several minor variants, and the praise poems of chiefs have formulas that can "interact with new and complicated political situations."

---

28. Ong, *Orality and Literacy*, 39.

29. Ong, 41.

30. H. Odera Oruka, *Sage Philosophy: Indigenous Thinkers and Modern Debate on African Philosophy* (Leiden: Brill, 1990), 28.

However, these formulas and themes are reshuffled rather than replaced with new material.[31]

Highly Relational

Oral people build relationships and enjoy interpersonal bonding. They focus on needing others to accomplish tasks and to become more efficient and productive. The feelings and happiness of those around them are key to accomplishing set goals.[32] Ong states that,

> In the absence of elaborate analytic categories that depend on writing to structure knowledge at a distance from lived experience, oral cultures must conceptualize and verbalize all their knowledge with more or less close reference to the human lifeworld, assimilating the alien, objective world to the more immediate, familiar interaction of human beings.[33]

Oral cultures, therefore, deal with human relationships rather than abstract categories. They prefer apprenticeships rather than how-to-do-it manuals. They are not too interested in preserving knowledge of skills "as an abstract, self-subsistent corpus."[34] Dialogue is paramount to their learning system[35] and has produced among them a sense of empathy, participation, and communal identification, action, and reaction.[36]

Combative Language

Oral language can sound to a literate person as "agonistically toned."[37] While writing is abstract and disengages people from direct interpersonal argument and struggles, orality embeds knowledge in life situations and subsists in the context of struggle. Since orality is verbal communication, it involves exchanging the dynamics of sound, interpersonal relationship, and antagonism. For example, proverbs and riddles "are not used simply to store knowledge but to engage others in verbal and intellectual combat: utterance of one proverb

---

31. Ong, *Orality and Literacy*, 41.
32. Motty, "Contextualizing Theological Education in Africa," 155.
33. Ong, *Orality and Literacy*, 42.
34. Ong, 43.
35. Moon, "Teaching Oral Learners," 147.
36. Ong, *Orality and Literacy*, 54.
37. Ong, 43.

or riddle challenges hearers to top it with a more opposite or contradictory one."[38] But this interaction must be placed in context. Proverbs generally are powerful tools in discussion and argument among oral communities. Emilie Towns suggests that proverbs could serve to explain human behavior, serve as a guides for moral conduct, explain social behavior, serve to censure or criticize conduct, give shrewd advice on how to deal with situations, express egalitarian views, and express finer human qualities or emotions such as generosity.[39] Akinmade also observes that proverbs are utilized to advise, rebuke, or praise or as a comment or in persuasion. Proverbs educate, warn, ridicule, console, encourage, resolve conflicts, and even perform legal functions. Ultimately the function of proverbs depends on the context of conversation and cannot be pinned down only to storing knowledge and prosecuting an argument.[40]

Another reason for the agonistic tone of orality is the celebration of physical behavior or violence, which may be the result of the physical hardships many early societies faced or an expression of early art forms. Lavishing praise on one hand and name-calling or vituperation on the other hand are highly characteristic of oral cultures.[41]

Active Words in the Present

Since oral cultures have limited capacity to store information because they do not write, from time to time they discard memories that have lost relevance. Also because they do not store up words in dictionaries, "the oral mind is uninterested in definitions," and "words acquire their meanings only from their always insistent actual habitat, which is not, as in a dictionary, simply other words, but includes also gestures, vocal inflections, facial expression, and the entire human, existential setting in which the real, spoken word always occurs."[42]

---

38. Ong, 43.

39. Emilie Towns quoted in Tex Sample, *Ministry in an Oral Culture – Living with Will Rogers, Uncle Remus, and Minnie Pearl* (Louisville, KY: Westminster John Knox, 1994), 3.

40. Arinola C. Akinmade, "The Decline of Proverbs as a Creative Oral Expression: A Case Study of Proverb Usage among the Ondo in the South Western Part of Nigeria," *AFRREV LALIGENS: An International Journal of Language, Literature and Gender Studies, Bahir Dar, Ethiopia* 1, no. 2 (April-July 2012): 131. See also W. Jay Moon. "African Proverbs: Stepping Stones within Oral Cultures" (accessed 10 October 2016).

41. Ong, *Orality and Literacy*, 45.

42. Ong, 48.

The concept of capacity to store information is not only a relative statement but one that needs to be further researched. John William Johnson in his work on oral poetry in Somalia discovered that the capacity to compose and recite whatever length of poems has nothing to do with literacy or orality. In his own words, "I have regularly been introduced to elders who recite poetry for me and who were described as completely unknowledgeable in any writing system. Their abilities at composition and recitation did not differ to any noticeable degree from other elders who were described as fully literate. Indeed the skills of both groups were the same after the literacy campaign as they had always been before it."[43] So in oral societies, information is supplied for the interest of the present members rather than being unnecessarily curious about the past.

Avoiding Abstraction

The speaker places more emphasis on objects and situations known directly than on abstract concepts. A. R. Luria compares oral and literate subjects in Uzbekistan and Kirghizia and concludes that an orally based thought is "prelogical" and "magical in the sense that it was based on belief systems rather than on practical actuality."[44] Godwin S. Sogolo strongly argues that such categorizations as prelogical, alogical, and antilogical are products of evolutionary thoughts that place almost everything within an evolutionary hierarchy. Identifying these categorizations with the writings of Levy-Bruhl, Sogolo also suggests that they might have been a product of doubt as to how a people supposedly devoid of reason have survived for such a long time. His conclusion is that traditional thought systems are socially acquired and not biologically or psychologically imposed.[45] Ong also adds that it is wrong to assume that oral people are essentially unintelligent or that their mental processes are crude. It is also wrong to assume that their thoughts are "prelogical" or illogical or to think they do not understand such things as causal relationship. He affirms that

> they know very well that if you push hard on a mobile object, the push causes it to move. What is true is that they cannot organize elaborate concatenations of causes in the analytic kind of linear

---

43. John William Johnson, "Orality, Literacy, and Somali Oral Poetry," *Journal of African Cultural Studies* 18, no. 1 (June 2006): 129.

44. A. R. Luria quoted in Ong, "*Orality and Literacy,*" 49.

45. Godwin W. Sogolo, "Logic and Rationality," in *The African Philosophy Reader*, ed. Coetzee and A. P. J. Roux (London: Routledge, 1998), 218–19.

sequences which can only be set up with the help of texts. The lengthy sequences they produce, such as genealogies, are not analytic but aggregative. But oral cultures can produce amazingly complex and intelligent and beautiful organizations of thought and experience.[46]

Luria's experiments have shown first that oral subjects identified geometrical figures by assigning names to them and never abstractly as circles or squares or any other shape. Second, they thought of a group of objects in terms of the practical situation rather than categorically. When asked to select three similar words from the group hammer, saw, log, and hatchet, they rejected the literate option of removing the log to produce a list of three tools because there is no use of these tools without the log. Logic is not their way of thinking, and illiterate people do not operate with formal deductive procedures.[47] This does not mean they cannot think "or that their thinking was not governed by logic, but only that they would not fit their thinking into pure logical forms, which they seem to have found uninteresting."[48]

By Sogolo's submission, no mind is "intellectually malstructured" such that it cannot reason based on universal principles. He affirms that the African mind has no structural differences from that of a Westerner. According to Sogolo, "the difference lies in the ways the two societies conceive of reality and explain object and events. This is so because they live different forms of life. And it is for this reason alone that an intelligible analysis of African thought demands the application of its own universe of discourse, its own logic, and its own criteria of rationality."[49] This task is largely undone and demands urgent attention. Many oral societies are among the poorest and most underdeveloped in the world. If there are working tools such as Sogolo envisioned that can uncover the complexities of the social systems that confront these societies and can liberate them into economic, infrastructural, and technological breakthroughs, the earlier they are discovered, the better.

Third, the oral subjects were not interested in definitions and self-analysis. When asked to evaluate self, they would rather speak of their external situations, and when asked to describe their character, they would want others to assess that, not themselves.[50] These and some of the characteristics above

---

46. Ong, *Orality and Literacy*, 56.
47. Ong, 51.
48. Ong, 51.
49. Sogolo, "Logic and Rationality," 221.
50. Sogolo, 53–54.

have caused some to conclude that oral people are unintelligent, but Ong observes unequivocally that intelligence is not measured by textbook quizzes. It is rather situated in operational contexts.[51]

Orality and Communication in Africa

That Africans live in predominantly oral societies is usually a given fact. Virtually all of the characteristics listed above find representation and expression in Africa. Bauta D. Motty succinctly states, "no matter how educated an African is, he or she is an oral being."[52] He reached this conclusion based on his observation of several book launches where the chief launcher would usually say, "If you keep money in the bank or a safe, someone may steal it. But if you keep money in a book, no one will steal it." This was not just an indictment of those present at such occasions who have a poor reading culture (though this is an African problem), Motty's point is that Africans generally, even when they are the "local intellectuals," are oral, and they love to remain oral.[53]

Grant Lovejoy once discussed the concept of orality with some university students. During a following midweek service in the church, one of the graduate students who was present in the discussion carried out a survey on the oral preferences of about thirty Africans who were university students and graduates. The result showed that they all had a preference for oral communication. Lovejoy opines that this result was not surprising because "African culture is strongly oral. Its oral forms of communication are aesthetically and relationally rewarding."[54] Margaret Doll also observed that even when Africans are educated, they love to hear their language rather than read it, which also brought her to the conclusion that "most African cultures are strongly oral and strongly relational."[55] Some more evidence of the nature of Africans as having oral societies will be enumerated.

---

51. Ong, *Orality and Literacy*, 51.
52. Motty, "Contextualizing Theological Education in Africa," 155.
53. Motty, 153.
54. Lovejoy, "That All May Hear," 3.
55. Margaret Doll, "Literacy and Orality Working Together: The Intersection of Heart and Mind," *Orality Journal* 4, no. 1 (2015): 5.

Evidence from Philosophical and Psychological Presupposition

For understanding orality, Hannes Wiher used an interdisciplinary approach to conscience, worldview, and identity which included models of theology, philosophy, psychology, and cultural anthropology. He posits that worldview is how one sees the world and oneself and how things really are. Worldview is therefore at the core of personality, culture, and religion.[56] Wiher cites Paul Hiebert who defines worldview as the "fundamental cognitive, affective, and evaluative presuppositions a group of people make about the nature of things and which they use to order their lives."[57] Then Wiher outlines two models – the stratigraphic model of creation and the model of the five basic soteriological concepts of God, human beings, sin, evil, and salvation. The stratigraphic model of creation is based on how a worldview organizes the elements of creation, visible and invisible, and the five basic soteriological model builds upon worldviews that evangelism and discipleship must work upon to transform to a biblical one.

These two models represent the cognitive aspects of worldview. A third model Wiher suggests, the model of conscience orientation, concerns the evaluative and affective aspects that represent the "deepest layers of personality, culture, and religion."[58] These are the areas with which orality is particularly linked. As conscience develops from childhood, depending on the context of culture, it produces different conscience orientations. American anthropologist Melford Spiro submits that when children are raised by few educators like only a father and mother, not only do the children integrate the norms they are exposed to, the educators are also ingrained in their conscience. Their lives are built around some set of rules, and they develop rule-centered personalities with such traits as organizing their lives with an agenda, being punctual, and pursuing objectives. They value work more than relationship and tend to become individualistic because their consciences function autonomously. Spiro calls this conscience "guilt-oriented conscience."[59]

However, when children are raised by many educators such as extended family, the norms are integrated into children's conscience but not the educators. The presence of many educators is needed for their conscience to

---

56. Hannes Wiher, "Worldview and Oral Preference Learners and Leaders," in *Beyond Literate Western Contexts: Continuing Conversations in Orality and Theological Education*, ed. Samuel E. Chiang and Grant Lovejoy (Hong Kong: International Orality Network, 2014), 110.

57. Paul G. Hiebert, *Transforming Worldviews: An Anthropological Understanding of How People Change*, 15, 25, cited in Wiher, "Worldview and Oral Preference," 110.

58. Wiher, 110.

59. Melford Spiro, *Children of the Kibbutz*, 408, cited in Wiher, 111.

function properly, and their relational personality is tied to group identity. Interaction becomes more important than work, except if it is team work, and status is more important than achievement and objective. When no one is around, no norm is functional. Having no norms is a basis of corruption because it thrives on the notion that "as long as nobody sees you doing it, you can always do it." But public knowledge of the violation of a norm leads to shame. Spiro calls this "shame-oriented conscience."[60]

Identifying these conscience orientations is very helpful in understanding worldview, but the causal factors go beyond the kind of homes and parents that raised children. Other influences are involved like formal education, peers, religion, and in modern times television and social media. However, Spiro's analyses are fundamental and make it easy to identify the differences between the Western and African worldviews. It is agreed that conscience orientation certainly affects identity and basic values. It also affects communication. While guilt-oriented communication is usually direct and does not need a mediator, shame-oriented communication is the opposite.[61]

Wiher's conclusion is that oral people, cultures, and religions are most likely to be shame oriented. This does not mean they cannot be literate, but their basic values are collectivism, indirect communication, vent orientation, person orientation, status focused, holistic in thinking, and fearful of losing face.[62] This largely describes Africa where the upbringing of children is communal and where, sincerely, many of the traits of shame-oriented conscience are in full manifestation. Africans believe that a family gives birth to a child, but the community raises him or her. The sense of community in most African societies is too palpable to be underestimated. Kunhiyop affirms that "the idea of 'we' and 'us' is entrenched in Africans right from childhood, so that as they grow they know that they belong to and must function within the community in which they are rooted."[63] Even the renowned African bishop Desmond Tutu analyzes the difference between Westerners and Africans. He observes that while Westerners are analytical, Africans are synthetic, and that while Westerners tend to be good scientists, they are not good at putting things back together like Africans. Africans may see the wood but not care to notice the individual trees. Also, Westerners have a tendency to be cerebral

---

60. Spiro, *Children of the Kibbutz*, 408, Wiher, 111.
61. Wiher, 115.
62. Wiher, 115.
63. Samuel Waje Kunhiyop, *African Christian Ethics* (Nairobi: WordAlive, 2008), 20.

while Africans lay more emphasis on feelings. While Westerners emphasize the individual, Africans are communal.[64] Africans are thus highly oral in nature.

Evidence from Empirical Studies

Much research on orality has been conducted on the soils of Africa. Barnes and Carmichael observe the fact that some of the best works on orality and literacy can be found in case studies from Southern and West Africa.[65] A few other works on oral status and nature from some regions of Africa are also worthy of mention. But in an editorial piece, Barnes and Carmichael submit that studying orality and literacy in the Horn of Africa region provides an enriching experience because sub-Saharan Africa's deepest recoverable literate tradition can be found there; it has robust and living oral cultures; and it better presents modern struggles over language and political identity. Even when Ben Knighton attacks the notion that oral cultures are struck in traditional time, Barnes and Carmichael still draw the following inference from his work:

> Indeed, despite the best efforts of the "literate" state, church and NGOs to rescue Karamajong society from perceived backwardness (e.g. very low literacy rates), "tradition" and orality remain strong. In short, rather than weakening Karamajong society as ideologies of literacy may suggest, orality – and especially the oral performance of prayer – contributes to the survival and welfare of Karamajong society. There, as elsewhere around the African continent and the world, the spoken word remains remarkably potent.[66]

These empirical studies provide strong indications that Africans are highly oral people. A similar conclusion is reached by Richard Reid in "War and Remembrance: Orality, Literacy and Conflict in the Horn." He uses the chronicles of the war between Ethiopia and Eritrea to identify the differences between those who connect to the village life which is the "repository of so

---

64. Kunhiyop, *African Christian Ethics*, 119.
65. Cedric Barnes and Tim Carmichael, "Editorial Introduction Language, Power and Society: Orality and Literacy in the Horn of Africa," *Journal of African Cultural Studies* 18, no. 1 (June 2006): 1. However, such work is not limited to Africa. Research has been conducted in several oral societies around the world.
66. Barnes and Carmichael, "Editorial Introduction Language," 6. Also see Ben Knighton, "Orality in the Service of Karomojong Autonomy: Polity and Performance," *Journal of African Cultural Studies* 18, no. 1 (June 2006).

much narrative wisdom" and those on whom globalization has taken its toll.[67] He observes that though Eritrea has an oral culture, there is a dangerous silence there because those who have the real chronicles will not speak, and those outside are not "permitted to enter."[68] In other words, those with the oral tradition have the life story, and when they are impenetrable for whatever reason, real facts are concealed for whatever good purposes they may be needed.

This example does not imply that oral societies are closed societies. Outsiders usually have access to poetry, songs, proverbs, stories, and other media of expression. But it seems that wherever literacy and orality are presented as in conflict or competition with each other, or the custodians of the tradition are jettisoned, those searching for original information will exert more energy than when the people's heritage is celebrated and appreciated.

Again in West Africa, Elisa Fiorio studied among the Tupuri group who occupy some extensive portions of southwestern Chad and northwestern Cameroun. She sees orality as "the vehicle for the transmission of tradition" and "the bearer of the totality of significations specific to an oral culture."[69] On this basis, she describes the narrative prowess of the Tupuris and warns that the chain of orality can be broken when there is a lack of "intergenerational communication." The Tupuris ensure that narration of a story or historical account is regulated or restricted by time, place, and people involved because of the social significance of oral tradition. For example, narration is restricted to March, April, and May corresponding to the very hot and dry seasons, shortly before the rain sets in. No recitation takes place until after sunset and when the evening meal is over. For the rest of the year, no one tells stories again except if they are heard among little children. This rule does not however, apply to historical accounts. Storytelling involves some aptitude to transmit. It was often done around the family fire for the purpose of being close to one's grandfather ancestors and for warmth and learning. The narrative of an account is seen as "willingness to preserve cultural identity as well as a willingness to adapt to changes."[70]

---

67. Richard Reid, "War and Remembrance: Orality, Literacy and Conflict in the Horn," *Journal of African Cultural Studies* 18, no. 1 (2006): 101.

68. Reid, "War and Remembrance," 102.

69. Elisa Fiorio, "Orality and Cultural Identity: The Oral Tradition in Tupuri (Chad)," *Museum International* 58, no. 1-2 (2006): 68.

70. Fiorio, "Orality and Cultural Identity," 74.

This "evolution" to suppress oral tradition, Fiorio states, "affects all oral cultures in African societies like those of the Tupuri where strong external pressures are beginning to undermine the determination of younger generations to preserve their oral tradition and to threaten their historical continuity and awareness of group identity."[71] This statement is not just a celebration of the oral heritage of Africans but an important alarm about the danger of losing an identity that has kept several African communities together for a long time.

Representing a modern form of orality, and from East Africa, James Odhiambo Ogone presented "Remediating Orality: The Cultural Domestication of Video Technology in Kenya."[72] The crux of his submission is that through an adoption process, video technology has become identified with African experiences and is giving more and more opportunities for people to participate in global discourse. Video has become a new means of expressing oral tradition as it is used and known in Africa. By this Ogone is asserting that Africans are oral, and even in the face of modernity, they struggle not to lose their orality. As in the case of Kenya, they would rather use a vernacular film to "remediate the oral traditions of local communities within the new technological medium of video" than lose it.[73]

This attitude may fit into Jonah Sach's classification of secondary oral learners who are termed "digitoral." The craze for home video in the vernacular has become a social phenomenon across Africa. In Nigeria, Nollywood has become the second largest movie industry in the world, raking in as much as $3.3 billion dollars in 2014 alone.[74] It is not the financial gain but the attention given to to these movies and the ways they affect popular culture. One of the best places to see Africa in its original oral form is the re-enactment of their culture in home videos. Nothing could be truer than Sach's word that "the oral tradition that dominated human experience for all but the last few hundred years is returning with vengeance."[75]

---

71. Fiorio, 74.

72. James Odhiambo Ogone, "Remediating Orality: The Cultural Domestication of Video Technology in Kenya," *Critical Arts* 29, no. 4 (2015): 480.

73. Ogone, "Remediating Orality," 480.

74. Jake Bright, "Meet 'Nollywood': The Second Largest Movie Industry in the World," *Fortune* (24 June 2015).

75. Jonah Sachs, *Winning the Story Wars: Why Those Who Tell (and Live) the Best Stories Will Rule the Future* (Boston: Harvard Business Review Press, 2012), 20, quoted in Moon, "African Proverbs," 56.

Evidence from Literacy Statistics

Literacy statistics also reveal the orality of Africa. Recent UNESCO statistics reveal that 38 percent of African adults totaling some 153 million are illiterate. Two thirds of this population are women. The report further reveals that the only continent in the world where more than half of the parents are so illiterate that they cannot help their children with their homework is Africa.[76] Further statistics from The African Library Project reveal that more than 1 in 3 adults cannot read, 48 million youth aged 15–24 are illiterate, 22 percent of primary aged children, about 30 million, are not in school.[77]

Yet literacy statistics all around the world have faults and are often underestimated for definitional, functional, and political reasons. Based on his research and assessment of the variables that determine the real statistics on literacy around the world, Lovejoy concludes that "5.7 billion people in the world are oral communicators because either they are illiterate or their reading comprehension is inadequate."[78] This number means that over 80 percent of the adults, teenagers, and children in the world have "low enough reading comprehension that they are highly likely to be oral communicators."[79] While statistics for Africa indicate 38 percent illiteracy among adults, other evidence shows that the 62 percent which may be literate are either in the categories of residual or secondary orality.[80]

Evidence from Diaspora

There is some evidence that African orality spans beyond the continent. Adetayo Alabi, in a study of Isidore Okpewho's *Call Me by My Rightful Name*, explores the power of epigraph, African drums, and panegyric poems as they were experienced by Otis Hampton, a young African American who lived in the United States but whose link to his African origins was unbreakable. Epigraphic codes "provide sociological, literary, and epistemological contexts for the episode or event to be narrated."[81] The calling of Hampton's name

---

76. UNESCO cited in "Literacy and Non-Formal Education" (accessed 7 October 2016).

77. UNESCO, *Adult and Youth Literacy: National Regional and Global Trends, 1885–2015* (Montreal, Quebec: UNESCO Institute for Statistics, 2013).

78. Grant Lovejoy, "The Extent of Orality: 2012 Update," *Orality Journal* 1, no. 1 (2012): 29.

79. Lovejoy, "Extent of Orality," 31.

80. See the discussion of these categories at the beginning of this chapter, pages 71–2.

81. Alabi Adetayo, "On Seeing Africa for the First Time: Orality, Memory, and the Diaspora in Isidore Okpewho's *Call Me by My Rightful Name*," *Research in African Literatures* 40, no. 1 (Spring 2009): 149.

was powerful enough to invite him from where he was to come home and perform a necessary traditional function.[82] These elements of naming and returning have been actively present in the oral traditions of the Yorubas of southwestern Nigeria until today. A traditional African-American spiritual conveys the concept of naming:

> Hush, hush, somebody's calling my name
> Hush, hush, somebody's calling my name
> Hush, hush, somebody's calling my name:
> Oh my Lord, oh my Lord, what shall I do?

Ifa chant is powerful enough to offer a remedy to existential crises Hampton was experiencing where he lived in the United States, and it came through a voice in the night:

> The strange tongue said, *Ifa* divination was done for Oyepolu, scion of those who performed cult rites at Ife. He was told it was because he had ignored the ancestral rites that his life was in disarray. He was told to visit his ancestral shrine and pay his respects. Once he did that, life would be good for him again. He did as he was told. Things became well for him.[83]

Then there is the power of *orikis* which are panegyric poems "deployed in the celebration of the history and achievements of individuals, their families and communities." An example cited is the following:

> Akindiji! Akindiji! Akindiji o o o!
> I hail you three times, son of Itayemi
> He who bore three sheaves of arrows to war
> Balogun, father of Akimbowale and the twins
> Chest like a gorilla's, broad and bristling with hair
> Who strode cheerily towards the enemy
> With bare chest and grinning teeth
> Whence to the end he sported a thousand welts
> Husband of Ashake, father of Akimbowale and the twins
> Scourge of the Tapa
> "I will traverse the earth to snare the mole in his burrow!"
> Son of Itayemi, barn sagging with yams
> Balogun, chest like a gorilla's, man of peace and war

---

82. Adetayo, "On Seeing Africa," 149.
83. Isidore Okpewho, *Call Me by My Rightful Name*, quoted in Adetayo, 150.

> Paternally, he hailed from a long line of warriors
> Maternally, he hailed from a long line of farmers
> Scourge of the Tapa, son of Itayemi, man of peace and war.
> *Tapa, eji nana baabo*
> *Taapa, eji nana baabo*
> *Tapa, eji nana baabo*
> *Taapa, eji nana baabo!*[84]

Alabi's conclusion is a profound indication that there

> is an affirmation of that strong umbilical cord and spirituality that link the various cultures of Africa and its diaspora. . . . Though separated by thousands of miles, people of African descent in various places still carry with them the spirituality of the continent. Even in real life, they still practice the various African traditional religions, such as Santeria and Candomble in Cuba, Trinidad, and Brazil, among others, and they still preserve African languages, especially in the traditional rituals of Trinidad, Cuba, and Brazil. The panegyric and other oral texts with which Okpewho structures his story show the overwhelming importance of orality to an understanding of the cultures and traditions of Africa and its diaspora. The texts embody the wisdom of the ages, the history of a people, and what makes them who they are long before European occupation of the various African nations and now after their independence from formal colonization.[85]

This connection is not just to African traditional religions. Even African-American folk preaching has been associated with oral elements in West Africa as background to their performance.[86] Walter Pitts has traced the roots of Black preaching styles to African praise poems like the Mande praise poems, griots, African panegyric poetry, one stroke recitation from Benin, African breathe-group principle, Diola-Fogny of the Senegambia extemporaneous performance, and the Bantu poems which survived as "a capella," "toasts," and "boasts."[87] His conclusion is that "over the span of 250 years, Afro-Americans were able to fashion new panegyric genres out of surviving remnants from the different

---

84. Adetayo, 151.

85. Adetayo, 153.

86. Walter Pitts, "West African Poetics in the Black Preaching Style," *American Speech* 64, no. 2 (Summer 1989): 139–40.

87. Pitts, "West African Poetics," 141–45.

regions of Africa that were their origins."[88] The oral form they took along from Africa stayed with them and metamorphosed into various creative genres of speech that have survived until today.

Evidence from Power Attached to the Spoken Word

Africans in oral communities attach great significance to the spoken word. Fiorio observes that "the spoken word in the most generic sense of the term, represents society's 'vision of the world,' and in particular reveals the criteria for interpreting and classifying observable phenomena."[89] A power and dynamism accompany human speech so that for several generations, oral literature is committed to memory and continues to be handed down purely by word of mouth.[90] Words are believed to have originated from God and to have been used to create the world. For instance according to a Mande folklore, there was a point when the world was created. From the time they emerged, the original Nummo pair who were the great ancestral spirits had the ability of speech. So when they observed the nakedness and speechlessness of their Mother Earth, they wove fibers that were full of water and words, used them to clothe her, and gave her a language. This was the first language ever spoken, very primitive and having elementary syntax with few verbs and an unpolished vocabulary. The sounds breathed out were thus unclear, but they were all that was needed to communicate, create, and perfect the earth.[91] Gleanings from various African communities like the Limba of Sierra Leone, Yorubas of southwestern Nigeria, Igbos of southeastern Nigeria, Isokos of Niger Delta, Dinka of Sudan, and others in Central Africa verify that words are a means of community identification; they demonstrate wisdom, intelligence, and maturity; identify personality; and are equated with action.[92]

---

88. Pitts, 147.

89. Fiorio, "Orality and Cultural Identity," 71.

90. Gus Palmer, "Power of the Spoken Word," *American Indian Quarterly* 38, no. 4 (Fall 2014): 519.

91. Ezekiel Adewale Ajibade, "The Potency of Words in African Philosophy: Its Relevance to Contemporary Christians," in *Theological Educators: Academic Papers in Honour of Rev. Prof. O. G. Adetunji and Rev. Dr. F. K. Babalola of the Nigerian Baptist Theological Seminary, Ogbomoso*, ed. Peter Ropo Awoniyi and G. O. Olaniyan (Ogbomoso: NBTS Publishing Unit, 2016), 336.

92. Philip M. Peek, "The Power of Word in African Verbal Art," *The Journal of American Folklore*, no. 94 (Jan–March 1981), 21–27.

The use of words is highly celebrated and revered especially among the Yorubas of southwestern Nigeria who consider them to be inherently potent.[93] For example such phenomena as *ase, ofo, ayajo, ogede* are potent tools that are believed to produce negative or positive physical effects just by the spoken word. *Ase* literally means authority, command, or power. Dennis Akomeah describes it as "the vital power, the energy and the greatest strength of all things." *Ofo* is incantations that involve the manipulation of natural or unknown forces to meet human desires. While some consider them as esoteric and weird, others consider them to be purely a literary genre that can be used to demonstrate the potency of words. Incantations can be in three forms and serve different purposes: *ofo* is used in emergencies; *ayajo* is used as precedents or "statements of a past mythical occurrence of a similar situation"; and *ogede* is a statement of promise which relies on nature's immutable laws that can be observed, verified, and experientially proven.[94]

Regarding the creative power of incantation, Pius O. Abioje shares an account, "When I was with some hunters in a hamlet, it happened one day that they needed to speak with one of their colleagues in a distant location about ten or more kilometres. One of them went into his bag of magic and brought out a horn. He blew it, and the person responded at the other end." Abioje had observed a similar incident in Ola Rotimi's play titled "Kurunmi" where Ogunmola, a leader of the Ibadan warriors, called the leader of Ijaye warriors from a long distance to come and count his losses. Abioje thus gives the challenge that if telephones are believed to be the product of science, then Africans might actually have what it takes to make human beings communicate with each other beyond the normal hearing distance. Others have simply not explored it. It is practically possible that telephones could come from Africa.[95] However it is pertinent to note that these oral assets of the Yoruba culture have not been channeled towards much creativity or productivity. They are still in most cases used negatively and shrouded in so much mystery. The ability to subject these oral powers to experimentation and empirical certification,

---

93. Ajibade, "Potency of Words," 338–39.

94. Dennis Akomeah, "Build Your ASE" (27 May 2005); S. A. Oriloye, "Contents and Features of Yoruba Incantatory Poetry," *Journal of Communication and Culture* 1, no. 1/2 (n.d): 32–44; Lois Fuller, *A Missionary Handbook on African Traditional Religion* (Bukuru: African Christian Textbooks, 2001), 84; Kofi Asare Opoku, *West Africa Traditional Religion* (Accra: FEP International Private Limited, 1978), 147.

95. Pius O. Abioje, "Magic and Science in Yorubaland: Towards Africa's Technological Development," in *Science and Religion in the Service of Humanity* (Ilorin: Local Societies Initiatives and NASTREN, 2006), 192. See also Ajibade, "Potency of Words."

to replicate them and turn them into instruments of physical and spiritual advancement of the African race, will be of great value. But that is yet to be seen.

Kofi Asare Opoku sees this phenomenon of the spoken word as a product of humans coming to terms with their environment through religion and magic. Submission and appeal to the forces of divine origin help them to control and manipulate nature and its forces at will.[96] Africans believe in the power of the spoken word, and that is a symbol of their orality.

Gospel Communication and Engagement with Orality

So far, the discussion has centered on the concept of orality, and efforts have been made to supply a series of evidence that Africans are predominantly oral in nature and culture. It is necessary at this point to establish a connection between orality and the preaching of the gospel in Africa, considering what has taken place so far and projecting what potential orality has for gospel proclamation on the continent.

Historical Background

While orality has always been, it began to take center stage in gospel proclamation, especially missions, in the last thirty years.[97] The current dimension of movement may be traced to the New Tribes missionaries who worked in Papua New Guinea and recognized the power of orally presenting Bible stories, which they documented in a Ee-Taow video. This method was adapted by the International Mission Board in the Philippines, relying much on Walter Ong's *Orality and Literacy*. Chronological Bible Teaching (CBT) was developed here. In an effort to put more emphasis on storying than teaching, they came up with Chronological Bible Storying (CBS), later Bible Storying (BS). Eventually Creation to Christ (C2C) replaced these.[98] Hundreds of methods are in use today because of the philosophy that orality is not just an

---

96. Opoku, *West Africa Traditional Religion*, 147.

97. Hill, "Conversations about Orality," 215. She wrote this article in 2011 and mentions that orality has come to the center of attention in the past twenty years. It has been ten years since then.

98. Hill, 215. But Tom Steffen's account seems to date the work among the Palowanos in the Philippines to over thirty years ago. Tom Steffen, "Tracking the Orality Movement: Some Implications for 21st Century Missions," *Lausanne Global Analysis* 3, no. 2 (March 2014).

initial step in literacy-based ministry but a substantive and legitimate means of communicating the gospel.

The umbrella body the International Orality Network (ION) that brings together several of the organizations involved in orality was founded in 2000. ION formed the Oral Bible Network to connect gospel communicators through orality, and because the body grew through many breakthroughs around the world, they now have an annual conference in the United States and other places and published the book *Making Disciples of Oral Learners*.[99] The network continues to grow with partners in Africa and Asia convening forums, carrying out research, and helping to fund field training, leadership programs, and theological education with the unique vision of reaching out with the gospel to oral communities.[100] As of today, the ION has a very functional website and has published different literature to further their goals and visions.[101]

But the orality movement has grown so large and spontaneously that it is beyond the scope of ION. Some other organizations involved in orality include the International Mission Board of the Southern Baptist Convention, E3 Partners, and One Story, a partnership between agencies that share the same vision like Wycliffe, Youth with a Mission (YWAM), and Pioneers.[102] Various theological institutions are now responding to the movement, and discipleship efforts are now flourishing through orality. According to Steffen, "The orality movement had moved from the country to the city, and from primary oral learners to secondary oral learners."[103]

Dimensions of Engagement

There are several dimensions to the engagement of orality with the gospel. Those who are persuaded that the gospel should take an oral form have several reasons and guiding philosophies ranging from theological, missiological, and hermeneutical to homiletical dimensions which dovetail into the process of contextualizing expository preaching.

---

99. Jennifer Jagerson, "The *Simply The Story* Method: Next Steps in Oral Strategies," in *Beyond Literate Western Contexts: Honor and Shame and Assessment of Orality Preference*, ed. Samuel E. Chiang and Grant Lovejoy (Hong Kong: International Orality Network, 2015), 114.

100. Randall Prior, "Orality: The Not-So-Silent Issue in Mission Theology," *International Bulletin of Missionary Research* 35, no. 3 (July 2011): 146.

101. The ION website is https://orality.net/.

102. Jagerson, "*Simply The Story* Method," 114.

103. Steffen, "Tracking the Orality Movement."

Biblical and Theological Dimension

A review of the historical books of the Old Testament, the Gospels, and Acts reveals that much of the Bible is written in narrative genres. Many of these narratives must have existed initially as oral stories which were later set in textual form.[104] Grant Lovejoy corroborates this idea when he opines that the Bible arose in oral contexts. The Old and New Testaments were written in times when the literacy level of those cultures was between 5 and 20 percent depending on the culture or subculture in question. Throughout this history too, these ancient people preferred the spoken word irrespective of their literacy status. Therefore it is not a surprise that almost half of the Bible is narratives with poetry making about another third.[105]

Many studies have been conducted in the last decade regarding the oral aspects of the four Gospels. The general discovery is that "rather than seeing the Gospels as texts read by Christians and seekers privately in the first century, New Testament scholars have recovered the important fact that the texts were orally read or performed to a gathering of the local community of believers (and seekers), most of whom were not literate."[106] Internal evidence abounds in both the Old and New Testaments to support the reality of this finding. For example, Moses told the priests to read the law to the assembly at the end of every seventh year (Deut 31:10–13). Joshua 8:34–35 records how Joshua read the entire law to the Israelites as does Nehemiah 8:1–3 of when Ezra did the same. The epistles of Paul include requests that his letters be read among the churches and is coupled with indications that they were orally dictated to a scribe (Rom 16:22; 1 Cor 16:21; Col 4:16, 18; 1 Thess 5:27; 2 Thess 3:17). In Revelation 1:3, a blessing is pronounced on "the one who reads aloud the words of this prophecy, and blessed are those who hear it and take to heart what is written in it."[107]

So likely many narratives in the Bible had an oral form before being converted to text, and oral performance is encouraged in the written text. These stories were told with a particular audience in mind – like Matthew was written to a predominantly Jewish audience and Luke to a predominantly Gentile audience. The same gospel content was in essence written and delivered

---

104. Damon So, "How Should a Theological Institution Prepare Students/Leaders Who Will go Out into the Fields to Train Local People (Storytellers) to Tell Bible Stories Effectively?" in *Beyond Literate Western Contexts: Contextualizing Theological Education in Oral Contexts*, ed. Samuel E. Chiang and Grant Lovejoy (Hong Kong: International Orality Network, 2013), 29.

105. Lovejoy, "That All May Hear," 3.

106. So, "How Should a Theological Institution," 30.

107. Lovejoy, "That All May Hear," 3. In the Greek, the "he" is singular and "those" is plural.

orally in slightly different forms to reach different audiences.[108] These stories may have circulated in oral form for a generation before they were written, and eye witnesses spread what they saw and heard, resulting in dramatic growth of the church as it expanded from Judea and Galilee into Asia, Africa, and Europe. According to Lovejoy,

> Ordinary believers were able to tell the stories that they knew. They used them to explain who Jesus was, why they were his followers, and why as Jesus' followers they lived differently. Though the Jewish leaders viewed Jesus' followers as "uneducated and untrained men" (Acts 4:13), his followers were remarkably effective. Led by God's Spirit, they went everywhere telling the stories they had heard and the experiences that they had had with God. Their example reminds us of the potential today for ordinary Christians to learn, internalize, and tell biblical stories as a means of proclaiming their faith. Those who have not been educated can still take a role in the Great Commission.[109]

The implication here is that just as most people in the Old and New Testaments encountered the word by hearing, oral transmission of the gospel is still critical to God's method of saving the world. But this should not obscure that Scripture indicates God also appreciates reading and writing. For example, he could have orally given Moses the Ten Commandments and told him to simply recite it to Israel and be sure that oral recitation remained the process. Using his hands to write upon tablets of stone is an indication of his interest in literacy (Exod 34:1, 27). Several Bible passages support reading and writing as legitimate means of communication (Deut 11:18–21; 17:18–19; Neh 9:38; Esth 8:8; Jer 30:2; 36:5–6; Hab 2:2; Rev 1:11).[110] For a very long time the only copies of the Old and New Testaments available were handwritten and inaccessible to the common people. Personal, silent reading of the Bible began over 1400 years after Jesus's ascension when printed materials became cheaper and more accessible through the invention of the Gutenberg press.[111] But it is continuously substantiated that literacy is never at war with orality. They both complement each other in fulfilling the Great Commission.

---

108. So, "How Should a Theological Institution," 30–31.

109. Lovejoy, "That All May Hear," 4.

110. Ezekiel Adewale Ajibade, *Treasure Mine: Living Gems from Searching the Scriptures* (New Bussa: Hope for a Generation International, 2012), 302–3.

111. Lovejoy, "That All May Hear," 4.

Advocates of orality have also emphasized its invaluable contributions to theology, especially systematic theology. A long-term error the West has been focusing on is one phase of Jesus's earthly life: liberal churches major on the life and conservatives on the death, with none telling the full story. This error corresponds to the dichotomy between "social action only" and "proclamation only."[112] The story form presenting the gospel covers all aspects of Jesus's life from birth to his universal reign, cutting the "Gordian knots" between Western liberals and conservatives.[113]

The story form has done the same for the divergence between biblical studies and systematic theology. While the story in the Bible remains the same for both liberals and conservatives, its interpretation has been different based on divergent theologies. Oral storytelling possesses the potential for uniting these two areas because students learn basically to "develop a biblical systematic theology from their biblical studies," unlike in the Western academy where the systematic theology being taught may not be truly biblical, or where biblical interpretation does not result in concrete systematic theology.[114] Sam Chan offers further insight when he observes that systematic theology begins from teaching speculative concepts, systems of thought, and propositional proof texts from the Bible and then moves on to some personal experiences and application. This method reverses the definition of theology from "faith seeking understanding" to "understanding seeking faith."[115] The best approach is to begin with Bible storytelling and case studies and elicit questions from the learners' thoughts and experiences. They can then integrate their questions and thoughts with historic and systematic theology.[116] This method can be illustrated by seventeen North Africans who were taught 135 Bible stories in sequence. After two years of study, the seminary professor gave them a six-hour exam. They succeeded in connecting stories with core doctrines and basic themes of the faith. When they were given a theological theme, they were able

---

112. So, "How Should a Theological Institution," 34.

113. So, 34.

114. So, 34–35.

115. Sam Chan, "Storytelling Seeking Understanding," in *Beyond Literate Western Contexts: Continuing Conversations in Orality and Theological Education*, ed. Samuel E. Chiang and Grant Lovejoy (Hong Kong: International Orality Network, 2014), 81.

116. Chan, "Storytelling Seeking Understanding," 81.

to use multiple stories for support, and when asked doctrinal questions, they had enough illustrations.[117]

Another valuable contribution of orality to theology is a reshaping of the concept. Randall Prior notes that "with the relative decline of the church within the Western world and the rapid increase in the membership of the church in areas of the world where oral cultures dominate, a question is raised about the very shape of theology itself."[118] Theology is no longer just what is written in books and studied by literate societies. "Oral theology" mediated through evangelizing, conversion, sermons and preaching, hymns and songs, praying, and conversation is now regarded as valid theology.[119] Some of the names given to oral theology include "village theology" (Malenasia), peasant theology (Philippines and Minjung), and people's theology (Korea). This oral theology is one of the contributions of Africa and other oral communities around the world. Without necessarily producing "theological treatise and tomes, systematically worked out volumes which stand on the shelves of libraries," a mere look at the sermons preached every Sunday is enough to showcase Africans' response to their hopes and fears in the light of God's revelation.[120]

Oral theology is taken very seriously today, not only in Africa but also around the world. For example in the South Pacific, the *Malenesian Journal of Theology* has a vision to "develop the indigenous theology in Malanesia" by drawing on existing oral sources of indigenous stories and songs, adaptation of myths, and discovering how practical problems are solved by prayer and consensus. The real-life settings are long discussions on the beach, under a tree, round a fire, while singing at festivals, or during worship.[121]

In 1996, over one hundred and fifty participants from all over the Pacific region gathered in Aotearoa, New Zealand. That conference included no tedious academic paper presentations. All they did was interweave the creative presentations of participants who were grouped according to culture. They also held discussions on marriage, death, hospitality, land, birth, and struggle. This was theology done in a different way to the amazement of those who attended. Indeed as Prior concludes, oral theology has become a rich source

---

117. Miriam Adeney, "What Is Enough? Oral Bible Teaching in Three Dimensions," in *Beyond Literate Western Contexts: Contextualizing Theological Education in Oral Contexts*, ed. Samuel E. Chiang and Grant Lovejoy (Hong Kong: International Orality Network, 2013), 95.
118. Prior, "Orality: The Not-So-Silent Issue," 144.
119. Prior, 144.
120. Prior, 144.
121. Prior, 144.

for literate and academic theologians even when it is difficult to pin down or systematize.[122] Succinctly he states,

> We should no longer be measuring authentic theology by the quality of a written piece of work done by an individual islander who has successfully gained the skills of a literate culture. Rather, theology – as a passionate engagement with the God who became incarnate in Jesus Christ, who seeks to be the giver of life for all people of all cultures and the head of local communities of the church across a diverse world – deserves a broader definition that will allow oral expressions of theology to find their place.[123]

Missiological Dimension
The greatest motivating force behind the gospel orality movement is missions. Armed with storying and other oral tools, missions have taken the gospel to people groups who may never have heard if learning of the gospel depended on literacy alone. Research reveals effective church planting among Muslim and non-Muslim groups using the oral method.[124] Oral strategies have led to greater acceptance of the gospel and better discipleship and raising leaders within cultures. The results are so tremendous that in 2009 the Mission Exchange, which represents some one hundred mission organizations and supports more than twenty thousand missionaries around the world, gave the orality movement its Innovation in Missions award.[125]

In the task of missions, orality enables the gospel bearers to contextualize their message by appreciating and using the communication styles of their target group and gives opportunities for the good news to "spread in locally reproducible, natural ways."[126] In Africa for example, Beatrice Kadangs observes that while there are no written records of God's dealing with African people, his dealings are nevertheless recorded in such living forms as oral communication, rituals, symbols, ceremonies, and community faith. She suggests that effective

---

122. Prior, 144.
123. Prior, 147.
124. Lovejoy, "That All May Hear," 1.
125. Lovejoy, 1–2.
126. Hill, "Conversations about Orality," 215–16.

ministries among oral people should use communication forms already in place within their culture.[127]

Storytelling also presents opportunities to change worldviews, which is one of the powers that storytelling, a form of orality, possesses. Societies live in the reality of their worldviews, and many times these worldviews are contrary to the demands and dictates of the gospel. Harriet Hill believes that if a culture is going to be changed, the first thing is to change the stories that are told.[128] Other values of orality in missions include the fact that it helps present the panoramic view of God and the revelation of his word, ensures community growth in Christ, gives room for creativity and interaction, and allows the working of the Holy Spirit as people discover spiritual realities through the narratives rather than by being told everything.

Very importantly, an oral strategy in missions helps deal with the problem of resistance to the gospel. Those initially labelled "resistant to the gospel" may actually be "resistant to literacy." Removing the literacy barrier could produce an incredible response. Some have actually come to conclude that, "there are no resistant people groups; only ineffective presentations of the gospel."[129] Lovejoy concludes,

> We seek to communicate God's message so that ordinary people can understand it, respond to it, share it with others, and live it out fully. To the extent that our audience learns best by oral means, we must adjust our communication to meet them. Faithfulness to Jesus' example compels us to this, as does the possibility of increased fruitfulness in his service. Churches and mission organizations worldwide have seen increased effectiveness for the past two decades as they have experimented with, and then embraced ever more fully, the use of oral strategies. People who had been marginalized in Christianity because they lacked literacy can now be once again full participants in Christ's body.[130]

Orality as a normative communication channel remains one of the best expressions of contextualization in missions and meets one of the parameters

---

127. Beatrice Kadangs, "A Case Study of Women and Widows as It Relates to Orality and How It Works with Them," in *Beyond Literate Western Contexts: Honor and Shame and Assessment of Orality Preference*, ed. Samuel E. Chiang and Grant Lovejoy (Hong Kong: International Orality Network, 2015), 137–38.

128. Kadangs, "Case Study of Women," 216.

129. Kadangs, 216.

130. Lovejoy, "That All May Hear," 7.

for measuring a contextualized church.[131] Other measurements enumerated by Hayward are local vernacular, expression of faith, worship patterns, theological reflections, local metaphors, symbols and images, ethics and values, assembly, leadership and politics, members of societies, and discipleship.[132] The principle is that the word of God is unchanging and eternal and should continually be made incarnate to everyone in every generation. Partnering with God in this communication task demands that the integrity of this word be preserved as it was given and be made "flesh" in every conceivable way.[133]

Hermeneutical Dimension

A big question then is how can illiterate people carry out effective hermeneutics and interpretation of the Bible if they cannot read or may be able to read but not efficiently? There are so many hermeneutical tools out there, but they lie in volumes of books, journals, DVDs, and on the internet which the oral folks may not have access to because they are not functionally literate. James R. Krabill tells the story of N'Guessan Benoit who ministered in an Ivorian village and whose preaching ministry lasted for eight decades. He had no formal schooling and only understood a very little of the nineteenth-century archaic French-language Bible (Louis Segond Version) which he took to the pulpit weekly. Therefore to prepare his sermons, he brought into his yard a young elementary school boy, gave him the Bible, told him to pick a passage and read to him. Then Benoit asked the boy what the passage meant to him as he read and from his understanding to translate it into the Dida language which Benoit would use to preach on Sunday. The boy was required to repeat the passage for up to three times, and as Benoit listened to the text, he committed it to memory for use in the coming week and for the future. This was the process Papa Benoit faithfully followed throughout his lifetime of ministry. He died in 2011 at the age of one hundred.[134] Though the steps are described in a corporate setting, oral interpreters could individually carry out their own

---

131. Douglas Hayward, "Measuring Contextualization in Church and Missions," *International Journal of Frontier Missions* 12, no. 3 (July-Sept 1995): 137.

132. Hayward, "Measuring Contextualization," 135–38.

133. Daniel C. Runyon, "God's Communication Challenge: Oral Preference and the Tribal Bible," in *Beyond Literate Western Contexts: Honor and Shame and Assessment of Orality Preference*, ed. Samuel E. Chiang and Grant Lovejoy (Hong Kong: International Orality Network, 2015), 6.

134. James R. Krabill, "Important Lessons from Indigenous Movements and Locally-initiated Churches in the Global South," in *Beyond Literate Western Contexts: Contextualizing Theological Education in Oral Contexts*, ed. Samuel E. Chiang and Grant Lovejoy (Hong Kong: International Orality Network, 2013), 116–17.

study after having enough stories in memory. Another source of biblical text for an oral interpreter is an audio Bible.

With the storying method projected by the orality movement, oral preachers or teachers do not necessarily have to follow the procedure of N'Guessan Benoit, though cues could be taken from it. In recent times, hermeneutical methods have been fashioned out that can be of help to oral interpreters of Scripture. An example is a methodology of Simply the Story (STS), one of the many organizations working to develop missionary strategies to reach out to oral communities with the gospel. They have established oral Bible schools in a number of countries which take participants through 296 Bible stories from Genesis to Revelation. This strategy can serve as a secondary level training with the potential to develop leadership, disciple believers, and grow planted churches around the world using the oral strategy.

The Simply the Story method uses the following three steps:[135]

1. Preparation: Participants learn to tell the story on the level of a "dynamic equivalence of the text," meaning they are to ensure that each sentence carries the same meaning as the sentence of biblical text. Nothing from the names of places to other minor details is to excluded or added. This level of commitment helps the participants investigate the original intention of the authors.[136]

2. Interpretation: Once participants know the story and can repeat it well without notes, they are taken through each section of the story using some basic questions to investigate the setting and the choices and motives of the characters as seen by what they do or not do, say or do not say, and what effects these have on the outcome of the story. Such elements as repetition, volume and description, order of thought and speech, development of the story, problems arising, and resolutions based on the interaction of the characters (including God) all help to give meaning to the story.[137]

3. Application: Participants are asked if the story and the issues it raises have significance for today. The process then moves from the world to their communities and personal lives. Research

---

135. Jagerson, "The *Simply the Story* Method," 109–10.
136. Jagerson, 110.
137. Jagerson, 110.

studies testify to the effectiveness of this method, as Jagerson reveals that

> Preliminary case study interviews conducted with STS leaders from seven nations suggest that the nature of narrative is such that the participants have often already begun relating the circumstance of the story to their own experiences, sometimes provoking profound emotional responses. By carefully breaking interpretational observations of the biblical text and personal application into two distinct sections, the STS method teaches participants to honor biblical meaning in its own context apart from their own opinions and experiences. This increases their ability to approach the word objectively so it can speak to the circumstances of other lives rather than reflect their own presuppositions and biases. Failure to make the distinction between right interpretation of the text and personal application puts the participant at risk of losing both.[138]

Not all proponents of narrative agree that there should be application after a story. As Jagerson observes, listeners often relate the circumstances of the story to their own experiences, so decisions should be left for them to make. This issue is a bone of contention, and the point of divergence is the pro- and anti-authority stances. People in oral communities like Africans can make meaning out of narratives, but part of the joy of learning is drawing out the lessons and applying them together or depending on the facilitator to bring out the lessons they can apply to their lives. Whereas in the Western and more literate world where people like Israel Galindo would state, "you can't teach anybody anything," Africans uphold the authority of their leaders.[139] Even when the lessons are not corporately derived, Africans still expect their leaders or facilitators to extract what message they can take home from the text and discussion. O'Donnell testifies to this importance of authority using Tanzania as a case study, though in a negative context. She states that in Tanzanian culture, "the authority of the pastor is given a divine legitimacy, regardless of whether or not his teachings are theologically sound. For many Tanzanians,

---

138. Jagerson, 112.
139. Israel Galindo, *The Craft of Christian Teaching* (Ibadan: Scripture Union Nigeria, 1998), 11.

as well as many other African cultures, truth is measured by the authority of the giver, not by truth itself." An evaluation of oral interviews conducted in the course of her research among seventy respondents also indicated a consensus that Tanzanians want lessons drawn out from a text or a story and applied to their life. Only two had alternative opinions.[140]

Another important dimension to oral hermeneutics is the need for discretion in the choice and development of stories. These choices should be made after a systematic analysis of the cultural context because different cultures approach Scripture with different questions which are developed by their local theologies.[141] Kadangs suggests that the stories and the manner of communication chosen should be aimed at transforming the worldview of the hearers and that the way to avoid syncretism is to communicate the gospel in the mother tongue of the people who are being reached.[142] There is a tendency in orality to be choosy about the stories to tell a people, and there is always a likelihood of sticking to narrative portions of Scripture. Every handler of God's word needs to be aware that they are charged with the responsibility of teaching the whole counsel of God and not just "snippets of Scripture, however interesting they may be."[143]

Homiletical Dimension

Much of the current work in orality in missions is centered on gospel presentation in evangelism, teaching, and discipleship. Jagerson notes that such orality methods as those used by the International Mission Board of the Southern Baptist Convention, E3 Partners, and One Story often deal with the initial proclamation of the gospel. The Simply the Story methodology is a good leap in between initial proclamation of the gospel and Bible college.[144] When it comes to gospel proclamation as preaching in its real sense, methods of using orality are just beginning to take shape.

This does not mean that preaching as an oral event is a new phenomenon nor that there have not been efforts in homiletical history to wrest preaching from the solely literate form. Paul Scott Wilson states that sermons, essentially, are spoken. While large sermon collections fill most theological libraries

---

140. Katherine O'Donnell, "An Investigation into how Tanzanian Christians Perceive and Engage with God's Word" (MA diss., Redcliffe College, 2013), cited in Doll, "Literacy and Orality Working Together," 72.

141. Adeney, "What Is Enough?," 97.

142. Kadangs, "Case Study of Women," 138.

143. Adeney, "What Is Enough?," 96.

144. Jagerson, "The *Simply the Story* Method," 115.

around the world, they only gained the name "sermon" after being preached. In Wilson's words, "a written document becomes a sermon only through its having being spoken. Sermons are events in time, God's word addressed to particular congregations in particular circumstances."[145] Dave McClellan goes historical to prove that preaching was actually oral before the advent of the printing press which changed the way information is processed. Hundreds of years ago when there were no word processors, hard drives, or printers, the idea of a sermon as words on a page was not an issue in homiletics because then sermons "lived inside the preacher and needed the preacher to voice them, the sermon flowed out of a different method of preparation and different model of communication." This earlier model of sermon communication has been identified by scholars of biblical studies and rhetoric as "orality," and their principles are being strongly reapplied to the theories of homiletics.[146] This reconnecting with orality indeed is the birthing point for the New Homiletic and the rise of narrative preaching as a concept. The point being made here is that the next phase in orality studies should be how to preach in a predominantly oral society like Africa by having a full understanding of what it means to be an oral learner or listener living in an oral community.

Storying is the gem of orality. But orality is not storying, and preaching is not always storying. Richard Lischer is of the strong opinion that storying has limits especially when it comes to preaching.[147] He identifies those limits as aesthetic, ontological, theological, and socio-political. Stories, like Bible parables, are sometimes treated as an end in themselves and not as means to an end, are reshaped so as to lose their historicity, or are considered as mere plots. Some preachers embrace storytelling because they consider it to be more ethical, less authoritative, and less manipulative than other rhetorical endeavors. But they quickly forget that "in any story the narrator is not the author but one of the actors," and that by maintaining "the narrator's ironic distance from the audience, the preacher is put at a further remove from the congregation."[148] Many also forget the deep non-narrative domains of human lives. These Lischer calls the storyless places in human life where episodes of complications do not connect with new ones anymore.

Lischer maintains that the theological limit of story has to do with faith. Faith transcends stories because it is the ability to trust God even when stories

---

145. Paul Scott Wilson, *The Practice of Preaching* (Nashville: Abingdon, 1995), 47.
146. Dave McClellan, "Preaching by Ear" (accessed 10 October 2016).
147. Richard Lischer, "The Limits of Story," *Interpretation* 38, no. 1 (January 1984): 26–38.
148. Lischer, "The Limits of Story," 29.

about him do not address an existential need or those non-narrative incidents of modern life. Stories form good raw material for faith, but actions will not follow stories until "Christians review the complicated mesh of stories and abstract from it the principle demanded by the present, be it God's faithfulness, mercy, or justice, and resolve to live by it."[149] This limitation is related to the social-political dimension. Stories may provide inspiration for a change, and like Lischer states, "stories set the tone for principled action. It may be the story of the exodus or the story of self-discovery in an Esalen lodge at Big Sur, the one radiating liberation for justice, the other exuding bourgeois narcissism" but "each story is incomplete as a vehicle for change until it is interpreted."[150]

Lischer's conclusion is instructive:

> Each of story's limitations – the aesthetic, ontological, theological, and socio-political – contains a positive and restorative element for preaching. The importance of "background" vis-à-vis aestheticism reminds us of the "thesis sentence," if we may call it that, which preachers and audiences bring to their dialogue, with the result that neither approaches the gospel *de novo* or without a shared context. The qualification of the ontological argument on behalf of story can sensitize preachers to the kinds of needs that resist storification, so that our preaching will become more vigilant in its advocacy of the forgotten people whose stories have ended. The theological shortcomings in story's expression of faith may call attention to the long-lost eschatological dimension of preaching. Story teaches us that faith is a living out; eschatology reminds us that faith is a slash across the symmetry or predictability of history. Finally, a socio-political critique of story exposes the ideological bent of our own sermons and invites preachers to take up all the rhetorical tools, and not just one aesthetic form, in service of social and personal transformation.[151]

Daniel Runyon discusses the importance of stories stating that they bring the listeners to a point where they reflect on such basic questions as "how do things happen? How are they related? What have they to do with us?"[152] But

---

149. Lischer, 34.
150. Lischer, 35.
151. Lischer, 38.
152. Runyon, "God's Communication Challenge," 97.

these questions are products of other probing questions after the story such as the following:

- What do you like best about this story?
- What do you struggle with or not understand?
- What do you learn about people?
- What do you learn about God?
- What needs to change in your life after hearing this story?[153]

Runyon indeed concludes that "Conversation is the natural aftermath of a story and serves to imprint the message on the minds of the listeners."[154] But this conversation would rather be like a Bible study, discipleship forum, or another informal gathering for sharing the gospel rather than a preaching event. When a preaching event is just a story told and questions asked with the congregation responding in a conversational form, we need to ask whether the event is preaching.

The question has therefore been raised as to whether expository preaching is possible within the corridors of orality. The answer is always positive once it is agreed that the content of expository preaching must be biblical but the form can be cultural.[155] Grant Lovejoy offers that the first option in preaching for oral listeners is using biblical narratives in such a way that the texts retain their narrative character. This option takes a preacher through approximately two-thirds of the Bible and is a way of reflecting the literary genre of Scripture as well as an attempt to uphold its communication dynamics in sermons. This does not mean, as some homileticians have suggested, that every sermon must be narrative since the Bible contains other genres that will be better presented using other methods.[156]

Lovejoy also cautions that care should be taken not to outline narrative texts in an analytical form. The thought should be of "plots" rather than "points."[157] This assertion is in the order of the work of Eugene Lowry, David Buttrick, and John C. Holbeert, some of which has been discussed earlier. Lischer disagrees that a story or narrative is all a plot. While agreeing that plot is an essential element because a narrative is "a sequence of episodes that moves with a sense of purpose through reactions, complications, and new

---

153. Runyon, 98.
154. Runyon, 98.
155. See the discussion on forms and contents of expository preaching in chapter two, pages 29–53.
156. Lovejoy, "But I Did Such a Good Exposition," 8.
157. Lovejoy, 8.

predicaments toward a conclusion," he opines that it is "the least variable and most dependent on a few mythic forms of development." The quality of mind which is reflected in the language of characterization, motivation, description, and commentary are more important than the narrative. In fact, the quality of mind is the soul of narrative, not the plot.[158]

According to Lischer, to reach oral audiences preachers need to develop sermon styles that are marked by "fulsomeness, repetition, high emotion, frequent use of formulaic language, inclusion of words and phrases because of their euphony rather than cognitive contribution, patterns of organization that are anything but syllogistic."[159] He also adds that such sermons should be sprinkled with pointed, pithy, and memorable sayings like proverbs. The suspense and drama of the story should be retained. But while trying to be accurate with the story, the presentation should not be dry, nor should the story be over explained. Instead, the listeners should be helped to relive the story.[160]

Handling non-narrative portions of the Bible is an issue of concern whenever orality is discussed. Stephen Kemp raises the question of the relationship between the epistles and narratives by observing that emphasis on story tends to lean toward texts like the Gospels and not much toward the letters and even their narrative portions. He therefore asks, "How does this fit with the fact that the early church meetings were essentially gatherings to hear and implement what was written in the letters and Gospels," bearing in mind that those Gospels were probably written with the letters in mind?[161]

Lovejoy suggests that preachers in oral contexts should learn to fit the teaching of the epistles into the story line of Acts in ways that promote understanding of the story and its teaching. For the psalms, proverbs, and poetic portions of the Bible, oral communities who appreciate their use should not have issues when they are explored.[162] Oral interviews conducted in researching this field reveal a preference for gospel parables, proverbs, and narrative portions of the Scripture and Psalms above other genres. Psalms seem to resonate more with some respondents because, like J. A. Oguntoye notes,

---

158. Lischer, "Limits of Story," 29.

159. Lovejoy, "But I Did Such a Good Exposition," 8.

160. Ivor Calvin Greer, *Orality and Christian Discipleship: Developing a 'Living' Word* (MA diss., Bangor University, 2011), 80.

161. Stephen Kemp, "Leadership Development of Oral Learners: A Case Study of Operation Agape Using BILD Resources," in *Beyond Literate Western Contexts: Honor and Shame and Assessment of Orality Preference*, ed. Samuel E. Chiang and Grant Lovejoy (Hong Kong: International Orality Network, 2015), 147.

162. Lovejoy, "That All May Hear," 5.

they talk about praising God, extolling his supremacy, and his ability to help Christians fight their life battles. Dele Oguntola sees the Psalms as giving voice to African problems and challenges, and Alice Olatunji sees the Psalms as a good prayer tool.[163] A few of those who preferred Pauline Epistles were highly educated at the masters and Phd levels. But they still wanted such material to be illuminated with adequate illustrations and stories so they would stay long in their memories.

Psalms can also be treated based on their historical background and the stories that surround them. Proverbs can be taught by seeking parallels in the local culture. But much is still at stake concerning the specific ways non-narrative portions of the Bible should be used to preach to oral listeners. For example, Greer used a portion of his work to discuss the place of songs in oral gospel presentation. But he is not specific about how the Bible songs can be used in the preaching event or what form their presentation should be.[164] That is not a problem in Africa. Niyi Adedokun is a popular gospel musician in Nigeria. For several years, he has used his music not just as a medium of praise, as many gospel musicians do, but to preach specific biblical themes. When invited by different local churches and denominations for revival services, what he did was sing because his songs are sermons in themselves. His lyrics are loaded with stories that convey biblical messages and their application.[165]

Another area of disagreement is whether or not oral listeners can access linear-logical presentations of the gospel as it is presented in the non-narrative portions of the Bible and are rich in instruction for the growth of the church and its members in any society.[166] It is of interest to note that many of those I interviewed in the course of my research for this work prefer that a sermon be outlined. The definition of outlining may differ. However, these listeners want some logical structure in the presentation, and sermons that are otherwise do not seem to be satisfactory. Even if a story is told, they want a presentation that they can logically follow. Some of those interviewed from rural areas who cannot read or write nor jot down sermon outlines or points still gave the impression that a preacher should give sermon points.

---

163. J. A. Oguntoye, interview by Mary-Ann Udemba, 5 September 2016; Dele Oguntola, interview by the author, 30 August 2016; Alice Olatunji, interview by the author, 9 October 2016.

164. Greer, *Orality and Christian Discipleship*, 53–56.

165. Samples of Niyi Adedokun's songs can be found at https://sonichits.com/artist/Evangelist_Niyi_Adedokun_(The_Glory_Singer).

166. Joseph Roger Webber, interview by the author, 25 November 2016.

These preferences do not negate their inclinations toward orality. But it is also possible that many who attend churches have been shaped by the methods their preachers have used to present the gospel over the years. Evidence for this can be seen in the information elicited from the pastors interviewed, most of whom are topical preachers who have to drive their sermons with points not coming from the text but from their thoughts and backed up with different Bible passages. Even when some of these preachers want to use narrative portions of the Scripture, they must still be outlined. One preacher interviewed, Joseph Roger Webber from Liberia, compared the use of storying or narrative to taking members to "Sunday school level." The missionaries who trained him did not like storytelling because they thought it wastes time. Sermon outlining is, therefore, a function of the mindset and not of efficacy. A number of those interviewed cannot remember those points after few days unless they are in touch with their jotters. An interview with Tolulope Akanbi, a master-level student, was quite revealing. She said she seldom jots down points because she does not get to use the points. What she takes home and acts on is the central idea of the sermon which she called "the message for me."[167]

Whatever methodology is to be used in preaching in oral societies, Belden C. Lane suggests three basic ingredients of an oral sermon. First, the sermon should be seen as oral art and prepared and presented in like manner. The preached word must be heard as nothing less than the "very word of God." Once this is neglected, preaching becomes like practiced reading that reflects the linearity of writing because the manuscript becomes the most indispensable tool on the pulpit, and the preaching sounds like the preacher writes.[168]

In his article "Preaching by Ear," Dave McClellan asserts that it is possible to plan a sermon completely orally, and he gives some tips for this. The sermon should begin from the preacher's own character and personal theology which has nothing to do with the hypocrisy of saying what we do not own or live. The sermon should use literate sources, particularly the Bible, but quickly moves toward an oral composition, with preparation including discussing the content with listeners before preaching and organizing sequentially but not with bullet points, and continues to evolve as the preacher confronts real life

---

167. Tolulope Akanbi, interview by author, 1 September 2016. See interview guides and respondents in Appendices 1–3 below.

168. Belden C. Lane, "The Oral Tradition and Its Implications for Contemporary Preaching" (n.d.): 22.

situations. The sermon should be delivered with good eye contact, conviction, and authenticity, and should be archived in the mind and soul of the preacher.[169]

As good as McClellan's ideas are, many of his views are subjective, and his biblical basis of Matthew 10:19 for a sermon like this stands on a faulty hermeneutics. Preaching by ear as analogous to playing music by ear has nothing to do with Jesus asking his followers not to be anxious about how they are to speak or what to say. The context and intentions are different. While McClellan encourages organizing oral sermons sequentially "so that one unit of thought leads naturally into the next" and it becomes "easy to maintain the order in delivery,"[170] he is still writing about logicality which oral listeners are occasionally alleged to avoid. The value of McClellan's article is for secondary orality and not primary, but his suggestions are quite helpful and may be adaptable even to non-narrative sermons.

Second, preaching should recover the parabolic dimension of the gospel as much as possible. Parables are provocative and agonistic, eliciting a response from listeners which makes their message memorable. The present overfamiliarity with parables as a result of their being recorded in writing should not be used as an excuse to jettison their original form and intention. Instead, the language of surprise and intrigue in parables should be allowed to engender interest, as well as their ability to complete and supply meaning as is customary in oral traditions.[171] But such meaning must be guided just as Jesus helped his disciples on many occasions to understand what he called the "secrets of the kingdom" (Matt 13:11).

The third ingredient Lane recommends is that the process allow for active listening, reception, communication, and a specially shared encounter between the preacher and the hearers. According to Lane, "Active listening is as important to the process as is active speaking. The storyteller makes use of a whole para-language of facial expression, tone of voice, phrasing of words, and body language. In turn, he or she is accustomed to receiving back from the listeners a response given through a similar para-language."[172] This interaction does not happen when a sermon is delivered as it was written during preparation and when it makes no difference if it is preached with or without the presence of a congregation. The life that manifests in a sermon is

---

169. McClellan, "Preaching by Ear," E-Book, https://www.scribd.com/read/389144615/Preaching-by-Ear-Speaking-God-s-Truth-from-the-Inside-out.

170. McClellan, "Preaching by Ear."

171. Lane, "Oral Tradition," 22.

172. Lane, 22.

an indication of a completed hermeneutical circle as the message goes from the ancient spoken word of God to the written biblical text and then is made alive and received in the oral preaching event.

The Pro- and Anti-Orality Stances

So many have come on the side of orality, spanning all disciplines of study and with participation from both those in highly literate and highly oral communities. Orality has a strong appeal at present because it addresses the needs of both the non-literate and postmodern societies whose interests in this generation cannot be overlooked. Nevertheless, the orality movement has been subjected to different kinds of criticism, some of which will be highlighted here.

E. S. William in his article "Beware of the Orality Movement" discusses, in strict terms, his aversion for the activities of the orality movement.[173] Among others, he emphasizes two areas of disagreement that need to be mentioned. First is the theory of Walter Ong upon which William believes the movement based their theoretical framework. He cannot understand why a book written by a Jesuit priest and humanist scholar whose aim for writing was to consider "the deeper implications of the contrast between orality and writing" should be anything for evangelical bodies to celebrate.[174] William accuses Ong of two fallacies. One is Ong's evolutionary view that falsely presents primitive human beings who lived with the spoken word alone as having the ideal form of communication. Therefore writing represents a "fall" from a "utopian, primitive world in which myth, fable and story were methods of communication," and primitive people who were without writing were a repository of wisdom.[175] William cannot agree with this view because he states, "the stark reality is that most oral cultures are ruled by superstition and ignorance."[176] The other problem William had with Ong is that he had created a false dichotomy between the spoken and written word, making the spoken word natural and superior to the written word which is artificial. This is false because speaking and writing are complimentary rather than competitive.[177]

However, it is not absolutely correct to conclude that the orality movement is fundamentally based on Ong's work. The movement has used several tools

---

173. E. S. Williams, "Beware of the Orality Movement," Bible League Trust (n.d.).
174. Ong, *Orality and Literacy*, 5.
175. Williams, "Beware of the Orality Movement."
176. Williams.
177. Williams.

and fieldwork to establish the needs of oral communities and the methods that should be used to reach out to them. Today, orality has found a place in the fields of narrative theology and hermeneutics and recently in homiletics which cannot be discountenanced. William's view that most oral cultures are ruled by superstition and ignorance is a misunderstanding. Superstition is a product of religion rather than wisdom or knowledge.

It has been proved over and over again that the attempt to differentiate oral and written mentalities "is the most debatable."[178] Literate mentalities are in no way superior to oral mentalities. Regarding the dichotomy between the spoken and written word, enough evidence abounds beyond Ong to show that each has its strong and weak points, but ultimately many agree that they complement each other. Guss Palmer beautifully presents the relationship this way:

> In terms of the oral tradition, speech is the fundamental apparatus to keep the people human and active within the human fold. The reliance on the technology of writing and literacy is important for advancing our civilization, but they are not the only systems needed. We also need the human voice and utterance to maintain the balance between orality and literacy, one not greater than the other or any less important, both possessing the power to advance our human societies and why we should honor and respect the two.[179]

While Ong is often greatly appreciated, supporters of the orality movement have been cautious to avoid what Harriet Hill calls "hyper-Ong tendencies," to hold to Ong's claims and go beyond them. As noted earlier, this tendency is to "claim that oral communicators are not able to think abstractly and so limit the canon to narrative, or re-write the epistles in story form so people with an oral preference can understand them."[180] For support, she cites research among the Vai of Liberia that showed it is education which affects a person's ability to think abstractly and not literacy itself. Other examples of oral people who thought abstractly include Panini in the third century BC in India. He analyzed Sanskrit grammar and developed a complex set of rules which he orally taught to his followers. Therefore, it is wrong to claim that oral people cannot think abstractly. It is indeed insulting. And when emphasizing story or storying, it should be remembered that both literate and oral people love stories.

---

178. Johnson, "Orality, Literacy," 130.
179. Palmer, "Power of the Spoken Word," 21.
180. Hill, "Conversations about Orality," 216.

William's second argument against the orality movement are the Oral Bibles. These Bibles contain accumulated Bible stories told in oral societies over time and typically contain between fifty and two hundred stories which are crafted to be sensitive to the worldview of the receiving society. Williams fears that each teacher and each disciple have their own version of the Oral Bible which changes as their memory fades. He also accuses the "Story Runner" of Campus Crusade for Christ (Cru) of asking Oral Bible crafters to avoid words and phrases used in the Bible which could be confusing in everyday use. So words like "sinner" and "repent" are not used in crafting a story like Luke 15:8–10. In conclusion, William warns adherents of his Reformed tradition that

> The actions of the Orality Movement represent a serious attack on God's Word. The tragedy is that many true Christians are being deceived and misled by the persuasive promotion of the storytelling agenda. As reformed Christians we must warn our brothers and sisters in Christ, especially those in the Third World, of the dangers of this movement. As Martin Luther opposed the darkness of Rome, so today we must oppose the darkness of Lausanne and its Orality Movement. We live in a time when there is a great hunger for the truth of God's Word and the doctrines of the truth [sic] faith.[181]

These condemnations are products of misunderstanding the orality movement that will be cleared up with time as more light is shed on the intentions and activities of the movement's adherents. However, this criticism is also a caution that no method of gospel presentation should in any way kick against scriptural principles and by doing so become counterproductive.

Williams is not alone in criticizing the orality movement. The website Discernment Group also accuses the movement of wanting to deprive people of their basic right of access to the Bible text which was once available only to elites and of wanting to return them to the pre-Reformation era.[182] What this group and others need to understand is that the use of orality is intended to create an incarnational presentation of the gospel for people who are not first compelled to be literate before being saved or growing in their faith. Second, it is an effort to help fill the ladder rungs between illiteracy and functional literacy. People who are taught and discipled with oral methods are likely to aspire to know more through literacy as they grow. Orality, therefore, remains

---

181. Williams, "Beware of the Orality Movement."
182. "Orality the Newest Heresy of the NAR," Discernment Group (4 May 2006).

a powerful tool to reach the world for Christ in a manner that is holistic and time efficient.

Not all who embraced orality do so with easy conviction. Larry Dinkins is a good example of a church planter and professor who was trained in Dallas Theological Seminary, United States, to be a critical thinker and who can analyze the content of texts in both Hebrew and Greek. He possesses all the traits of an expositor – being logical, purposeful, and abstract – and he is obviously obsessed with the doctrinal sections of the Epistles.[183] But his experience when he attempted to teach at Bangkok Bible College, Thailand, changed his orientation completely. While officially Thailand has a high literacy rate, it is a predominantly oral culture. Thai people enjoy communication through narrative, drama, proverbs, and music over and above Western propositional and analytical thought systems. It took Dinkins twelve years of teaching narrative in a PhD program at Biola University, United States, a return to Thailand for qualitative research on his dissertation, seven years of field testing, several interviews and ground evaluations all over Thailand to be convinced that Thai people are oral learners and can best be reached through orality. At Biola University, Dinkins met Tom Steffens who was once frustrated while trying to reach the Ifugao tribe of the Philippines. According to Steffen, "The Ifugao wanted stories and I gave them systematic theology, they wanted relationships and I gave them reasons, they wanted characters and I gave them categories." He particularly convinced Dinkins of how valid orality could be for communication.[184]

Here is Dinkins' testimony:

> For the first time in my ministry I am seeing people consistently emote as they identify with Bible characters. In the past, if Thai people were crying during my sermons it was probably due to my bad Thai language. Now when I pause at the application stage of a story like Blind Bartimeus, I find that the Spirit often softens and prepares hearts for a personal discovery of truth, a truth that penetrates to a deep level in the human heart.[185]

Dinkins argues that people should not disparage this method of preaching to an oral culture, and of preaching to a typical Western literate culture, he states,

---

183. Larry Dinkins, "My Bumpy Road to Orality" (accessed 17 October 2016).

184. Tom Steffen, "My Reluctant Journey into Orality," Address to the 4th Conference on Reaching Oral Communicators, Anaheim, California, 13 July 2005, cited in Dinkins, "My Bumpy Road to Orality."

185. Dinkins, "My Bumpy Road to Orality."

Over the years I had used my exegetical scalpel to dissect hundreds of sections of holy writ, analyzing them in the original languages and then arranging them in sequential, logical fashion for teaching or preaching purposes. I had done this so often that I could diagram most any passage and construct a detailed outline with points and sub points in a few minutes. This time tested method is a valid and proven approach which expositors have used for centuries. It was developed within highly literate cultures and continues to resonate with print oriented societies.[186]

The point here is that the Thai are not very print oriented, and like so many of the unreached people in the world who prefer oral learning, "when wrapped in an oral package Scriptures retain a vitality and ability to jump and move in the life of oral learners."[187]

Implications for Expository Preaching in Africa

The working definition of expository preaching in this book is the incarnational communication of the text of God's word considering its historical, grammatical, and literary intention in a form that is faithful to the genres of the text and that is meaningful to the hearers in their sociocultural contexts, with the ultimate aim of enhancing total transformation to Christ-likeness. Juxtaposed against orality are certain implications that need to be enumerated for expository preaching in Africa.

First, African orality is not the same as attempts to communicate with a postmodern world. The roots of advocacy for orality in the West are not often statistics of literacy or the history of orality, though it may include such elements. Advocacy is more often for a paradigm shift from modernity to postmodernity. To reach a society that revels in absolute relativism, rejects objective truth, and is skeptical and suspicious of authority, one of the solutions homileticians have offered is to take a dialogical approach to preaching. This inductive preaching promotes the use of storytelling, audiovisuals, drama, and art.[188] These are vital elements of orality that have been studied so far. But the

---

186. Dinkins, "My Bumpy Road to Orality."
187. Dinkins.
188. Graham Macpherson Johnson, *Preaching to a Postmodern: A Guide to Reaching Twenty-first Century Listeners* (Grand Rapids: Baker Books, 2006), 26. See also Michael J. Quicke, *360-Degree Preaching* (Grand Rapids: Baker Academic, 2003), 73.

question I raised in a previous work is whether Africans are postmoderns in the real sense.

> Does Africa have a share in postmodernism? Is Africa in anyway close to a postmodern continent? If this were to be a question raised in a class setting, perhaps the chorused answer will be "No." Africa has always been synonymous with poverty, corruption, bad governance, poor infrastructure, political instability, war, ethnic cleansing, terrorism, religious fanaticism, and dependence on the western world for survival. Africa is far from being technologically advanced and its economy is largely dependent on imports. In the real sense of it, while modernity is giving way to postmodernity, Africa can be viewed as having yet to experience any full sense of modernity.[189]

What Africans may share with the world is the universality of globalization, but this is not enough to classify them as postmodern. Nhiwatiwa gives a sense to this when he states, "if modern is defined by the level of industrial and technological development, then postmodern thought is irrelevant to Africa." Africa's contribution to a postmodern world for now is to offer what postmodern people yearn for, community against individualism and a sense of the sacred, if these will be appreciated in the light of biblical spirituality.[190]

The second implication and related to the first is the fact that African orality is not an escape from authority. Orality is simply a mediation of authority through the communication language and experience of the people. To use storying or other oral means of communicating in a sermon just because "it appears less authoritative or less sophisticated and therefore less manipulative than straightforward analysis and proclamation" will not sell to an African preacher's conscience.[191] Lovejoy corroborates this when he states that "narrative sermons seemed less authoritarian than traditional sermons, utilized a format familiar to television and film viewers, and preserved more of the literary qualities of biblical narratives. Narrative sermon structures seemed better suited to the parables of Jesus, for instance, than analytical,

---

189. Ezekiel Ajibade, "The African Preacher and the Demands of Postmodernism," ed. E. E. Nihinlola, *Ogbomoso Journal of Theology (OJOT)* 20, no. 1 (2015): 16.

190. Eben Kanukayi Nhiwatiwa, *Preaching in the African Context: Why We Preach* (Nashville: Discipleship Resources International, 2012), 40. See also Marguerite A. Peeters, "Postmodernity and Africa: In the Balance," *Faith Magazine* (April 2008): https://www.faith.org.uk/article/march-april-2008-postmodernity-and-africa-in-the-balance (accessed 22 February 2021).

191. Lischer, "Limits of Story," 29.

outlined approaches did."[192] Deflecting authority should not be a reason why a preacher does not engage in expository preaching because "in Africa persons are still regarded with respect and as authorities because of their positions. Similarly, the Bible occupies a place of high honor and will not be brought under human scrutiny and questioning."[193] Expository preaching in Africa, even when employing orality, should recognize that preachers and the word of God they are carrying are authoritative.

The third implication from the foregoing is that expository preaching should be done with proper audience exegeses. While Africans are predominantly oral, it should be recognized that literacy is as high as 62 percent. The majority of these literate people may belong to the residual or secondary oral class, but there are still communities of highly literate listeners who do not have a problem with the linear-logical method of expository preaching. Examples of these are some university students, core urban dwellers, people who have been conditioned to abstractness as a result of their professions and careers, people who constantly travel out of Africa to the West, and others. This sense of stratification in orality is also mentioned by Harriet Hill when she advises that

> rather than blanket statements about how orality works, orality enthusiasts would do better to think of oralities and literacies. Every society is different and needs to be researched. Rather than polarizing oral people with literates, it is more correct to think of all people as oral, with some also literate. In most communities in the world today, both orality and literacy are present.[194]

An effort must be made in preaching to reach all strata. While it is suggested that African theologians and in essence African preachers develop village theology – a theology that considers "the rural situation of the majority of African people"[195] – the tools for audience analysis available to African preachers are very helpful to use to discover how to make their sermons reach

---

192. Grant Lovejoy, "Narrative Preaching in Recent North American Homiletics," Paper adapted from Grant Lovejoy, "Shaping Sermons by the Literary Form of the Text," in *Biblical Hermeneutics*, ed. Bruce Corley, Steve Lemke, and Grant Lovejoy (Nashville: Broadman & Holman, 1996), 327–34 and from a lecture given during Scholars in Ministry Week at Southwestern Baptist Theological Seminary, Fort Worth, Texas, 1997.

193. Nhiwatiwa, *Preaching in the African Context*, 40.

194. Hill, "Conversations about Orality," 217.

195. Nhiwatiwa, *Preaching in the African Context*, 20.

every ear and heart.[196] Then a model needs to be develop for a village oral expository sermon for completely oral preachers and to reach oral listeners and model for an African oral expository sermon that is oral but carries components of linear-logical and is useful to the preachers and listeners whose thought system has been significantly shaped by literacy.[197]

The fourth implication is that narrative preaching remains the greatest option for African preaching. Narrative preaching is where African orality can find full expression considering Africans' heritage of celebration, participation, dialogue, expression through myths, songs, stories and drama, prophetic utterances, and faith healing.[198] The burden is to make narrative preaching expository – ensuring that the historical, grammatical, and literary sense of the text is made clear. Grant Lovejoy offers several options in his survey of some of the types of narrative sermons in the literature:[199]

- In recited narrative sermons, preachers purely recite a Bible story, but this type may not directly qualify as a sermon even if it communicates God's word.
- In pure narrative sermons, preachers retell a biblical story with their own words but do not apply or exhort.
- In framed narrative sermons, preachers also retell a Bible story but cast a frame around it, brief introductory and concluding comments but which do not explain the story.
- In the narrative plus lessons type of sermon, preachers retell a biblical story and at the end tie it to the hearers' lives by stating lessons, principles, or applications.
- In the delayed narrative sermon, preachers delay by simply using the introductory time to give biblical background or prepare the people to listen to the story by stating a problem, its causes, effects, and probable solutions before taking them through the story.[200] In

---

196. Nhiwatiwa, 20. Discussions on audience exegesis or analysis can be found in Michael Milco, "Exegeting your Congregation," in *Moody Handbook on Preaching*, ed. John Kossler (Chicago: Moody, 2008), 351; and Keith Willhite, "Audience Relevance in Expository Preaching," *Bibliotheca Sacra* 149, no. 595 (Jul 1992): 370.

197. An attempt will be made to provide these models in chapter 6.

198. These substances were gleaned from studying the history of preaching in Africa in chapter three.

199. Lovejoy, "Narrative Preaching in Recent North American Homiletics." He extracts these narrative sermon types from the work of such authors as Thomas E. Boomershine, John Holbert, Eugene Lowry, and Richard A. Jenson.

200. Lovejoy, 5–11.

the suspended narrative type of sermons, preachers retell a biblical story and suspend it at a point because a certain aspect of it takes them outside the text to attempt to complete the message.
- In segmented narrative sermons, preachers tell a story one scene or episode at a time and pause between each segment to explain, illustrate, and apply.
- In multiple story narrative types of sermons, preachers use two or more stories, each serving as an indirect commentary on the other.
- In constructed narrative sermon, preachers attempt to lead listeners through sequences of experiences.
- In nonbiblical narrative sermons, preachers use nonbiblical stories as a substitute for biblical stories.

Put together, the narrative plus lessons sermon and the segmented narrative sermon stand out as most relevant to African preaching.[201] The former is relevant to the "Village Oral Expository Sermon," given in chapter 7 below, because while it is purely retelling a Bible story, it allows for application to the life of the hearers. The latter is useful to the African oral expository sermon because it allows for skillful weaving of biblical backgrounds in the Bible story, as well as explanations, illustrations, and applications which are the gems of expository preaching.

Lovejoy's reservations on narrative plus lessons sermons are understandable but not tenable within African contexts. He states, "admittedly there is risk in this approach. If we have told the story well, the listeners may have already had an encounter with God. Our comments could diminish the sermon's impact by belaboring what God has already made obvious to them. We may insult their intelligence. We may distract them from lessons God wants to teach them but which we did not include in our application."[202] Many of these risks are assumed. Typical Africans are glad to know that there are some lessons they can take home from the preacher's message. Lovejoy's reservation on the segmented narrative sermon is that it breaks the biblical story apart and may make it difficult for oral communicators to remember. But as he admits, "This act of breaking the story apart is very natural for literates."[203] This is why I suggest that the narrative plus lessons sermon be used in modelling the village

---

201. Lovejoy, 11–17.
202. Lovejoy, 8.
203. Lovejoy, 8.

oral expository sermon and the segmented narrative sermon be used for the African oral expository sermon.[204]

I coined the titles "Village Oral Expository Sermon" and "African Oral Expository Sermon" for this work. The first is developed in the next chapter as a model for preaching in the rural, non-literate, and oral communities in Africa, and the second is developed, also in the next chapter, as a model for preaching in general African communities where there are often mixed congregations of literate and non-literate people as well as residual and secondary oral listeners. The village concept is derived from Eben Kanukayi Nhiwatiwa who recommends that Africa theologians must develop what he calls "village theology." He states,

> By village theology I mean theological reflection that considers the rural situation of the majority of African people. It is a theology that faces the glaring reality that the problems of our people cannot be solved by endless presentations of learned papers at conferences and workshops in Africa and abroad. Village theology demands that African theologians be where the people are. . . . If we African theologians and preachers are not living within earshot of what is going on in the village, then we miss vital themes for preaching. . . . After mingling with the people during the week and listening to such affirmations of faith in prayer, the preacher will do well to reaffirm the people's theologies from the pulpit. But if we live in isolation from the people's daily experiences in the village, then our call for contextual preaching is in vain.[205]

Akwasi O. Ofori made a similar effort of developing a contextualized sermon for Africa by adapting the New Homiletic which he calls "The New Ghanaian Sermon." There is further discussion about this sermon type in chapter six.[206]

The fifth implication worth commenting on is the need for faithfulness to the genres and subgenres of the Bible. Not all Scriptures are narrative, despite the volume of narratives in the Bible. African preachers will have to devise means of preaching the books of Proverbs and Psalms, apocalyptic literature, and the highly didactic Epistles without forcing these texts into a narrative mold and yet making them meaningful to predominantly oral-culture listeners.

---

204. Lovejoy, 12.
205. Nhiwatiwa, *Preaching in the African Context*, 20.
206. Akwasi O. Ofori, *Recovering Storytelling for Ghanaian Preaching: An Adaptation of the New Homiletic for an African Culture* (Bloomington, IN: WestBow, 2015), Kindle edition.

Preachers must also bear in mind that African orality does not defy or deny logicality. Walter Ong observes that oral communicators "cannot organize elaborate concatenations of causes in the analytic kind of linear sequences which can only be set up with the help of texts. The lengthy sequences they produce, such as genealogies, are not analytic but aggregative. But oral cultures can produce amazingly complex and intelligent and beautiful organizations of thought and experience."[207] Sogolo corroborates Ong by stating that "it is for this reason alone that an intelligible analysis of African thought demands the application of its own universe of discourse, its own logic, and its own criteria of rationality."[208] The question then is in what rational way can these non-narrative genres of Scripture be presented to and understood by Africans with an oral culture?

The value of the oral elements of stories, songs, drama, proverbs, and folklore becomes relevant at this point. They are the channels of communication in Africa. None of them is qualified to take the position of a sermon, but the concept of orality does not regard them as mere tools. Therefore, it becomes evident that preachers in Africa might consider a shift from the traditional monologue sermon to a variety of styles that incorporate orality or express content through orality.

For example, dialogue is part of African orality. This dialogue is not in the context of Thompson and Bennett who see dialogical preaching as "an act within the context of public worship in which two or more persons engage in a verbal exchange as the sermon or message."[209] It is also not in the sense of Doug Pagitt who in advocating dialogue in preaching sarcastically renamed preaching as "speaching."[210] Gerald T. Kanye defines dialogical preaching as "involving the congregation in a question and answer or discussion approach to the word of God which has been proclaimed in that particular liturgical celebration." He then lists some advantages of this kind of preaching: it invites the celebrating community to reflect, challenges participants to understand and respond to God's word, and makes sermons have a cultural context. Dialogical preaching also helps in direct application, increased interest, communication of new ideas, active listening, and prevention of sleep during the sermon.[211]

---

207. Ong, *Orality and Literacy*, 56.

208. Sogolo, "Logic and Rationality," 221.

209. William D. Thompson and Gordon C. Bennett, *Dialogue Preaching: The Shared Sermon* (Valley Forge, PA: Judson, 1969), 29.

210. Doug Pagitt, *Preaching Re-Imagined* (Grand Rapids: Zondervan, 2005), 29.

211. Gerald K. Tanye, *The Church-as-family and Ethnocentrism in Sub-Saharan Africa* (Berlin: LIT Verlag, 2010), 404.

An objection to dialogical preaching is that all of these said advantages can be achieved without using the kind of dialogue these authors advocate. Moreover, dialogical preaching makes it difficult to achieve unity in a sermon, may leave some people in the congregation out, may engender some controversies and debate, and may result in some individuals dominating a discussion.[212] The real root of dialogical preaching remains rebellion against authority. There are other ways that African preachers who are held in high honor and accorded much authority can employ participation in such an important discourse as a sermon. Eliciting and receiving responses can be almost spontaneous and not based on an arranged round table conference over God's preached word.

Finally, there are no obstacles to the use of stories because narrative sermons incorporate them. But critical consideration of how orality elements can be used and yet satisfy the working definition of expository preaching is the task ahead. The challenge of development is of utmost concern when orality is critically examined. Many predominantly oral societies are still backward technologically, economically, and politically, Africa being a typical example. If orality is considered to be a first step in reaching those who are not educated and cannot read the Bible or write, a great missiological advantage is gained. But use of orality cannot stop there. If it is the effective means of communication that it is emphasized here to be, then it should become a means of challenging the continent into a better life. It is not enough to tell a Bible story and assume a sermon has been preached. Richard Lischer's insight on this topic is pungent:

> Stories may be the inspiration for change and set the tone or historical background for change, but they are not equipped to make the kinds of discriminations necessary for informed ethical decisions; nor by their nature can they issue the direct proclamations and exhortations which, historically, have galvanized the process of social and ecclesiastical reform. For example, the black tradition of preaching, rich as it is in the art of biblical storytelling, made a greater contribution to black endurance than to social change in the United States. The effectiveness of Martin Luther King as a preacher and agent of social change lay not in his ability to tell a story but in his incisive analysis of the situation in America and his prophetic call to justice. In his style of oratory he did not desert the

---

212. Tanye, *Church-as-family*, 405.

black tradition, but the content and structure of his sermons are not organized around Gospel narratives but gospel principles.[213]

Any means of communication in sermons that does not lift Africans up and help promote their sociopolitical and economic development is deficient. African sermons must anticipate the question asked on the day of Pentecost in Acts 2:37: "When the people heard this, they were cut to the heart and said to Peter and the other apostles, 'Brothers, what shall we do?'" Embedded in sermons should also be those principles that will lead to the actions that ultimately produce transformation.

Discussion Questions

1. Has it occurred to you, beyond what you read in this chapter, that Africans are predominantly oral in their communication? In what ways has it occurred to you?

2. Discuss your experience about storytelling and the type of responses you have received from your hearers.

3. Take a look at the narrative preaching forms shared by Grant Lovejoy. Which of them would you consider appropriate for your congregation and which would you love to experiment with?

---

213. Lischer, "Limits of Story," 35.

5

Using African Orality to Contextualize Expository Preaching

Orality has been defined and discussed, and it has been presupposed to be a communication vehicle to reach the heart of Africans. This is where context comes in. Context is defined as "the circumstances or events that form the environment within which something exists or takes place."[1] The African context encompasses all situations and circumstances that surround Africa and make it what it is. The question then is, what is happening in the hearts of Africans today that needs to be reached with the word of God in expository preaching mediated by orality?

Africa is a complete paradox. It contains a mix of all that can be found almost anywhere in the world, but perhaps in their extremes. In a famous speech marking the commemoration of the movement called "African Renaissance," Thabo Mbeki, the former president of South Africa, expressed this tension and paradox:

> I am born of the peoples of the continent of Africa. The pain of the violent conflict that the peoples of Liberia, Somalia, the Sudan, Burundi and Algeria is a pain I also bear. The dismal shame of poverty, suffering and human degradation of my continent is a blight that we share. The blight on our happiness that derives from this and from our drift to the periphery of the ordering of human affairs leaves us in a persistent shadow of despair. This is a savage road to which nobody should be condemned. This thing

---

1. "Context," *Encarta Dictionaries*, Microsoft Encarta (2009).

> that we have done today, in this small corner of a great continent that has contributed so decisively to the evolution of humanity says that Africa reaffirms that she is continuing her rise from the ashes. . . . Whatever the difficulties, Africa shall be at peace! However improbable it may sound to the sceptics, Africa will prosper! Whoever we may be, whatever our immediate interest, however much we carry baggage from our past, however much we have been caught by the fashion of cynicism and loss of faith in the capacity of the people, let us err today and say – nothing can stop us now![2]

This is the paradox that characterizes Africa, and this is the context in which African Christian preachers find themselves. More specifically, two of these paradoxical contexts are described below.

Religiosity and Religious Plurality

Africans have been described as overly religious.[3] Traditional religion was the first, but several others, especially Islam and Christianity, came in later. These all affect the worldview of Africans and become a challenge to anyone who will preach in Africa. Africans are exposed to a worldview that acknowledges God and the things of the spirit which assists in their understanding of the Christian message either as a means to salvation or Christian growth. Khunhiyop opines that African traditional religious belief "provides an important bridge to a meaningful discussion of a theology that makes sense to Africans."[4] He further asserts that these "beliefs and the African worldview are not lost when Africans become Christian. They affect everyday life, whether in terms of marriage, farming, career choices, or even such mundane matters as travelling."[5]

But African preachers have several issues to contend with as a result of the influence of other religions. One of the challenges they face is a conception of the Bible as an instrument for divination or of fortune telling. Another is that Africans see the Bible as having such incredible power that it can protect

---

2. Thabo Mbeki quoted in Khaya Dlanga, "'I am an African': Thabo Mbeki's Speech. Possibly the Greatest African Speech Ever," *Afrika* 1, no. 1 (accessed 11 December 2016).

3. Samuel Waje Kunhiyop, *African Christian Ethics* (Bukuru: Africa Christian Textbooks, 2008), 15.

4. Samuel Waje Kunhiyop, *African Christian Theology* (Nairobi: WordAlive Publishers, 2012), 43.

5. Kunhiyop, *African Christian Theology*, xv.

people from harm including car accidents, untimely death, dreadful dreams, and attacks from demons, sorcerers, witches, and wizards.[6] The Bible may be seen as something to "use" rather than something to open, interpret, and apply to daily life. For some it is a magical book that can be kept under the pillow, inside the car, or placed on a demon-possessed individual while conducting an exorcism, popularly known as deliverance. Some portions of the Psalms, especially the imprecatory parts, are read against the enemies at different prayer grounds and gatherings, or before sleeping or embarking on a journey. So shaping the African paradigm with the word of God is an indispensable task for African preachers.

The religious inclination of Africans is one of the catalysts for the growth of Christianity, and Africa has become a bastion of church growth in the world. It is on record that the church in Africa grew from ten million in 1900 to over two hundred million by the early 1980s. Four hundred million was projected before 2000.[7] By 2010, the church had grown to over 516 million, and a study in 2018 put the number at 631 million.[8] As of 2016, between twenty-five thousand and thirty thousand were being added to the church daily, which amounts to an estimated ten million in a year.[9] In 2020 it was estimated that Christians form 49 percent of Africa's population.[10]

But there is a tension here: the reported and observed growth is not commensurate with the life of Christ manifested in the continent. There exists disunity, interdenominational strife, leadership tussles, and splitting of churches. Newspaper headlines carry information about the scandalous sins of church members including sexual immorality among church leaders and members alike. It is ironic that Christians are involved in intertribal wars, killing and maiming each other. Christian politicians are in the governments of several nations, and at times head such nations, yet the continent continues to wallow in deep poverty and wretchedness because of the corruption and compromise of believers who are not living as salt and light. Armed robbers now daringly visit churches to rob, and occasionally investigations reveal that

---

6. Sam Oleka, "The Authority of the Bible in the African Context," in *Issues in African Christian Theology* (Nairobi: East African Educational Publishers, 1998), 87.

7. Geoff Waugh, "Astounding Church Growth," *Renewal Journal* (28 February 2016).

8. "Global Christianity – A Report on the Size and Distribution of the World's Christian Population," Pew Research Center: Religion and Public Life (19 December 2011). "Christianity in Africa," Wikipedia (accessed 14 January 2016).

9. Waugh, "Astounding Church Growth."

10. "Christianity in Africa," Wikipedia (accessed 14 January 2016).

one or two of the robbers' gang were members of the church, or they had an informant in the church. Many churches in Africa need revival.

Relative Backwardness

Africa is a land of historical blessedness and cultural richness and has been a source of moral light to the entire world. Even in the face of the realities of globalization and postmodernism, Marguerite A. Peeters still sees Africa as a land of great opportunities. She has compared what Africa possesses but has been lost in the Western world and made some analysis.[11] The first African asset is sound anthropology. Its cultures have yet to radically divorce reason from conscience or the heart, and therefore they retain a high level of rationality, wisdom, and intelligence of the heart.

Second, Peeters believes that most African traditions are still deeply rooted in a sense of reality and concreteness, with such aspirations as are born out of a healthy common sense. This she considers to be antithetical to postmodernism and technological advancement which threaten to enslave humanity in a world of dream and less of reality. Third, against Western rationalism, deism, and naturalism which have led to humanism apart from God, indigenous Africans uphold the sacred and the sacredness of life. Nature is still considered to come directly from God. Fourth, Africans possesses a nature of receiving and giving without payment or obligation, a nature of love in human relationships which can be shared as a gift to the rest of humanity who are yearning for a reintroduction of love in their cultures. And finally, Peeters opines that Africans can lead a return to brotherhood, fatherhood, and motherhood. African societies are still places where a neighbor is primarily a brother, a father, or a mother and not just a citizen seeking for rights and empowerment. The family is still the basic cell of the society, and in some parts of Africa, each woman, known or unknown, married or not, is called "mother" and each man "father."[12]

But all is far from being well with Africa. It remains a continent bedeviled with intertribal and ethnic wars, famine, epidemics, HIV/AIDS, poverty, corruption, selfish leadership, illiteracy, and gross underdevelopment across the board and has a long way to go in convincing the world it has something to offer. Enyinnaya captures this reality when he states that "apart from

---

11. Marguerite A. Peeters, "Postmodernity and Africa: In the Balance," *Faith Magazine* (April 2008): faith.org.uk/article/march-april-2008-postmodernity-and-africa-in-the-balance.

12. Peeters, "Postmodernity and Africa."

bad leadership, system instability, social and political violence, and ethnic conflicts, the contemporary African political situation is characterized by brazen corruption by public officers and economic misadventure on the part of succeeding governments." These characteristics, he concludes, are the "obstacles on Africa's path to development."[13]

Many of these issues must have cropped up in the mind of the London-based Nigerian pastor Matthew Ashimolowo when he wrote his book *What is Wrong with Being Black?*[14] He raises a series of questions from his observation that "wherever Black people are, whether it is Australia – among the Aborigines, Africa, Europe, Latin America, the Caribbean, or North America, we seem to belong at the bottom pile, or the bottom of the pyramid, economically, socially, physically, mentally, etc."[15] Below are some of the questions Ashimolowo raises:

- What is responsible for these two thousand years of "black backwardness"?
- What is responsible for Africa being the richest continent and yet inhabited by the poorest people?
- Why do black nations constitute the biggest group of borrower nations?
- If blacks are not cursed, is their land cursed?
- Africans are religious by nature, and where they have become Christians, they have been committed. Why are they still not making progress?
- Why is there such a gap between white-dominated and black-dominated nations?
- Some African nations have high numbers of educated citizens, yet Africa in modern times has not contributed significantly to discoveries or inventions.
- When will the black person's day of manifestation come?[16]

These are great questions that must ring in the heart and mind of an African preacher. Ashimolowo is only one among several who have tried to think hard about the causes of the problems of Africa and probable solutions. Basil Davidson in *The Black Man's Burden: Africa and the Curse of the Nation-*

---

13. John Enyinnaya, "A Theological Approach to Political Transformation in Africa," *Ogbomoso Journal of Theology* 11 (2006): 80.
14. Matthew Ashimolowo, *What is Wrong with Being Black?: Celebrating Our Heritage, Confronting Our Challenges* (Shippensburg: Destiny Image, 2007).
15. Ashimolowo, *What Is Wrong*, 7.
16. Ashimolowo, 7–11.

State considers the problem of Africa to be nation-statism, a model which he opines was imposed on Africa by colonial masters.[17] Martin Meredith considers the problem of Africa to be basically leadership and states that "Few countries have experienced wise or competent leadership. . . . Africa has suffered grievously at the hand of its Big Men and its ruling elites. Their preoccupations, above all, have been to hold power for the purpose of self-enrichment."[18] At a holistic level, the African problem predates colonialism, as evidenced by the ability to connect it to the problems of the Africans in the diaspora, especially African Americans in slavery. But something was equally wrong when many of these slaves were betrayed by their fellow Africans who connived with the white slave buyers. Leadership has been a big problem in Africa as Meredith rightly observed.

Whatever the diagnoses or solution, Africa has hope. According to Ashimolowo, all Africans need to do is turn their hearts to Jesus, climb above their inherent weaknesses through education, love each other, and build a healthy self-image. Ashimolowo further suggests that Africans should be devoted to the study of God's word and follow up with great dreams, planning, creating, and encouraging each other to trust in God.[19] Finally, he states that

> Blacks must take pride in the fact that they truly built the first civilization, and that in that first 3,000–4,000 years of humanity they were not the ones considered backward or barbaric. Egypt was a land of advanced architecture – the world's oldest stone structures are found in ancient Egypt, the great pyramids constitute one of the seven wonders of the world.[20]

The foregoing paints a picture of the context in which African preachers find themselves, as well as their need to make the necessary impact. As African preachers interpret the revelation of God in Scripture, so should they respond to concrete human situations in their preaching.[21] Preachers need to address many of the issues hitherto mentioned so many Africans will not think they have to return to the African traditional religions from whence they came.

---

17. Basil Davidson, *The Black Man's Burden: Africa and the Curse of the Nation-state.* (New York: Times Books, 1992), 13.

18. Martin Meredith, *The State of Africa: A History of Fifty Years of Independence* (London: Free Press, 2006), 686.

19. Ashimolowo, *What is Wrong*, 348.

20. Ashimolowo, 348.

21. Emiola Nihinlola, *Theology Under the Mango Tree: A Handbook of African Christian Theology* (Alausa-Ikeja, Lagos: Fine Print and Manufacturing, 2013), 41.

Anyone who will preach within an African context must be ready to deal with people who operate within the paradoxes that have been described here, bringing in the gospel as the ultimate solution to African existential problems by sound exposition of God's word through the channels of communication provided by orality.

Oral Resources for Contextualized Expository Preaching

Several oral elements have been alluded to so far including songs, drama, drumming, dancing, poetry, folktales, myths, storytelling, art, proverbs, and idioms. The list is not exhaustive considering several perspectives from which writers on African oral communication have viewed it. For example, Sulaiman Osho adapts the word "oramedia" to describe elements such as gongs, drumbeats, drama, festivals, town criers, puppet shows, dance, singing, stories, artwork, traditional clothing, and masks.[22] Sticking to the goal of contextualized expository preaching in Africa, only the use of songs, drama, proverbs, poems, folktales, and storytelling will be examined. A journey into categorization may be a distraction as several of the elements are intertwined. Songs may be used in drama, and drama may be used in songs. Folklore is often a story and has its academic classifications. Poems may be sung or recited, and proverbs may be engaged in songs, drama, and storytelling. Details of such classifications go beyond the scope of this work. At the risk of oversimplification, Akinyemi's assertion may suffice here:

> The continent of Africa hosts the largest reservoir of varieties of verbal arts, which could be classified into two categories, namely, literary and historical. While the literary category includes poetic genres such as praise poetry, sacred chants, songs, and the verbal formulae like incantations, parables, and proverbs, the historical

---

22. Sulaiman A. Osho, "The Uniqueness of African Means of Communication in Contemporary World," Seminar on Cultural Diplomacy in Africa, from the Institute for Cultural Diplomacy, Kurfurstendamm, Berlin, Germany, 11 July 2011, 3. Also see Steve Agilenko, "A Re-assessment of the Relevance of African Culture to the Church in London with Particular Reference to Predominantly African Churches" (accessed 15 July 2015); Rob van Poelje, "Consultancy Training in Communication Strategy Development and Materials Production," Mission Report (New Bussa: Nigerian-German (GTZ) Kainji Lake Fisheries Promotion Project, 1996), 5; Kenneth Inyani Simala, "Orality, Modernity and African Development: Myth as Dialogue of Civilizations," Abstract, *CODESRIA* (December 2011): 2.

type, on the other hand, includes such forms as narratives based on myths, legends, folktales, and historical genres like epics.[23]

The emphasis is on the role these elements can play, which can either be supportive or substantive, in the contextualization process. The supportive role is generally accepted, but the substantive role may be viewed as radical and objectionable in some homiletical quarters. Supportive roles can be using these oral elements for introducing, illustrating, or concluding a sermon, while the sermon content is pure biblical exposition. Substantive roles are when any of the oral elements become the direct medium through which exposition is done. Striking a balance is a highly required task.

The battle line for this discussion was drawn by John Piper when in an interview he expressed his fears about using video clips and drama during worship services. He expressed the liberty that believers have in Christ and acknowledged that the New Testament does not explicitly forbid airing visuals during worship services, then he went on to express his reservations and indeed warnings:

> I'll be gone in a few years and you can do whatever you want to do, but I believe profoundly in the power and the till-Jesus-comes-validity of preaching. And by that I mean the spirit-anointed exposition of the Scripture through clear explanations and applications of what's there. There's something God-appointed about that. I think the use of video and drama largely is a token of unbelief in the power of preaching. And I think that, to the degree that pastors begin to supplement their preaching with this entertaining spice to help people stay with them and be moved and get helped, it's going to backfire. It's going to backfire. It's going to communicate that preaching is weak, preaching doesn't save, preaching doesn't hold, but entertainment does. And we'll just go further and further. So we don't do video clips during the sermon. We don't do skits. I went to a drama at our church four days ago. I believe in drama. I believe in the power of drama. But let drama be drama! And let preaching be preaching! Let's have the arts in our churches, but don't try to squash it all into Sunday morning. So I get worked up about these things. That's where I

---

23. Akintunde Akinyemi, "African Oral Tradition Then and Now: A Culture in Transition," *Centrepoint Humanities Edition* 14, no. 1 (n.d.): 27.

am on that. Free. Nobody is going to go to hell because of this, in the short run.[24]

It is not clear if John Piper is referring to situations where drama plays a supportive role to the sermon or it is the sermon. But it is clear that anything short of a formal sermon presentation, which he regards as "the spirit-anointed exposition of Scripture through clear explanations and applications of what's there," is not acceptable to him.

However, the context of orality is far different from that of entertainment in which John Piper responded in this interview. The whole idea of content and form come into play again. The content of expository preaching remains the truth derived from the techniques of exegesis and the principles of biblical interpretation. Expository preaching must arise from an honest engagement with the text and place the gospel at its center.[25] But the form can be varied. In the words of Robert Allen,

> Accepting a view which makes a distinction between expository content and organization enables the preacher to maintain fidelity to Scripture by means of a historical-grammatical hermeneutic, while adapting to an audience in the way those biblical truths are communicated. In this way narrative preaching, dialogue preaching, debate, drama, storytelling, and inductive preaching can serve as viable communicative styles while at the same time the preacher faithfully exposits the God-given meaning of any text. The expository method of preparing content is demanded by Scripture and should not be abandoned. The method of organization commonly called expository preaching is not demanded by Scripture and is therefore only one of many styles of preaching available to the preacher today.[26]

For a contextualized expository preaching, the oral elements in view are mostly considered to be supportive, but it is recommended even if not all the time that some are substantively used to expound the word based on the creativity and dexterity of the African preacher.

---

24. John Piper, "What Are Your Thoughts on Drama and Movie Clips in Church Services?" desiringGod (15 July 2009).

25. Robert A. Allen, "The Expository Sermon – Cultural or Biblical?" *Journal of Ministry and Theology* 2, no. 2 (Fall 1998): 213.

26. Allen, "Expository Sermon," 229.

Use of Songs

Music and the word are highly complementary. That music can be a vehicle for communicating the word of God is implied in Colossian 3:16 where believers were admonished, "Let the word of Christ dwell in you richly; in all wisdom teaching and admonishing one another with psalms and hymns and spiritual songs, singing with grace in your hearts unto God" (ASV). Citing Robert Shaw who states "let us see to it that music shall be as worthy an act of worship as the spoken word," Olford and Olford point out that "God has married preaching and praising; and what God has joined together, let no man put asunder!"[27] Like the word of God, music remains a potent tool in converting many to Christ. The singing of the early church fathers is known to have converted many hostile and barbarous tribes who had never heard the name of Jesus.[28] During the Great Awakenings in the United States, it is also on record that "when sinful men who were bent on murder, could not be tamed by the austere utterances of John Wesley or the powerful oratory of George Whitefield, the singing of spiritual songs by Charles Wesley humbled them."[29]

If singing is this powerful and is one of the elements in African orality, then singing can play several roles in the preaching task. It can serve the purpose of introducing a sermon. A theme song by a musician or the preacher can prepare the hearts of the people. This role is often performed by church choirs in Africa who sing shortly before the preacher preaches, and some of those interviewed in the course of this research confessed that those choir songs stay longer in their memory than the sermon. Many interviewees said that sermons stay long in their memories. But J. A. Oguntoye sincerely affirmed that songs stay longer, and most of the respondents stated that a sermon stays longer in their memories when it is backed up with songs as well as other elements of orality hitherto mentioned.[30]

A song can illustrate a sermon, conclude it, or be used for the invitation. But songs have also been used in Africa to directly preach the gospel message and to expound Scripture, and they are still being used. Reference has been made to Niyi Adedokun.[31] Another singer, J. A. Adelakun, gave an exposition of

---

27. Robert Shaw cited in Stephen F. Olford and David Olford, *Anointed Expository Preaching* (Nashville: B&H Academic, 1998), 331.

28. Olford and Olford, *Anointed Expository Preaching*, 323.

29. Olford and Olford, 326.

30. J. A. Oguntoye, interview by Abimbola Abosede Odejobi, 25 October 2016.

31. See chapter 4, page 112–113. Noteworthy among the collection is *Esan ko gboogun* (Nemesis has no remedy), *Olorun Semi* (God offended me), and *Won kilo folode* (The hunter was warned). The albums are well illustrated on the back covers to reflect the content.

Luke 17:26–27 and Genesis 6:9–7:24 to a Nigerian (Yoruba) audience, and they have savored his album track *Amona Tete Wa* for decades. Thirty-two years after the release of the album, many still sing the lyrics off hand on the streets in southwestern Nigeria. The lyrics stand as a complete sermon with introduction, exposition, illustration, application, conclusion, and invitation.[32] If this song is viewed as an inductive sermon, which it really is considering its features, it is possible to identify the movement. Though it starts with the refrain, which is typical of his genre of African gospel music, Adelakun introduces the problem, highlighting serious issues of concern in the world and especially the nation of Nigeria at that time. Then he brings in Scripture describing the events of the flood in Noah's time. An excerpt from the album sings,

> *Ará ẹ jẹ́ á rántí ìgbà ayé Noah,*
> (Brethren, let us remember the times of Noah)
> *Ẹ́ má jẹ́ á gbà gbé o gbogbo wa*
> (Do not let us all forget)
> *Ìkún omi tó kọjá*
> (The flood that once took place)
> *Olówó ayé ń wí, wọ́nńí rọ́ ni Noah ńpa*
> (The rich of the world said Noah was lying)
> *Tálíkà ńsọ tirẹ̀*
> (The poor said their own)
> *Wón ní bo lòjò ti ń bọ̀wá*
> (They said, "Where is rain coming from?")
> *Láláì jiyàn rárá, seni Noah tèsíwájú*
> (Without any argument, Noah just continued)
> *Láláì bìkítà, ọmọ Ọlọ́run ọ wẹ̀yìn wò*
> (Without worrying, the child of God never looked back)
> *Pẹ̀lú ìrànlọ́wọ́ Olúwa, ọkọ̀ Noah parí*
> (With the Lord's help, Noah's ark was completed)
> *Ẹranko ńwọlé, èèrà ńwọnú ọkọ̀*
> (The animals came in, the ants entered the ark)
> *Àwọn ẹyẹ ojú ọrun gbogbo*
> (All the birds of the sky)
> *Gbogbo wọn ló sáré wọlé*
> (All came in with haste)

---

32. Segun Oikelome, "Amona Tete Mabo.flv," YouTube (28 June 2011).

> *B'ẹ́lẹ́dẹ̀ ti y'ọ̀bùn tó síbẹ̀ ó r'áyè wọlé*
>> (As dirty as the pig was, he got a chance to enter)
>
> *Níbẹ̀ la r'ọ́mọ ènìyàn, wọ́n njẹ tí wọ́n nmu*
>> (There we saw human beings, wining and dining)
>
> *B'éwúrẹ́ ti j'áláìgbọrọ̀n tó, kíá ló sáré wọlé*
>> (As stubborn as the goat was, it quickly ran in)
>
> *Ibẹ̀ la r'ọ́mọ ènìyàn, wọ́n sọ pé 'rọ́ ni*
>> (Still we saw human beings saying it was a lie)
>
> *Wọ́n nkó mọ jáde, nwọ́n sè 'gbéyàwó kiri*
>> (They were christening babies and doing wedding ceremonies all over)
>
> *Wọn o bẹ̀rù òfin Olúwa ọba wa*
>> (They did not fear the law of the Lord our King)
>
> *Gbogbo wọn ló njayé*
>> (They were all enjoying life).

After the refrain the sermon lyrics continue:

> *Ẹranko gbogbo wọlé tán, à t'ẹyẹ ojú ọ̀run*
>> (After the animals came in and the birds in the sky)
>
> *Noah pẹ̀lú ìdílé rẹ̀ wọ́n nkó jíje mímu*
>> (Noah and his family kept gathering food and drink)
>
> *Nígbà tísé parí tán Noah bá wo 'nú ọkọ̀*
>> (When they were through Noah entered the ark)
>
> *Ó wọnú ọkọ̀ lọ tàràrà pẹ̀lú ènìyàn meje*
>> (He entered straight into the ark with seven people)
>
> *Ènìyàn meje wọ̀nyí, ìdílé Noah ni gbogbo wọn*
>> (These seven people were Noah's family)
>
> *Nígbà tí wọ́n wọlé tán, Ọ̀gá ògo ti 'lẹ̀kùn*
>> (After entering the King of Glory shut the door)
>
> *Óku àwọn aláigbọràn lati gbàdájó wọn*
>> (It was now left for the disobedient to receive their judgment)
>
> *Ọ̀kán kígbe títí, ó ní Noah, Noah*
>> (One of them cried and cried, saying, Noah! Noah!)
>
> *Noah jọ̀wọ́ sí 'lèkùn,*
>> (Noah, please open the door!)
>
> *A b'óò mọmí mọ́ ni, èmi ni wọ́n bí lé yèyé rẹ*
>> (Or don't you know me again? I am your uncle!)
>
> *Mo ló ti pé ó ti jù, mo l'ẹ́pa ò b'óró mọ́*
>> (I say it was too late. Their fate was irreversible)

Ìlẹ̀kùn ọkọ̀ ti tì, ọ̀nà ìgbàlà ti dí
(The door of the ark has been locked. The way of salvation has been blocked)

Adelakun then compares the biblical situation with current happenings and affirms Jesus's prophecy that the end times will be as it was in the days of Noah. He challenges listeners to repent because whether the world likes it or not, it will not be long before Jesus comes to judge the world.

The nuances that Adelakun introduces to the song are quite insightful. His description of how the dirty pig and the stubborn goat all got into the ark while humans never cared is an example. One of the beautiful and highly imaginative moments is when he pictures people trying to knock on the ark's door after it was shut by God. He describes someone crying "Noah, Noah, Noah please opened the door! Or don't you know me? I am your uncle. But it was too late. Their fate is irreversible. The door of the ark has been locked." This is a highly emotional moment for the listeners to the album. Unfortunately, it has been edited in several of the versions available on YouTube, because it is not impossible that someone challenged him that this part is not actually in the story and is his own addition (or he personally thought over it).

Adelakun has also been criticized for his use of *Amọ̀nà* for Jesus Christ. *Amọ̀nà* is literally "the one that knows the way." The argument is that Jesus is not just the one that knows the way; according to John 14:6, he is the Way. But perhaps the transcription of Adelakun's recent update of the album on social media indicates what was on his mind thirty-two years ago. He translates *Amọ̀nà* as The Omniscience. That is also not correct because in Yoruba language, Omniscience means *a mọ ohun gbogbo* (knower of all things). But these issues do not reduce the powerful impact Adelakun's album has made and is still making.

The dexterity of Adelakun reminds this writer of Carman, an American gospel artist who is greatly skilled in the art of using music to expound the word this way. In his song titled "Lazarus Come Forth," Carman sings a rich narrative of the events of John 11. He introduces what could be called the central proposition or the big idea using the words of Jesus himself in John 11:25,

> I am the resurrection and the Life:
> He that believeth in me,
> Though he were dead,
> Yet shall he live.

Carman goes on to sing the following:

> A certain man had died
> In the town of Bethany
> And Lazarus was his name
> The Bible says he was
> A man that Jesus loved
> And his sisters thought
> It was a shame
> Mary and Martha longed
> For Jesus healing touch
> To come and raise their brother
> Cause they loved that boy so much
> But Jesus had a plan not known to any man
> That would soon take away their pain
> They was waiting for Jesus
> To come and say
>
> *Chorus:*
> *Lazarus, Lazarus, Lazarus Come Forth*
>
> When he died he went to where
> The saints of God did stay
> In the holding place
> They lived beyond the tomb
> And there he saw Elijah, Moses, Samuel, even Ruth

From this point Carman goes into a highly imaginative session where he pictures a long conversation between Lazarus and the saints – many of those referred to as the "cloud of witnesses" in Hebrew 11. As Lazarus begins to share his own testimony about who Jesus is, Carman narrates what takes place at the grave as Jesus calls Lazarus to come forth. Lazarus excuses himself from the saints, and Carman closes with the good news:

> Mountains be moved
> When he said, Lazarus Come Forth
> Mary don't weep Martha don't moan
> Here come your boy Comin' Forth[33]

---

33. Carman, "Lazarus Come Forth." See full lyrics at https://genius.com/Carman-lazarus-come-forth-lyrics. See also "Lazarus Come Forth (Unofficial Music Video) by Carman." YouTube (17 March 2015). https://www.youtube.com/watch?v=XvAqvr8_TP8.

While there are a number of such musicians who practically sing Scripture to exhort, evangelize, and teach their hearers, many more are needed in the task of reaching Africans with the word of God.

Ultimately singing the word is an act of faithfulness to some of the genres of Scripture. Jeffrey D. Arthurs poses the challenge that "the Psalmist used music; why shouldn't we?"[34] While submitting that music is powerful rhetorically, stating that the biblical poets intended their poems to be accompanied by music, and reiterating that "there is no such thing as sermon form," Arthurs suggests that a sermon on a Psalm could end with a hymn or praise song based on the Psalm, and the preacher could begin or end with special music that coordinates with the emotional and ideational content of the sermon. He also suggests that a congregational song or special music could be inserted in the middle of the sermon, or a musical background could be used as the text is read, or the preacher could insert an original own singing into the sermon.[35] Africans love music, and according to Kunhiyop, singing is a part of everyday African life.[36] Using it to preach and teach the word will be highly effective.

Use of Drama

Kelli Worrall describes drama as a powerful communication tool and asserts that while a sermon tells, a drama shows.[37] Drama can bridge cross-cultural gaps and even communicate without the need for language. As a supportive tool for sermons, drama can be used as props and employed in reading Scripture. Dramatic Scripture reading can be done by one good reader or multiple readers who share reading one or a combination of passages in artistic and significant ways. Choral reading can be done by two to twelve readers where several Scriptures are combined on one topic and creatively distributed among readers to express the voices and genders in the passages. In readers theatre, readers enter and exit by raising and bowing their head. Actors can portray a specific character, or each of them can take on multiple characters.[38]

---

34. Jeffrey D. Arthurs, *Preaching with Variety: How to Re-create the Dynamics of Biblical Genre* (Grand Rapids: Kregel, 2007), 57.

35. Arthurs, *Preaching with Variety*, 57.

36. Kunhiyop, *African Christian Ethics*, 12.

37. Kelli Worrall, "Drama and the Sermon," in *The Moody Handbook of Preaching*, ed. John Koessler (Chicago: Moody, 2008), 300.

38. An example of readers theater is "Because He Lives – an Easter play based on a true story" by Bob Allen at The Scripture Story Teller (16 February 2016), http://scripturestoryteller.blogspot.com/2016/02/because-he-lives-easter-play-based-on.html. A collection of over one

Monologues involve an actor taking on a single character and telling the character's story to the congregation. The preacher can also assume character and tell the story. These forms gradually move drama into a substantive role, beyond the supportive. Representational theatre is the typical full drama.[39] But while Scripture can be read and dramatized, the sermon should not end there because of the need to explain, apply, and invite people to make a decision.

Drama is a favorite of oral people. Some of the methods of Scripture dramatization described above would be greatly celebrated in any oral community and especially where many cannot read the Bible themselves because of illiteracy. Drama can be and has been used to communicate the word of God both in oral and literate communities. What needs to be confirmed in each instance is whether the drama is a reenactment of God's word as in Scripture reading or recasting, dramatizing the Bible story with or without emphasizing the nuances, acting a drama about a scriptural theme, or acting a drama like a parable, which is common among Christian dramatist and movie makers in Nigeria.

An example is a drama titled "The Forerunner of Destruction." *Oníférè Àtàtà* (meaning Precious Flutist) is a gifted flutist who plays for the king and makes the entire palace happy. One day the king asks the flutist if he can teach this skill to younger people in the kingdom so that many more could play like him, and the king could have someone to replace him when he is no longer there. The flutist tells the king that nobody taught him the skill, and he cannot teach anyone. Also, the younger people in the kingdom are not brilliant enough and therefore cannot even comprehend the skill. The king is appalled, but he keeps quiet. Another day, the gifted flutist asks his wife to go and tell the king he is dead. The wife is reluctant and asks questions. But he prevails on her forcefully, and she goes to tell the king. His intention is to test his popularity and indispensability. When the king and the entire palace hear the news, they all became sad and moody – who will bring joy to their lives like *Oníférè Àtàtà* again?

Suddenly beautiful music begins to emerge in the background, the king's spirit is lifted, and he begins to dance again. Then one of the chiefs comes in with a young, unknown flutist. When asked who taught him how to play, he replies it was his father and some else along the way. When asked if he can teach others in the kingdom, he gladly agrees to do. The king announces

---

hundred and sixty dramas and stories which Allen has used in several years of ministry are available at this blogsite.

39. Worrall, "Drama and the Sermon," 304.

him as the new palace flutist. While this is going on, *Oníf̀er̀e Àtàtà* the flutist emerges from nowhere with an envious look at the new flutist and surprise at the announcement of his replacement. The king is surprised at his appearance. "We were told you were dead? What are you then looking for?" *Oníf̀er̀e Àtàtà* says he is sorry. He just decided to test his popularity and indispensability. He begs not to be replaced, but it is too late. The king banishes him and his family from the kingdom.

Pastor Victor S. Ogundipe put this drama together and presented it in a worship setting instead of a normal sermon. When interviewed, he said his motivation was his discovery over the years that probably only thirty out of one hundred members remember a sermon one week after it is preached. But drama sticks fast and longer in their memories. Once they remember the main character, the whole story is brought to their memory. Ogundipe emphasizes that when drama is used in a sermon, there is always the need to make some comments so there will be no misinterpretation. Moreover, a drama must elicit some kind of response, so there should be an invitation.[40] If a drama will go beyond a supportive role of introducing, illustrating, or concluding a sermon, it must show the character of biblical exposition that can make people see Scripture, hear it explained, and make certain concrete decisions.

A step beyond merely dramatized readings of Scripture is found in this portion of my book, *Treasure Mine: Living Gems from Searching the Scriptures*. It was created as another way to enjoy reading 1 Samuel 15:13–31, but it is dramatic. Note the nuances coming from an African background and the concluding challenge that invites those who listen (or watch) to take a step on the passage's lesson.

> **Saul**: Sir, I have carried out the Lord's instruction.
>
> **Samuel**: What then is this bleating of sheep and lowing of cattle I am hearing?
>
> **Saul**: Really, it is the soldiers that spared and brought them. They want to use them for sacrifice.
>
> **Samuel**: Hun . . . hun . . . But God is annoyed with you. He told you to destroy the Amalekites completely, but you have disobeyed.
>
> **Saul**: No sir, I obeyed and I destroyed them. It was the soldiers that brought the sheep.

---

40. Victor S. Ogundipe, interview by the author, 6 October 2016.

Samuel: Ah! Ah! Saul, you are still arguing? Anyway, obedience is better than sacrifice. Since you chose to be disobedient and you have enough excuses for it, the Lord has rejected you as king!

Saul: Ah! Baba Samuel. Please sir. I know I have sinned, but it's not my fault. It's because I was afraid of the people.

Samuel: It's okay. Carry on with your excuses. I am going away.

Saul: No sir, you can't go away like that. You want me to be disgraced among these people? Please stay with me while I worship the Lord . . .

Samuel: No, I can't stay. God has rejected you as king. (As Samuel began to take his leave, Saul grabbed his cloth and it got torn.) Ah, you tear my cloth? *O ti pari!* (It is finished). Your kingdom has been torn and given to another person.

Saul: (Without a show of remorse). Ehn, I know I have sinned and you said the kingdom has been torn, but it's still not my fault. So please still stay with me and honor me before these elders . . .

Postlude: Samuel went home and mourned for Saul. "And the LORD was grieved that he had made Saul king over Israel" (1 Sam 15:35).

My friend, what does it cost you to say "I am sorry"? Why do you enjoy excuses even when you are confronted with the facts? What has it produced in your job, your studies, or your marriage? Are you not using your pride to gradually destroy your destiny? Throw away those excuses! When you are at fault, admit it, confess it, and put your past behind. Exaltation only comes from humility. And don't excuse your failures. Men who make excuses never make anything out of life. We may have 40 million reasons for failure, but not a single excuse (Rudyard Kipling).[41]

But a full drama can also be based on Scripture and be expositional. An example is another presentation titled "As It Was in the Days of Noah." I watched this drama sketch one fellowship day at Evangelical Christian Union, Obafemi Awolowo University, Ile Ife, as an undergraduate more than twenty-five years ago. I could not lay hold of the script but was led by some youths to act the drama at different times in the course of my ministry. The drama not only shows

---

41. Ezekiel A. Ajibade, *Treasure Mine: Living Gems from Searching the Scriptures* (New Bussa: Hope for a Generation International, 2013), 83–84.

a skillful way in which Scripture can be expounded, the beauty of moving from the world of the Bible to the contemporary one is also demonstrated.

I modified and re-scripted the drama for the purpose of this research as a sample of a "homiletical drama." The full version of this re-scripting is in Appendix 1. It was staged on 25 January 2017 for twenty minutes in the Chapel of Nigerian Baptist Theological Seminary, Ogbomoso, with about two hundred people participating from both within and outside the seminary. Fifty assessment forms serving as interview guides were distributed to some of the live audience (see Appendix 2). Forty-three of the forms were returned. Every respondent agreed that the drama explained the text that was read – Luke 17:26–37. They also said that the drama gave a clearer meaning of the passage and bridged the world of the Bible and the contemporary world. Every respondent agreed that this drama was a good way to minister to an African audience for some of the following reasons:

- Some African audiences hardly have time for preaching but can spend the whole day watching drama (movies).
- The cultural background, context, and current events in Africa are reflected in the drama.
- Visuals have a way of enhancing in-depth communication.
- Drama remains longer in memory.
- Africans like something practical and visible.
- Drama strengthens the sermon heard.
- African culture is image rich and strongly related to emotional cognition.

When asked if the drama presentation was enough as a sermon for the day, or if there was still a need for someone to come and preach a full-length sermon, most agreed that the drama was enough because the message was clearly received, and any attempt to preach further might diminish the impact. Only three respondents felt there was still a need for either a short or full-length sermon. On how often a homiletical drama like this should be performed in the church, twenty-four respondents (55.8 percent) responded "as often as possible." Eighteen respondents (41.8 percent) responded "once in a while," and one respondent (2.3 percent) responded "every Sunday." No respondent checked the option of "never" staging such drama in the church.

Drama has been a strong evangelistic tool in Africa. The man known as the "father of Nigerian theatre," Hubert Ogunde (1916–1990),[42] is the pioneer

---

42. "Hubert Ogunde Nigerian Playwright, Actor, and Musician," *Encyclopedia Britannica* (accessed 18 November 2016).

of Nigerian drama and dance known as Native Air Opera.[43] He came out of the missionary church to be part of the Aladura church (African Independent Church) where apparently he had more freedom to demonstrate his skill as an African dramatist. It is on record that the missionaries indeed came with drama as one of their tools for evangelism. The Catholics, Church Missionary Society, Baptists, and Wesleyans all actively participated in drama, but it was not until 1881 that a non-denominational theatre group, "The Rising Entertainment Society," was inaugurated. This group sought to project biblical lessons in a cultural mode, and at the time there was a real freedom to do it in the African way. Bible stories were set to music and dance as drama, and this is the setting from which Hubert Ogunde emerged.[44]

Interestingly, Ogunde's first folk opera was "The Garden of Eden and the Throne of God" which he successfully staged in 1944. It was a mixture of biblical theme with traditional Yoruba dance-drama. Though his latter themes were more of an effort to address the evils of the society such as colonialism, dangerous party politics, and corruption, which he did successfully and for which he was recognized throughout West Africa, Ogunde was able to set the stage for Christian drama that is truly African. Today, Nigeria is replete with independent and church-based groups that not only stage dramas across the continent but also produce home videos that have gone all over the world.[45] These groups need to see themselves as foot soldiers for both evangelism and the exposition of God's word for the transformation of Africa.[46]

Use of Poetry

Oral poetry in traditional Africa is known to be produced by specially trained poets who had connections with kings, chiefs, spiritual figures, or secret societies. Some groups like hunters, warriors, farmers, and cattle breeders may also have designated poets.[47] These poets are often descended from family lineages and are very powerful. They are held in high esteem because they

---

43. Ingrid Monson, ed., *African Diaspora: A Musical Perspective* (New York: Routledge, 2003), 216.

44. Yinka Ololade, *Drama as Catalyst in Christian Worship and Evangelism* (Ibadan: Ola-Oluseye, 2013), 31–32.

45. Ololade, *Drama as Catalyst*, 33.

46. This motive is displayed by Ernst Wedland in *Sewero! Christian Drama and the Drama of Christianity in Africa* (Zomba: Kachere Series, 2005), 13–14.

47. African Poetry, "Oral Traditions" (accessed 13 December 2016), https://www.enotes.com/topics/african-poetry/in-depth.

possess a special ability and effrontery to say what ordinary people in the society avoid saying. They are believed to have immunity before kings because they are regarded as the piper of the Supreme Being.[48] They are variously known as *griot* (Mandinka), *kwadwumfo* (Asante), *imbongi* (southern Africa), *azmaris* (Ethiopia), and *umusizi* (central Africa).[49] Their genres include praise, pleasure, survival, relationships, gods and ancestors, protest, satire, and epic, but the most striking of African oral poetry is the praise poems.[50] Praise poems are known as *oríkì* (Yoruba), *maboko* (Tswana), *izibongo* (Zulu), and *ìjálá*, the poetry of professional Yoruba hunters. But the praise poem is not the only genre among the oral poetry in Yorubaland. "*Ewì* (literally poems), *Ìjálá* (hunters' chants), *ẹ̀sà* (masquerades' chants), *ẹkún ìyàwó* (bride's farewell song)," and several others are also recognized.[51]

The power of these forms of poetry are worthy of note if they will be engaged in the exposition of the word of God. Falade states that,

> Poetry in any language is a respected literary genre and the people of Yoruba-land are no exception. Although it is mostly enjoyed as a form of entertainment and relaxation, poetry also serves other purposes such as the propagation of traditional norms, customs, values and the transmission of a people's cultural history from one generation to another. Amongst the Yoruba, poetry, depending on the genre can be used as a means of preserving historical occurrences and experiences.[52]

They not only possess much entertainment value and the ability to be deployed in the propagation and preservation of traditions and customs, they also serve to transform society. Some of these poems are didactic in nature, teaching history; expositing human names, family, or compound backgrounds; and passing down instructions about moral values. One popular poem in Yorubaland is *Ise Logun Ise* (Work is the Antidote for Poverty).

---

48. Adeoye Dennis Falade, "Oral Tradition in Africa: Poetry as a Means of Preserving Cultural Heritage and Engendering Social Change among the Yoruba," Academia (September 2013).

49. Falade, "Oral Tradition in Africa."

50. Mbongeni Malaba, "Review Article: African Oral Poetry," *English in Africa* 15, no. 2 (October 1988): 101–11.

51. Falade, "Oral Tradition in Africa." For an example of a rich collection of *ijala* poetry, see Sayo Alagbe, *Ijala Ogundare Foyanmu . . . Ijinle Ede Ohun Enu Yoruba* (Ogbomoso: Astra J. Creations, 2006), 1–78.

52. Falade, "Oral Tradition in Africa."

Iṣẹ́ Lògùn ìsẹ̀
    (Work is the antidote for poverty)
Múra sí sẹ̀ rẹ, ọ̀rẹ́ mi
    (Work hard and work smart, my friend)
Iṣẹ́ la fi ńdẹni gíga
    (Hard and smart work brings success)
Bí a kò bá rẹ̀ni fẹ̀hìn tì
    (When there is no one to rely on)
Bí ọ̀le là rí
    (It's like we are lazy)
Bí a kò ba rẹ́ni gbẹ́kẹ̀lé,
    (When there is no one to trust)
A tẹ ra mọ́ ṣẹ ni
    (We focus more on our work)
Ìyá rẹ́ lè lówó lọ́wọ́
    (Your mother might be rich)
Bàbá rẹ́ lè lẹ̀sin lẹ́kàn
    (Your father might own a thousand and one horses)
Tí o bá gbójúlé wọn
    (If you rely on them)
O té tán ni mo sọ fún o
    (In truth, you might be on sinking ground)
Apá lará ìgúpá ni yè kan
    (Families are like the arm, extended family are like the elbow)
B'áiyé bá fẹ́ ọ loni
    (If you are loved by the world today)
Tí o bá lówó lọ́wọ́, wọn á tún fẹ́ ọ lóla
    (If you are still rich, they will love you tomorrow as well)
Àbí ko wà nípò àtàtá
    (If you have an esteemed position)
Aiyé á yẹ́ ọ sí tẹ̀rín tẹ̀rín
    (You will be honored with "fake" laughter)
Jẹ́ kí o dẹni tí rá ngó
    (If you unfortunately lose your money or position)
Ko rí bí wọ́n ti nyín mú sí ọ
    (They'll turn their back on you)
Ìyà mbe fọ́mọ ti kò gbọ́n
    (There is suffering for the foolish child)

Ẹkún mbẹ fọ́mọ tí nsáré kiri
(And there is sorrow for the child who has no plan or vision)
Máfòwúrò seré ọ̀rẹ́ mi
(Don't waste your formative years, my friend)
Mura sísẹ́ ọjọ́ nlọ.
(Work hard and plan well now, because time waits for no one)[53]

Christians in Nigeria have caught on to these oral genres to propagate the gospel. Job Alabi, a Nigerian Baptist evangelist, was well known for his knowledge and use of Ifa oral verses and other elements of African cosmology in his sermons. For example in a sermon he preached at the ten year remembrance service of Chief (Mrs) Faderera Aabeke-Akintola in August 2012, he tried to prove the reality of death to Africans in these words:

> Death is so real that even those who mock the dead would eventually die. But who is death? Listen to what I did not say, I did not say what is death? Death in Yoruba traditional belief is a being. He is one of the eight beings called *Ajoguns*. An Ifa oracle says: "*Ebo ni ko o ru bi o ba fe e bo lowo ajogun. Ohun lodifa fun ondese pupa oke apa ti iku ati arun ngba ile re re tajogun gbogbo n gba ile won ni lilo ni lilo*" meaning that if you want to escape from the *ajoguns* you must make sacrifice. The *ajoguns* are the eight spirit beings who are direct messengers of Satan through whom the world is afflicted. Their names are Disease, Stroke, Loss, Curse, Imprisonment, Trouble, Sin and Death. Africans know that all of the above are not abstract nouns. They are real nouns. Death is real to Africans.[54]

Like other oral elements discussed so far, poetry can be used to illustrate a sermon and presented before, in the middle, or after the sermon. But poetry can also be used substantively for a sermon once in a while. Matthew Adebare Ayanyemi wrote a Yoruba poem on Acts 3:1–11. It is a good example of sermon preached in poetry form. Due to the length, it is in Appendix 3. Poetry can potentially be used for biblical communication, explanation, illustration, application, and even invitation. Whatever the beauty of poetry (or any other resources used in a sermon) and the excitement it generates, Cornelius Plantinga warns that "Everything depends on whether the quotations and phrases serve to make the gospel of grace sound more urgently alive or whether

---

53. Curious Wumi, "A Yoruba Poem – Ise Logun Ise (Work is the antidote for poverty)," Curious Wumi (9 April 2012). The author is actually unknown. The accents were added.
54. Job Adegboyega Alabi, "Memorial Service and its Lessons" (accessed 12 December 2016).

they serve merely to make the sermon more aesthetically pleasing. When the sermon is over, does the preacher want hearers to say 'Thanks be to God!' or 'How lovely that was, really'?"[55]

Beyond Plantinga's warning, the need for great discernment in the use of some oral elements from African religion and culture is worth mentioning, and some have suggested the need to distinguish between the two. Not just any poetic or dramatic device rooted in African culture and religion can be directly used in preaching or other spiritual exercises. For example, Dabi Ayanlola Kanyinsola mentions some uses of *oriki* for purposes of poetry and entertainment. They serve as a means of identifying the right to the household one belongs to and its history. They also serve as a means of establishing and understanding one's ancestry. *Oriki* tells of the weaknesses and the strengths of someone's ancestors and can help reveal family traits and behaviors, past achievements, health issues, antecedents, family migration patterns, and where they have some other family ties to other towns and villages.

But *oriki* also has a spiritual connotation. According to Kanyinsola, "It is believed that a person who does not know his *Oriki* loses his spiritual essence." He then cites two stories. One is that of a young man who always loved to fight and create problems wherever he went. When his *orikì* is investigated, it is discovered he descended from a lineage of warriors, and it was their nature to fight. He now lives where there are no wars, and the solution they found for him is to get him engaged in combat sports. Another young man was known to be troublesome and hot tempered. When his temper flares up, a woman who is an *orikì* specialist is often engaged, and as she recites his *orikì*, the tempers calm down. Kanyinsola concludes that "The *Oriki* is viewed as a spiritual means of transmitting the collective consciousness of ancestors to children of the next generation."[56]

The above has to do with the power of words in the African worldview as discussed in chapter three. Just as Scripture affirms, words have power to create, make, or mar. Words are not just sounds and syllables when it comes to efficacy. In an interview, Kehinde Ajibade revealed his experience as a theatre art student at the University of Ilorin in Nigeria, that when acting some dramas that include some oral elements of African religion like incantations or other poetic devises, strange things like spirit possession took place on the stage. It

---

55. Cornelius Plantinga, *Reading for Preaching: The Preacher in Conversation with Storytellers, Biographers, Poets, and Journalists* (Grand Rapids: Eerdmans, 2013), 5.

56. Dabi Ayanlola Kanyinsola, "Oriki: The Yoruba-Praise-Poetry," (accessed 22 December 2016).

would become so real that those skilled in deliverance prayer (or exorcism) would have to be brought in to normalize the situation.[57]

This does not in any way connect African culture with demonism or give credence to those who consider anything African as fetish or demonic. The emphasis in this research is that engaging oral communication elements that are void of any demonic connection when communicating the gospel is possible and result-oriented, as evidenced by how they have been effectively used by several Christian musicians, dramatics, poets, and storytellers and can be successfully used by African preachers, too. The content of the word, its meaning, the vessel or channel of communication, and the context of the speaker are all vital to determining the result of communication.

Use of Proverbs

Jeffrey D. Arthurs cites Thomas Long's submission that "people need the kind of portable and memorable wisdom of the nuts-and-bolts variety that a proverb is designed to provide. The question is not will people live by proverbs, but what kind of proverbs they will cherish."[58] Proverbs are the face of culture and the channel for transmitting the spirit of the age. They serve as building blocks for worldviews.[59] Some work has been done on the use of African proverbs for preaching and teaching. An example is Abba Karnga's *Bassa Proverbs for Preaching and Teaching*.[60] Karnga believes that,

> Proverbs reflect the historical experiences of a people, and the wisdom gained from those experiences. The gospel is more effectively presented when it is expressed and practiced in the context of the people. Among the Bassa, as indeed among other African peoples, one of the best vehicles through which the gospel can be communicated is the proverb. This is what contextualization is all about.[61]

---

57. Kehinde Ajibade, interview by the author, 15 September 2016.
58. Thomas G. Long, *Preaching and the Literary Forms of the Bible* (1988), 53, quoted in Arthurs, *Preaching with Variety*, 130.
59. Arthurs, 130.
60. Abba Karnga, *Bassa Proverbs for Preaching and Teaching* (Accra: Asempa, 1996). This book is one of the series titled the "African Proverb Project." With grants from the Pew Charitable Trust, Philadelphia, Joshua Kudadje from Ghana, Abba Karnga from Liberia, and Daniel Mphande (Zambia?), who all have a long experience in preaching and teaching, were recruited for the project to produce annotated proverbs in their own language. Others involved in the project are John Mbiti (Kenya), Laurent Nare (Burkinabe), John Pobee (Ghana) and Willem Saayman (South Africa).
61. Karnga, *Bassa Proverbs*, 10.

Since the ultimate purposes of using proverbs are to impart wisdom, teach good morals and social values, deter against foolish acts, guide toward good conduct, and help toward success in life, they would suffice for a Christian preaching engagement. Support for their use comes from the example of Jesus who profusely used stories and proverbial lessons from his days to influence people from the outside as he appealed to their hearts and minds in his teachings.[62] Unfortunately, as useful and powerful as proverbs are as tools for communication, they do not contain the power for salvation and spiritual transformation. The question then is how can African proverbs be engaged in expository preaching?

First, they can be used to illustrate or buttress a biblical point. If one is teaching that we have no need to be anxious, a Yoruba proverb like this may be relevant: *Ilé njó ní Sókótó, olè njà ní Kàfànsàn, ọba òkè ọ̀hún ní òhun fẹ́ kú wí pé ayé sú oun. Èwo ló kàn án níbè?* (Houses are burning in Sokoto, thieves are robbing in Kafanchan, the king of an upland distant territory says he wants to commit suicide because he is fed up with life. What is his concern in this matter?) Sokoto and Kafanchan are in the far northern parts of Nigeria. Literally, the proverb is puzzled at how a king in the southern part of the nation would be so worried about the news in the north that he would want to commit suicide when the trouble has not come somewhere close to him and when he has not taken any administrative action to prevent it in his own kingdom.[63]

The second way in which proverbs can be used is what Arthur calls "dueling proverbs," comparing and contrasting modern proverbs with biblical ones which is a way of "evaluating culture's repository of wisdom against God's."[64] The exercise can be done by pairing proverbs to see which truth in a culture compares or contrasts sharply from biblical truth. For example Proverbs 19:21 states, "Many are the plans in a person's heart, but it is the LORD's purpose that prevails." A complimentary Yoruba proverb is *Rírò ni t'ènìyàn síse ni t'Ọlọ́run* (Man proposes but God disposes). Proverbs 10:4 states that "Lazy hands make for poverty, but diligent hands bring wealth." This proverb is complimented by the Yoruba proverb *Bí ènyàn bá mú isẹ́ jẹ, kò le mú isẹ́ jẹ* (If someone escapes work, he cannot escape poverty).

---

62. Karnga, 16–17.

63. See Raphael Odekunle, *Yoruba Proverbs* (Ibadan: Daystar, 1985); and S. O. Bada, *Owe Yoruba ati Isedale Won* (Ibadan: University of Ibadan Press, 1985).

64. Arthurs, *Preaching with Variety*, 146.

Some proverbs need to be tested and scrutinized for theological and homiletical accuracy.[65] Therefore, a biblical proverb can be used to correct some of the African proverbs that negate the teaching of Scripture. These proverbs can be related to such issues as the inferiority of females, sexual accusations against women, or selective truth telling. An example is the Ga proverb *Anokwale ni jwaa maa awieee* (Truth that can destroy the town or community is not to be told). Another is *Adowa se rrii poe* (The antelope's back does not get wet), meaning the evils of an elder or important personality do not easily leak out. Similarly is *Blo he ngmohuw hu we ngmo kpekpee* (One who farms by the path does not keep a crooked farm), which means that a wealthy person is never guilty.[66] These are proverbs that need to be scrutinized for their scriptural compatibility and which can be corrected with other proverbs from the Bible.

Proverb dueling can also be used to teach the conservative and radical wisdom of the Bible. For example, it can be used to preach the full theology of success or suffering.[67] Generally and in relation to the preaching of the word, proverbs are powerful in speaking to the intellect, soul and heart, understanding, and will. According to Kudadje, people are interested, stay awake, and pay attention when proverbs are used because proverbs stimulate their imagination. They remember the message and find themselves agreeing with the truth.[68]

Use of Folklore

In Africa, folklore serves the purposes of mirroring the familiar details of culture and incorporating common situations of everyday living. Folktales justify rituals and institutions for those who perform and observe them, and they serve as pedagogic devices. Ogre tales are used in the discipline of young children, and lullabies are sung to make them enjoy some good humor. Later in life, fables or folklore are used to incorporate such morals as diligence and piety and to ridicule laziness, rebelliousness, and stubbornness. Riddles are also engaged to express a threat which may not ultimately be carried out.[69]

---

65. Arthurs, 146.

66. Joshua N. Kudadjie, "Using Ga and Dangme Proverbs for Preaching and Teaching," *WAJIBU* 14, no. 1 (1999): 17.

67. Arthurs, *Preaching with Variety*, 146.

68. Kudadjie, "Using Ga and Dangme Proverbs," 13.

69. William Bascom, "Folklore, Verbal Art, and Culture," *Journal of American Folklore* 86, no. 342 (Oct–Dec, 1973): 374–81.

Deborah G. Plant in her analysis of Zora Neale Hurston's *Dust Tracks on a Road* also lays strong emphasis on the humor value of folktales. She states that the folklore Hurston uses is characteristically humorous, and she believes, as did the folk preachers, that humor is a vital part of the folk community, any representative of the people must have a sense of humor.[70] Bontemps writes that the folk preacher had to be entertaining and "comic when comedy was needed." A good sense of humor made the preacher "one of the folk," but he also had to be authoritative. His role as shepherd of the flock required him to teach, inform, admonish, and lead his congregation as well as inspire and uplift them. "What he gave, and what they picked up was hope, confidence, a will to survive."[71]

Folklore can basically serve illustrative purposes in the task of expository preaching, but generally should not be substantive. An exception may be when a folktale is parallel with a biblical story, and the preacher decides to use it to establish the authority of the Scripture or the universality of God's general revelation, or when the parallel is just good enough to complement the biblical story.

It is helpful that many African folktales have been gathered over the years by scholars and even coded for easy reference.[72] So African preachers have ready resources for their assignment. Many folktales are also available on the Internet, some produced with good animation and made much more meaningfully for modern audiences.[73]

One example is "The Talking Skull Refuses to Talk." A barber who barbs for the king discovers a horn on the king's head and reveals the secret, so he is banished from the king's land. While passing through the forest, he sees a white and dry human skull. He asks the skull, "Who brought you here?" and the skull replies, "It was my mouth that brought me here." The barber returns

---

70. Deborah G. Plant, "The Folk Preacher and Folk Sermon Form in Zora Neale Hurston's *Dust Tracks on a Road*," *Folklore Forum* 21, no. 1 (1988): 4.

71. Bontemps, *The Book of Negro Folklore* (1983), xiii, cited in Plant, "The Folk Preacher and Folk Sermon Form in Zora Neale Hurston's *Dust Tracks on a Road*."

72. Some of these collections include William Bascom, *African Folktales in the New World* (Bloomington: Indiana University Press, 1992); Jan Knappert, *African Mythology: An Encyclopedia of Myth and Legend* (London: Diamond, 1995); Daniel Butrus, *Legacy of Wisdom: Stories and Proverbs from Africa* (Bukuru, Jos: Africa Christian Textbooks, 2007); Olagoke Ojo, *Ijapa Tiroko* (Ikeja, Lagos: Longman Nigeria, 2005); and D. O. Fagunwa, *In the Forest of Olodumare*, trans. Wole Soyinka (Ibadan: Nelson, 2010).

73. Examples are Rashidat Hassan, "African Tales (Ijapa Ologbon Ewe)," YouTube (27 May 2013); West African Folktales Full Audiobook Unabridged, YouTube (16 July 2014); and "The Deamon, the Woman and the Bird – African Fairy Tale from Senegal," YouTube (11 April 2013).

to the king to tell him what happened, and the king says the barber is lying. The barber responds that they should check out his story, and if it is a lie, he should be killed. The king sends people to investigate, and when they get to the skull, it will not speak. The barber is brought back to the king and executed. The tale concludes that "it was his mouth that killed him with so much talk."[74]

The lessons from this tale include the need to be circumspect in speech; not everything one sees should be spoken. The barber has a problem with the king because he cannot not hold his tongue when he sees that the king has a horn on his head. The barber is banished for revealing the king's secret. Yet he is not disciplined enough. His first experience ought to have taught him a lesson, but gossip seems to be in his character. He also does not discern when the skull tells him, "It is my mouth that brought me here" that his mouth will eventually kill him, too.[75]

In an interview with Dele Oguntola in the course of this research, he mentioned a version of this folktale as his pastor told it a few years ago and which he never forgot. When his pastor, Philip Oyelaran, was contacted, he confirmed using that folktale while preaching from James 3:1–12 on the use of the tongue, and he narrated his version this way: A slave called Alaba was talkative. On his way to the farm one day, he saw a dead man on a kola nut tree. While he greeted him "Good morning," the dead man told him, "Focus on where you are going; it is your mouth that will kill you." Alaba went back home and told the king and all the villagers what he saw. They told him they were going to see for themselves if he really saw a dead man that spoke. They warned him that if what he told them was not true, he would be killed. They all followed Alaba to the kola nut tree. When he called the dead man, he did not show up. They all called Alaba a liar, and he was killed. Then the dead man appeared and said, "I have told him that his mouth would kill him."

Folktales are a simple way of illustrating some Scriptures in the Bible. Proverbs 11:13 states, "A gossip betrays a confidence, but a trustworthy person keeps a secret." Proverbs 13:3 states, "Those who guard their lips preserve their lives, but those who speak rashly will come to ruin." God expects believers to be disciplined and self-controlled. A New Testament rule that matches this tale is James 1:19, "My dear brothers and sisters, take note of this: Everyone should be quick to listen, slow to speak and slow to become angry." One more lesson is that one's life should never be used to swear or guarantee uncertainties.

---

74. Bascom, *African Folktales in the New World*, 23.
75. Dele Oguntola, interview by the author, 20 September 2016; Philip Oyelaran, interview by the author, 10 November 2016.

Even with some elements of certainty, except for issues of faith, it is still okay to doubt one's doubts.

In this interview, Philip Oyelaran admitted using stories including folktales in his preaching because his members, 50 percent of whom are literate, love it so much, and he hears them reuse those stories in Sunday school and in their daily conversations. Oyelaran's use of stories and folktales to buttress his sermon points helps make the messages clear, makes his hearers remember for longer, and helps them retell the messages to others.

Use of Stories

Storying and storytelling have been mentioned at several points in this work. It is even noted that some have erroneously equated orality with storytelling and argued that storytelling is not synonymous with orality, rather a component of it. But how storytelling should be applied to expository preaching in the African context still needs to be discussed. First is the need to decide whether a story should simply play a supportive role for instances as an introduction, illustration, or conclusion. Both biblical and non-biblical stories can serve this purpose if they are appropriate. Folklores, historical events or narratives, stories from daily lives, and news stories are all useful, and they excite a typical African when they are well used.

The second consideration for storytelling regards preaching the narrative sections of the Bible. Michael Rydelnik suggests that doing justice to historical narrative begins with "relating the timeless principle of the biblical story to their contemporary audience."[76] Preachers must also be armed with a homiletical idea that is memorable and addresses the audience, so they do not just tell a story and leave it there. Preachers should not forget an introduction that creates interest, raises need, and orients to the text. These elements are then fashioned into an inductive structure knowing that the resolution of a story often comes toward its end. The inductive sermon does not rule out a structure, one that at least guides the preacher but not necessarily one for the listeners to memorize. Such structure serves as a roadmap that guides the preacher-storyteller in telling the story, declares the principle and applies it to the situation of the people.[77]

Telling the parables as stories has its own dynamics. Jeffrey D. Arthurs does not regard parables as pure narrative because of their concise nature.

---

76. Michael Rydelnik, "Preaching Historical Narrative," in *The Moody Handbook of Preaching* (Chicago: Moody, 2008), 134.

77. Rydelnik, "Preaching Historical Narrative," 134–38.

Like non-biblical parables worldwide, most parables are an average of 150–250 words and are best considered as folk stories because they are rooted in oral communication.[78] So preaching parables involves interpreting them at the literal and dialectic levels, translating them into modern language, and transplanting them into an audience culture. It also involves stating the main idea in the conclusion, making the point of the parable clear, reproducing the effect of the text, and following the step of the Master who chose to shock, confirm, perplex, and enlighten the crowds as he told them the stories.[79]

Prepared materials are available for those who would engage in Bible storying to evangelize and disciple. A good example is *S-T4T: Storying and Church Formation Training for Trainers*. The scope of this work is preaching and not evangelism or discipleship, though there may be some interconnections. The writers suggest the following steps for those who want to craft Bible stories for oral learners:

1. Read the full biblical passage at least three times from at least three different versions.

2. Identify words or concepts that are strange or difficult in other languages and cultures and research the passage in commentaries, dictionaries, and other exegetical material to see how to bridge the gap and express the difficult words in your context. Give background information when necessary.

3. Think through and break the story into scenes which provides you with an "oral outline," and keep a summary inside of you, guiding you as you tell the story in full when meeting the audience.[80]

Whatever kind of stories are to be told, be they Bible stories or stories from other sources, Michael Duduit has some suggestions about what characterizes good storytelling. He begins with Fred Craddock's submission that good story telling should speak for the congregation and evoke their own stories, and it should be realistic. By this Craddock means the telling should have such a smell, sound, and taste of life that it makes the listeners identify with the story. Also, good stories should create an experience as the storyteller takes a trip and does not rush to the destination. The story should fit the sermon. Besides

---

78. Arthurs, *Preaching with Variety*, 109.

79. Arthurs, 120–28.

80. Stephen Stringer, ed., *S-T4T: Storying and Church Formation Training for Trainers* (WigTake Resources, 2010), 20.

Craddock's submission, Duduit encourages that best stories are drawn from the world of the listeners and should not need so much explanation. Details may only be added to generate interest and add credibility.[81]

Stories can be powerful, moving, and involving and are integral to everyday living. According to Scott Hoezee, stories bring "reality and the living presence of God into sermons because that reality is fundamentally perceived by us – and talked about by us – in narrative terms."[82] This reality has no cultural or geographical boundaries. But what needs to be stated is that whatever oral elements are employed in expository sermons, the message of the Bible must be held sacred and sacrosanct. Duduit warns,

> Don't turn the focus of your sermon into amusing the crowd. If you are a good storyteller, people will enjoy listening to your stories, and you'll enjoy telling them. It is possible to lose your bearings in such a situation and let the sermon become a time of entertainment rather than a time when you bring biblical truth to bear on the lives of the people. It is not bad to entertain people along the way – that keeps them focused and attentive – but the entertainment must be a strategic tool, not the purpose. Your purpose in preaching must always be to communicate biblical truth in order to set the stage for life change.[83]

Discussion Questions

1. As an African preacher, which of the pictures painted about the context of Africa appears most real to you and why?

2. Out of the oral resources discussed in this chapter, which ones resonate with your context of ministry and which ones are of less relevance?

3. Plan a sermon, incorporating the use of at least three of these oral elements. Preach it and find a way of getting feedback about its effectiveness.

---

81. Michael Duduit, "Doctrine that Flies: Using Story to Communicate Truth," in *Our Sufficiency is of God: Essays on Preaching in Honor of Gardner C. Taylor*, ed. James Earl Massey, Robert Smith Jr., and Timothy George (Macon, GA: Mercer University Press, 2010), quoting Fred Craddock, "Preaching as Storytelling, 490–91.

82. Scott Hoezee, *Actuality: Real Life Stories for Sermons That Matter* (Nashville: Abingdon, 2014), xx.

83. Duduit, "Doctrine That Flies," 77–78.

6

Antecedents from Korean, African-American, and Ghanaian Experience

The attempt to develop contextualized expository preaching is not unique to Africa. There are antecedents from other parts of the world where people have decided not to preach in blind replication of the way it was done by those who evangelized them but have attempted to develop their own preaching based on their own experience, culture, and indigenous communication channels.

Examples will be discussed from Korean and African-American preaching. To bring the case closer to home, a preaching model once proposed for the Ghanaian community which has a lot of bearing on contextualized preaching in Africa will also be discussed. Korean preaching was chosen not because it has many relationships with orality but because it has a contextualized flavor. African-American and the Ghanaian preaching have more of the orality content under discussion.

The choice of these three geographical areas is significant. Asia shares something in common with Africa. Church historians Andrew Walls, Lamin Sanneh, and Phillip Jenkins have noted for decades that Christianity is shifting to the South in terms of numerical strength and evangelistic passion. Albert Strydhorst succinctly observes that, "the gravitational center of Christianity is moving from the global North – understood as Europe and America – to the global South, or majority world – understood as Africa, Asia, and Latin America – and eastward. The 'gravitational center of world Christianity' is that point on the globe with equal number of Christians to the north, south and west."[1] Therefore, Africa and Asia share in what God is doing currently in world missions, and they are both formulating localized theologies that can sustain this movement so it lasts the test of time.

The African-American community is a point of reference because not only have they consistently claimed their origin from Africa, but they have also developed a contextualized method of preaching based on their African roots and stuck to it, so much that other homiletic communities are now learning from them. The choice of Ghana brings the concept being developed much closer home. It is based on the work of Akwasi O. Ofori who attempted to develop a "New Ghanaian Sermon" based on an adaptation of the New Homiletic for Africa.[2]

Korean Preaching

Oliphant Old observes that in Korea, preachers have been more important than sermons.[3] There is a background for this, and Allen acknowledges this reality when he expresses that "a culture which has a history of Christian influence should be able to use life stories, from its own history rather than illustrating messages from the culture of the American missionary."[4] For support he cites Jung Young Lee who states, "It is important to make a conscious effort to incorporate the life stories of Korean figures as much as possible into Korean preaching so that it becomes truly indigenous and accountable to the Korean cultural context."[5]

The context in question includes the Confucian hierarchical structure of Korean society. This cultural structure respects kings, leaders, and fathers so automatically holds pastors as authoritative figures. In the rural areas, since the pastors are the most educated people, they often serve as the community

---

1. Albert Strydhorst, "Emerging World Christianity," *Calvin Theological Seminary Forum* (Winter 2015): 3–4. Also see Jack Hayford, "Foreword," in *We are the Church: The Untold Story of God's Global Awakening*, ed. Leonard Sweet and James O. Davis (Orlando, FL: Billion Soul, 2014), xi.

2. Akwasi O. Ofori, *Recovering Storytelling for Ghanaian Preaching* (Bloomington, IN: WestBow, 2015). Kindle edition.

3. Hughes Oliphant Old, *The Reading and Preaching of the Scriptures in the Worship of the Christian Church*, vol. 7 (Grand Rapids: Eerdmans, 1997–2004), 645.

4. Allen, "Expository Sermon," 222. The stories of the Christian martyrs under Japanese occupation serve to motivate contemporary Christians to faithfulness. Bruce Shield, "Preaching and Culture," *Homiletic* 22, no. 2 (1997): 4.

5. Jung Young Lee, *Korean Preaching* (1997), 87, quoted in Allen, "Expository Sermon," 222.

leader.[6] Bruce Shield gathered from his research that there is variety in the "linguistic usages by which Koreans show respect of status and age in society and family. They have different words for older brother and younger brother; they also have honor suffixes which are used in addressing teachers, elders, etc. Such honor extends also to preachers, so that Christians are accustomed to listening attentively to preaching."[7] Pastors were the leaders of the Independent Movement against the Japanese colonial empire in the early history of the church, during the struggle against the military governments in 1970/80s, and in other mass movements. So the authority of preachers extends even to the sphere of public life.[8]

The second context is Shamanism. The traditional culture rates pastors as people of the spirit, so they are Shamanistic figures. As leaders of the oldest religious tradition in Korea, shamans are regarded as messengers of the spirit. Therefore, "pastors are viewed as messengers from God – persons filled with the Holy Spirit who preach with Spirit's power."[9] Pastors are seen to focus more on emotions and feelings above reason and intellectual doctrine.[10] It is common to see weeping, singing, shouting hallelujah, and expecting a vigorous "amen" from the congregation. Audible individual prayers are heard, and congregations are engaged in shouting "O Lord!" and raising their arms in praise.[11]

Similarities in the passion with which Koreans approach worship and that of Africans can be seen. Emotion plays a prominent role. Just like in Africa, the revivalist sermon is one of the types of Korean preaching. These revivals are between three days to one week, and the meetings involve their entire being –

---

6. Daniel J. Adams, "Korean Preaching from a Western Perspective," *Journal of Korean American Ministries and Theology* 2 (Spring 2009): 44.

7. Shield, "Preaching and Culture," 4.

8. Adams, "Korean Preaching," 44.

9. Adams, 45.

10. This is in contrast with the Japanese context where the term for preaching is *sekkyo* which comes from a Buddhist background and denotes an exposition of *sutra* used for public instruction in the temple. The term *sekkyo* was transplanted into the Christian context, and preaching came to mean "to expound and teach." So while Korean preaching is more topical in style, that of Japan relies on biblical exposition. A Japanese sermon may run for up to forty-five minutes, but the Korean preacher uses a shorter time. Robert Mikio Fukada and Tsuneaki Kato, "Homiletics and Preaching in Asia," in *Concise Encyclopedia of Preaching*, ed. William H. Willimon and Richard Lischer (Louisville, KY: Westminster John Knox, 1995), 233.

Old however opines that Koreans love exposition of Scripture and they have great respect for scholar-pastors. He describes them as careful expositors but not very colorful. A good preacher, he submits, ought to blend the intellectual and exciting elements of preaching. Old, *Reading and Preaching*, 665.

11. Adams, "Korean Preaching," 45.

loud and confrontational preaching, shouting and exclaiming hallelujah and amen, group prayers accompanied by weeping and deep emotion, and shaking of bodies as they cry in prayer. The preacher invites people to respond to salvation in Christ and challenges them to repent and turn away from sin while imbibing faithful Christian living.[12]

Fukada and Kato see the heritage of a strict ethical and pious life in Asia to be a product of the work of early Protestant missionaries. According to them, "What the early Protestant missionaries implanted in the process of forming churches set a pattern not only for general church life but for Christian preaching. The early missionaries emphasized an evangelistic zeal common in nineteenth-century North America, aiming at a life of strict ethical standards and a passionate piety."[13] In the specific case of Korea, however, they acknowledged that a strong Confucian orientation affects the context of their preaching.

A third context of Korean preaching is conservatism. Preachers have a simple gospel message that is a straightforward, non-critical doctrinal, historical, and literal presentation of Scripture miracles. This message is rooted in the traditions of their forebears like Kil Sun-Ju (1869–1936) and Chu Ki-Chol (1897–1944). Kil Sun-Ju, who was the founder of the Korea tradition of dawn prayer meetings, was known to have preached in a revivalist tradition. His theology was fundamental, and he had a literal belief in Christ's second coming and was deeply involved in politics.[14] But while their theology may be considered conservative, the lives of Korean preachers are noted for being rooted in Korean society and the struggles of the Korean people. Preachers are known to preach powerful social justice sermons which are clear calls to the hearers for action.[15]

Daniel J. Adam's conclusion is that "it becomes increasingly clear that there is a dialogical relationship between the Confucian and Shamanistic tradition in determining not only the authority of the pastors, but also the style of preaching."[16] Therefore Korean preaching has arisen out of the sociocultural and indeed political milieu of the Korean people and has been used to meet these needs since Christianity took root on their soil. While many changes are currently taking place in the globalized world and especially in an era of strong

---

12. Adams, 49.
13. Adams, 47.
14. Adams, 46.
15. Adams, 47.
16. Adams, 50.

Korean-American alliance and influence, recent efforts have been made to maintain the positive influences of culture on Korean preaching and to dispense with those that are inherently dangerous. An example is the connection of Shamanism with modern materialism and other worldly escapism.[17]

These issues are well discussed in Jung Young Lee's book *Korean Preaching: An Interpretation*.[18] According to reviewer Yung Suk Kim,

> Lee approaches Korean preaching from the point of a Korean culture. That is to say, Korean preaching is evaluated and understood through the vantage point of culture. This culture of Koreanness has been shaped and was handed down through the ages of religious, cultural synthesis of Shamanism, Buddhism and Confucianism. Because of this kind of cultural approach to Korean preaching, Lee sees both the positive and the negative influence of Korean culture on Korean preaching. By positive side he affirms Korean cultural root and asks Korean preachers to reaffirm that inherited Koreanness in a way that Korean preaching can contribute to the multicultural society. By negative side he warns Korean preachers to change the practice of Korean preaching, because Korean preachers' shamanistic orientation of visible, materialistic blessings is distant from the gospel preaching. That kind of preaching alienates Korean churches from the other social religious groups.[19]

African-American Preaching

African-American preaching is proof that it is possible to understand a preaching process and to articulate the etymology, evolution, and development of a homiletical methodology. It is also proof that while some things cannot be

---

17. Seungyoun Jeong, "Korean Preaching, Han, and Narrative" (American University Studies. Series VII. Theology and Religion)," *Asian American Theological Forum* (31 October 2014).
    Also see Church Hyunchul Henry Oh, *Preaching as Interaction between Church and Culture: With Specific Reference to the Korean* (PhD Thesis, University of Pretoria, 2004).

18. Jung Young Lee, *Korean Preaching: An Interpretation* (Nashville: Abingdon, 1997).

19. Yung Suk Kim, "Review of Korean Preaching," Dr. Kim's Old Blog (accessed 11 January 2017).
    Also see Sangyil Park, *Korean Preaching, Han, and Narrative* (New York: Peter Lang, 2008) who attempts to develop a Korean preaching that is rooted in the Korean culture but based on narrative preaching.

learned in a book but must be experienced, "preaching can be enhanced not by imitation but by association and assimilation of other preaching traditions and homiletical art forms."[20] This is a way of describing African-American preaching as a brand of its own which has reached a stage where it can be a model for others who want to borrow from the repository of skill. For example Robert Smith Jr. refers to David Buttrick who confessed he has been influenced by the black homiletical tradition and considers it as probably the finest preaching in America today.[21]

But Henry Mitchell does not agree that there is something like a monolithic preaching style in the African-American tradition. While he believes that the majority share a style with African influence, some argue that the majority of the middleclass are influenced by the Anglo culture. But whatever is the case, African-American preaching has become a cross-cultural bridge as blacks are now being earnestly sought to fill homiletics vacancies in seminaries, and the prospect is maturing where the strength of the two American preaching cultures, black and white, "will so shape worship as to make ethnic inclusivity a common thing, and the church of Jesus Christ a reliable foretaste of the praise services in heaven, where in the presence of God may be found every kindred and people and tongue."[22]

The beauty of African-American preaching as it relates to the discussion here is its orality. Richard Eslinger observes that "preaching in the African-American tradition is narrative preaching," drawing from Scripture stories and insisting that preachers must know and tell the story.[23] In Eslinger's words, "there is a fit between the biblical witness with its strong communal fabric and the oral art of preaching within the black church."[24] Henry H. Mitchell describes the structure of these sermons as imaginative, narrative, and prone to generate experiential encounter. This structure is unlike the Euro-American traditional sermon which is more of the cognitive, essay-type sermon designed to inform and convince through the use of logic or reason.[25]

---

20. Robert Smith Jr., *Doctrine that Dances: Bringing Doctrinal Preaching and Teaching to Life* (Nashville: B&H Academic, 2008), 40.

21. Smith, *Doctrine that Dances*, 40.

22. Henry H. Mitchell, "African-American Preaching," in *Concise Encyclopedia of Preaching* (Louisville, KY: Westminster John Knox, 1995), 3, 8.

23. Richard L. Eslinger, *The Web of Preaching: New Options in Homiletic Method* (Nashville: Abingdon, 2002), 104.

24. Eslinger, *Web of Preaching*, 105.

25. Mitchell, "African-American Preaching," 3.

Antecedents from Korean, African-American, and Ghanaian Experience 163

The sources of African-American preaching provide the context in which it was developed. African-Americans brought much of their culture with them from Africa – drumming, sophisticated systems of signal, medicine, and gathering for worship, all of which the whites outlawed. It was not too difficult for the African slaves to imbibe the Christian faith because of their African traditional religion backgrounds. They already knew the Omnipotent (*Olodumare* in Yoruba) and the Omniscient (*Brekyirihunuade* in Ashanti) with all his praise names and hundreds of proverbs which expresses his justice and which parallel with the Pauline expression in Galatians 6:7.[26]

African-Americans understood shrines, holy places to encounter divine spirits, and continued their tradition of special praying grounds. They loved oratory and meaningful narrative which involved community participation. Several African folktales were well known and simply waiting for use in the new faith to which these Africans were exposed. These stories were rich in symbolic meaning and performed with powerful imagination.[27] The beginnings of expression in America were in the "Invisible Institution" – the underground church of the South where they practiced their own adaptation of the Christian faith which was "authentically Christian and unashamedly African American."[28] Many large black churches have their roots here.

Another suggested source of African-American preaching is the Second Great Awakening. The famous revivalist preacher George Whitefield appealed greatly to African Americans because of his sonorous voice, passionate proclamations, and deep emotional response from listeners. The connection occurred because many African native languages are tonal and have an unrestricted emotional utterance. Whitefield's influence led to the first African-American Baptist Church at Silver Bluff, Aiken, South Carolina.[29] But neither George Whitefield nor the influence he had on African-American preaching was mere emotionalism without reason. According to Eslinger, "In the Great Awakening, an expression of Christian faith that spoke to the whole person touched and attracted African Americans, both by virtue of its appeal to reason and emotion and the message of God's word to the downtrodden. George

---

26. Mitchell, 4.

27. Mitchell, 4. O. C. Edwards Jr. also observes that African-American preaching can be compared to the oral literature of the Homeric epics, Beowulf, African chant, and Serbo-Croatian guslars. O. C. Edwards Jr., "History of Preaching," in *Concise Encyclopedia of Preaching*, ed. William H. Willimon and Richard Lischer (Louisville, KY: Westminster John Knox, 1995), 224.

28. Edwards, "History of Preaching," 224.

29. Mitchell, "African-American Preaching," 5.

Whitefield built a bridge over which the gospel could travel to a spiritually hungry and brutally oppressed people from Africa."[30]

O. C. Edwards Jr. also asserts that African-American preaching, aside from being influenced by the Second Awakening, has much in common with the Welsh folk preaching to which the First Awakening can be traced. But he submits that the form began in the African-American churches where there developed a skillful tradition of oral art where preachers regularly "commit poetry" and at the same time powerfully present the gospel message.[31]

Several characteristics of African-American preaching have been identified. Robert Smith Jr. states that the structure used from generation to generation consists of six movements. These steps were adapted from a British tradition following this rhyme:

> Begin low;
> > Proceed low;
> Rise higher;
> > Take fire;
> When most impressed
> > Be self-possessed;
> To Spirit wed form
> > Sit down in a storm.[32]

In the context of jazz music which Smith observes was influenced by the African experience, he discusses such elements that can be compared to preaching in the African-American style including call and response, improvisation, syncopation, polyrhythms, and ostinato.[33]

However generally, some characteristics are identified with African-American contextualized preaching. The first is rhythm which has to do with intentional timing in the use of words, phrase, and sentences. Words are shaped with "vocal percussiveness" which is also called "hitting-a-lick," a term adapted later from the idioms of jazz and blues musicians.[34] The second characteristic is the melody of "The Hum" which has to do with tonal quality. It is like a sermon being sung and is rooted in the song-like recitals of African storytelling or folk singing. Jon Michael Spencer's examination of hundreds of sermons revealed

---

30. Eslinger, *Web of Preaching*, 106.
31. Edwards, "History of Preaching," 229.
32. Smith, *Doctrine that Dances*, 41.
33. Smith, 148–49.
34. Eslinger, *Web of Preaching*, 108.

that the tuning of African-American sermons is pentatonic – a scale common to African folk songs and traditional black spirituals.³⁵

A third characteristic is call and response, the most dynamic and exciting aspect of the African-American preaching. Like the antiphonal song of the cherubim in Isaiah 6:3, call and response involves someone speaking, playing, or singing and a group responding. It is natural for African-American preachers to expect responses when preaching. Starting from a conversational tone, the call and response lifts to a cantillation, and before long, the congregation and the preacher are doing the job together.³⁶ The call and response, though characteristic of the African-American tradition, is not unique to them. Smith admits that the "Welsh folk preacher was not a helpless soloist or a liturgical dictator but affirmed and authenticated the hearers as valued partners in the preaching process by dialogically participating with the elders in the 'amen corner.'"³⁷

Call and response is also a common feature of African singing and preaching, though not in the artistic and highly developed form of African-American preaching. Many of the common choruses sung in churches involve someone saying something and the congregation responding. For example, one popular chorus in Nigeria is "My God Is a Good God."

> **Lead**: My God is a good God
>
> **Response**: Yes he is
>
> **Lead**: My God is a good God
>
> **Response**: Yes he is
>
> **Lead**: He lifts me up
>
> **Response**: He lifts me up
>
> **Lead**: He turns me around
>
> **Response**: He turns me around
>
> **Lead**: He places my feet
>
> **Response**: He places my feet

---

35. Eslinger, 110–11. Mitchel refers to this as "whooping," in "African-American Preaching," 3.

36. Smith, *Doctrine that Dances*, 147. See Ezekiel A. Ajibade, *Common Pulpit Errors and Solutions* (Ibadan: Baptist Press, 2016), 38.

37. Robert Smith Jr., "Call and Response," in *The New Interpreter's Handbook of Preaching*, ed. Paul Scott Wilson (Nashville, TN: Abingdon, 2008), 297.

Lead: Upon the solid rock

Response: Upon the solid rock

Lead: I feel like shouting . . . dancing . . . clapping, etc

Response: (Everyone shouts, dances, and claps in response to whatever the chorus leader suggests).

These kinds of responses are reflected in preaching, too. African-American preachers love to carry their listeners along with such words as "Amen?" and "Halleluyah," and "Is someone following me?" and "Tell your neighbor . . ." Some sermons actually carry many prayers in them, and typically people respond with a loud "Amen!" as a sign of keying into the prayers or prophecies.

Smith traces the roots of call and response to West Africa. The structure was improvised when African Americans encountered European music as they used the lining out technique to sing Isaac Watts songs and hymns which were their favorites. According to Smith,

> Dr. Watts had metricised his songs and made them a lot more singable. By lining them out, they had space and long passages where they could improvise, stretch the notes out, and add vocal embellishments. So there was an encounter between European hymnody sung in a line-out West African technique combined with sensibility. This was the birth of the musical form called the Spirituals.[38]

However, Elsinger states that the dialogical response can be audible or silent, using such non-verbal responses as gestures or body language.[39] But there is always a caution that such responses should not become a mere display of negative mannerisms.

The congregation is crucial to the experience of African-American preaching. Along with the preacher, they create the genius. They enjoy the unfettered participation, treasure the Bible together, and respond with gratitude for fresh insights gained and as a testimony to the truth and power of the word in their lives.[40] What results is a display of spiritual power and not mere emotionalism as some outsiders may imagine. Quietness is not often an option in a normal preaching situation. Quietness among hearers may mean that

---

38. Smith, "Call and Response," 148.
39. Eslinger, *Web of Preaching*, 111.
40. Mitchell, "African-American Preaching," 7.

the sermon is dull or uninspired, the listeners are not part of the tradition, or an undercurrent of strife is hindering the Spirit.[41] According to Mitchell, "the Black preacher is more of a broker of spiritual power than a teacher."[42] As preachers play down their talent and let the Holy Spirit do the work, the ultimate dimension of the worship is experienced in the Spirit's possession. But this experience is controlled by the Holy Spirit himself who provides "unconscious parameters beyond which no person possessed may properly go."[43]

A final characteristic of African-American preaching is celebration. Eslinger calls this the final arrival – the "glory hallelujah." Smith describes this celebration using the jazz element polyrhythms which is represented in the dynamics of the preacher, the members, and the musicians with groans, moans, and vocal shouts. This celebration helps to bring the message to a climax and to end on the mountain, not the valley. The congregation "joins with the preacher at the mountaintop, sees the promised land, and a proleptic celebration is the only appropriate outcome of the shared experience of the Word."[44]

African-American preaching is not without criticisms. But it has survived well in the midst of an onslaught of elitist criticism. Its strength is in the holistic approach it employs which includes cognition, intuition, and emotion but not emotionalism. Faith, hope, and love are intuitive and emotive, and a good preacher from any culture needs to address these factors in human life.[45] African-American preaching is not all about ecstasy. It is about empowerment. For example, the major advances by civil right movements in the United States are very much on the initiative of the black churches. Civil right leaders like Martin Luther King Jr. engaged the power of the gospel to motivate people to take unimaginable risks. Other preachers were practically involved in social actions like the construction of the Underground Railroad and organizing

---

41. Mitchell, 3.
42. Mitchell, 7.
43. Mitchell, 7.
44. Eslinger, *Web of Preaching*, 133. Also see Henry H. Mitchell, "Celebration," in *The New Intepreter's Handbook of Preaching*, ed. Paul Scott Wilson (Nashville: Abingdon, 2008), 297–98; and Cleophus J. LaRue, "African American Preaching Perspectives," in *The New Interpreter's Handbook of Preaching*, ed. Paul Scott Wilson (Nashville: Abingdon, 2008).
45. Mitchell, "African-American Preaching," 4. The extensive influence of African-American contextualized preaching was observed during an interview with Joseph Roger Webber of First Baptist Church, ELWA Community, Liberia. He indicated that there is a strong connection between Liberians and the African-American heritage. Some Liberian cities are even replications of US communities. But most noteworthy is the fact that the African-American flavor of preaching is very noticeable when you enter some Liberian churches. Joseph Webber Roger, interview by the author, 22 September 2016.

boycotts of vegetables raised by slave labor. Some were even hanged for revolution. Others partook in the construction of schools, contested for political offices, fought for voting rights, improved inheritance for women, and advanced public welfare legislation.[46]

Today, African-American homiletical characteristics have greatly influenced white Protestantism. Little wonder why Thomas Long challenged the title of "Dean of Black Preaching" given to Gardener C. Taylor, a highly celebrated Black American preacher. He rather titles him the "Dean of All Preaching in America."[47]

Ghanaian Preaching

Closer home is the effort of Akwasi Ofori to develop a Ghanaian model of preaching that can serve as a template for African preaching. In spite of inadequacies, it is a great attempt toward contextualized preaching for Africa.[48] Ofori rightly observes that in Ghana and many other African countries, church growth is being witnessed, but there is a discrepancy between quantitative and qualitative growth. He identifies three major problems which informed the foundation of his homiletical submissions.

First is the search for relevance. Ofori observes that part of the impact that white missionaries left behind is an identity crisis that raises some questions including, what is truly Christian culture, and what is Westernized? What is authentic African Christian identity including names, language, and rites of passage? What is an authentic model of preaching?

The second problem Ofori observes is economic and social concern. Many people live below the poverty line, and there is corruption, bad leadership, a lack of industrialization and economic diversity, tribalism and nepotism, and a lack of infrastructural development. Therefore, the need to craft sermons that "people can identify with and which also address their needs and lead to a call for social reform" is critical.[49] Ofori suggests story preaching which is in "keeping with the ways in which traditional storytelling has from one generation to another helped the people of Ghana find ways to respond to life's hope, fears and aspirations."[50]

---

46. Mitchell, "African-American Preaching," 7–8.
47. Smith, *Doctrine that Dances*, 40.
48. Ofori, *Recovering Storytelling*, Kindle.
49. Ofori.
50. Ofori.

The third concern of Ofori is Pentecostalism which engaged drumming, dancing, loud and hysterical prayers, and speaking in tongues as it permeated Christianity in the country. Mainline churches lost members until they began to become "Pentecostal" too. The influence of Pentecostalism is never inconsequential, and sermons must be crafted to keep with this new approach and reality.

Ofori's suggestion of a storytelling style of preaching is further based on the fact that a vast majority of Ghanaians still live in the rural towns and villages and still gather in the evenings to tell what he calls the *Anansesem* stories (spider tales). These stories are told in turns, and others may interrupt with probing songs (*mmuguo*) to ensure everyone remains focused on both the story and the teller. According to Ofori, "The Ananse stories personify the collective consciousness of Ghanaians in the recognition that in any society there abound social vices but in the final analysis what one ought to work for is the common good of the community in which one lives."[51] Every story ends with an object lesson, something which people are cautioned to refrain from. Finally, Ofori develops what he tags "The New Ghanaian Sermon" based on the presuppositions above. This sermon is quite close to the efforts at producing a model of a "Village Oral Expository Sermon" and an "African Oral Expository Sermon."[52] The full-length sermon Ofori developed is in Appendix 4.

One of the inadequacies of the sermon produced by Ofori is that it is not purely expository. His selection of Psalms 35:22, 83:1, and 50:21 is already an indication that he was not ready to do justice to the text because he isolated single verses from passages that ought to have been exposited in context. Whenever a preacher cannot sit with a pericope and expound, there is the usual problem of moving all around the Bible to find supporting verses for the subject of discussion. That is why Ofori has to inject 2 Peter 3:8–9, Luke 18:1–8, Psalm 50:22, and Isaiah 49:8a in some parts of the sermon. Also his adaptation of the New Homiletic, while he saw its inadequacies, became a moral problem for him. In his words, "It is interesting to note that after fifty years the New Homiletic has critiqued itself particularly as relates to narrative preaching. Long has surmised that the narrative format has not lived up to that depth required of it with many stories simply being sentimental in substance. He recommends a return to strong exegesis accompanied by strong exposition or delivery." The sermon is also not very Christocentric in content. Still, Ofori

---

51. Ofori.
52. See both model sermons in chapter 7.

has made a great contribution to the subject of African Christian preaching and must be credited for this.

Discussion Questions

1. Having studied the effort to contextualize preaching among the Koreans and African Americans, and thinking through the Ghanaian experience, discuss how orality could be used in contextualizing expository preaching within your specific culture.
2. With the roots of African Americans in Africa, can it be said that preaching among the two people is related? Why or why not?

7

Sample Expository Sermons Based on African Orality

Below are two attempts to create sermons that bring together some of the key elements of orality and the needs of Africa, modelling what oral expository sermons may be like. The idea of modelling here is not to create one-size-fits-all sermons. Sermons are living and dynamic, and the place and leadership of the Holy Spirit should not be jettisoned. Moreover, genre plays an important role in the form of a biblical sermon, and biblical genres vary, many at times having subgenres within them. But this book has posited along the way that narrative and storytelling are the best ways to communicate with oral listeners. The two sermons below are developed with these factors in mind. They were preached to live audiences, and inputs from listeners were well considered in fashioning the final forms. The "Village Oral Expository Sermon" was preached in the vernacular, Yoruba in this case, because of its peculiar target and the clamor for mother-tongue sermons in getting the meaning of the Bible to reach people at the grass roots. Like Mitchell opines, "People hear the good news in their own mother tongue – their own idiom, images, and cultural communication style."[1]

Village Oral Expository Sermon

This sermon follows the narrative plus lessons method of narrative preaching as mentioned in the last chapter. The basic characteristics of this kind of sermon are to retell the Bible story and at the end bring out lessons, principles, and applications. Proponents of the narrative plus lessons method do not think a good story should be explained or applied. But research on the preferences of

---

1. Mitchell, "African-American Preaching," 2.

African audiences, the example of Jesus, and existential need all show the need to explain and apply a biblical lesson after narrating it.[2] Therefore this sermon includes a retelling of the Bible story and its application without necessarily drawing out points as in the linear-logical method of expository sermon preparation. Since this sermon was developed with primarily oral listeners in mind, the assumption was that many of them did not have a Bible in their hands, and even if they did, they could not read, nor could they jot any sermon points from the message. Much of what they would take home depended on how the preacher told the story and let them see how it applies to their lives and situations. So the first part of the sermon is a recast or paraphrase of the biblical passage in such a way that nothing is missing from the original, and the second part is the explanation and application. This sermon is also shorter in length than most because of the attention span of the target audience.

* * *

Sermon Title:

From the Beautiful Gate into a Beautiful Life

Sermon Text: Acts 3:1–10

The Passage Recast

It happened one day that Peter and John, the disciples of Jesus Christ, were going to the temple at three o'clock in the afternoon to pray. The temple gate was called Beautiful, and there was a man who had been lame from the time he was born. He was dropped at the Beautiful Gate every day to beg for alms from those going into the temple. As soon as he saw Peter and John about to enter the temple, he begged for money. Peter looked at him and said, "Look at us." He looked at them. And while he was expecting them to pull out money and give it to him, they told him, "We do not have silver or gold, but we will give you what we have. In the name of Jesus Christ of Nazareth, walk!" Then they took him by the right hand and lifted him up. And immediately, the man's ankles and feet became strong, and he jumped to his feet and began to walk. That moment, the man went into the temple with Peter and John, walking, jumping, and praising God. When everybody saw him walking, jumping, and praising God, they all recognized that it was that same man who was always sitting at

---

2. Grant Lovejoy, "Narrative Preaching in Recent North American Homiletics." Paper adapted from Grant Lovejoy, "Shaping Sermons by the Literary Form of the Text," in *Biblical Hermeneutics*, ed. Bruce Corley, Steve Lemke, and Grant Lovejoy (Nashville: B&H, 1996), 7–8.

the temple gate called Beautiful and begging, and they were all surprised and wondered what had happened to him.

Explanation and Application
What would God want us to see in this story? It is a story of helpless limitation. I don't know how long this man had been laid at the Beautiful Gate, but for him to have been born lame, we can only imagine how long. I don't know what went on in his mind each time they carried him and put him at this gate. Did he appreciate the life, the clothing, the joy, and whatever radiates from the lives of those going into the temple? Did he desire or dream to cross over into this temple one day? Was he content with staying at the gate asking for alms all day? Or was he resigned to fate, accepting his destiny as we used to say? Maybe being crippled and begging all his life was his *àyànmọ́* (what he chose) when he was making his journey from heaven to earth.

You know in African cosmology we are all believed to have come from heaven with an *orí* (head). Before coming to the world, each one had to visit the home of *Àjàlá* – the head sculptor who also happens to be a debtor and has to occasionally hide in the roof when his creditors visit. Unfortunately because of his unstable behavior, he makes some heads good by baking them well, and he makes some others bad by not completing them or not baking them well. And remember he might have to abandon some heads when some of his creditors come knocking on his door! When you get to his chambers and you pick a head, the journey from heaven to earth will test it. There is usually a heavy rainfall in the course of the journey. If your head is a good one, congratulations! because you will arrive in the world with *oríire* (a good head, a successful destiny). If, however, you chose a bad, unfinished, or not well-baked head, the rain will beat down on you and erode your head. Then you will arrive on the earth with an *oríburúkú* (bad head or bad destiny).

So, which kind of "head" did you bring to the world? And where do you find this in the word of God? I met a woman with a set of twins in a motor park one day. She was healthy and nothing was wrong with her kids. But she was begging that we give alms to the twin she was carrying. I got mad inside of me and questioned her: "Why would you subject these innocent children to the hardship of bringing them out in the sun to beg for alms? Can't you work and take care of them?" Surprisingly, this woman was ready to insult me. She said, "If you have something to offer the twins, give me, and if you don't have, please don't talk to me that way." Later someone in a vehicle told us that it is the custom of some of those women around there. She must have gone to consult the gods on behalf of the kids, and that might have been what their head or "destiny" demands. That was really an unfortunate but unforgettable experience for me. I love it when we sing this song:

> *Orí mi kọ̀ ọ́*
> (My head rejects it)
> *Orí mí kọ̀ 'yà*
> (My head rejects suffering)
> *Ẹlẹ́da mí kọhun tí ò da ò*
> (My destiny rejects what is bad)
> *Orí mí kọ̀ 'yà*
> (My head rejects suffering)
> *Orí rere lorí mi o*
> (My head/destiny is a good one)
> *Response: Orí rere*
> (Good head/destiny)
> *Mo ti kékeré mọ 'sẹ́ Olúwa*
> (I knew the work of the Lord from my childhood)
> *Response: Orí rere*
> (Good head/destiny)
> *Mo sì tún dà 'gbà sí 'nú ìmọ́lẹ̀*
> (And I grew up in the Light)
> *Response: Orí rere*
> (Good head/Good destiny)

God created us for a purpose. He had good thoughts and plans for us when he created us because everything he creates is good. Yes, there are times he takes us through hard and challenging circumstances, but ultimately he makes all things work together for our good. I see him making all things work together for your good in Jesus's name (Amen!).

Whatever happens, he has not created you to be a beggar. Do you know that physically challenged people do great things in life? I have seen places where the lame, the blind, and other physically challenged people produce great arts and crafts, and carry out wonderful projects that those who are able-bodied celebrate and may not even be able to do. Maybe you need to watch the Paralympics where the physically challenged perform great feats and make their nations proud. God has not destined you to beg. He destined you to bring out ability from your disability and make your star to shine in spite of your limitations.

Now, while this is a story of human limitations, it is also a story of divine intervention. This man might have remained like this all his life if there had not been a divine intervention from God. He lived most days at the Beautiful Gate, but his life was not beautiful. This gate was described as one among others that was well decorated with Corinthian bronze. Yet the value of the bronze was far greater than others that were decorated with silver and gold. In fact, it was said that when you looked at this gate at times, the bronze shone as if it was gold. So what is the value of sitting in such a beautiful gate every day, when your life is not beautiful?

God decided to visit this man. He sent Peter and John to him. While the man ought to have asked them, "Please how can I get out of this limitation and join you in this temple, or live a better and more meaningful life than this?" all he asked for was money. Now tell me, how long will he take to gather five naira and ten naira to do any good in life? Even if he eventually succeeded in doing any "good," where is the dignity? What some of us are asking for is just too small compared to what God wants to do with our lives. And do you know one irony about life? As long as this man wanted just crumbs, there are tens and hundreds of people who will keep giving him crumbs for the rest of his life. At least "the barking of dogs does not reduce the beggar's daily allotment," like the Arabs would say. If you have settled for a life below the line, you keep getting help only at your level.

But God won't bear with the myopic request of this man. While he asked for money, Peter and John gave him Jesus. Jesus is the ultimate solution to all human problems. Once a person opens his or her heart to him, Jesus saves. Perhaps Peter and John had once or had usually given this man alms, but not today. The man must have been disappointed. Oh, may God disappoint you so that your disappointment could turn to appointment! If God did not "disappoint" some of us in the past, we wouldn't be where God has helped us to be today. They told him, "Man, you can't afford to sit here forever. There is a better life behind this gate. Rise up and walk!" The man was struggling. Perhaps his faith didn't carry him. Verse 7 says they took him by the right hand and helped him. Oh, we need to pray. Lord, send helpers who will encourage me to my destiny. Send helpers who will help me to my destiny. Maybe more aggressively now, send a helper who will force me to my destiny. Remember this song we use to sing:

> Ìrànlọ́wọ́ alaìní rànmí lọ́wọ́
>   (Helper of the needy, help me)
> Ìwọ nìkan ni mo ní láyé àti lọ́run
>   (You are the only one I have in heaven and on earth)
> Ẹní bá ní ọ, ó ti lóhùn gbogbo

>   (Anyone who has you has all things)
>   Ìrànlọ́wọ́ alaìní ránmí lọ́wọ́ o Bàbá
>   (Helper of the needy, help me Father)

I see help coming for you also (Amen). When help came for this man, he crossed the barrier. They pulled him up. The Spirit entered into him. He walked, he jumped, he started praising God. He crossed from the gate that was beautiful into the temple that was beautiful. He crossed from the temple that was beautiful into a life that was beautiful. How do I know it's a life that was beautiful?

For the first time this man became an object of celebration. No one ever celebrated this man before. He was an object of scorn: an unrecognized, abandoned, dejected, and rejected beggar dumped at the gate every morning to beg for alms. Nobody ever ran toward him before, only away from him. Today he was the cause of wonder and amazement (v. 10). Like the Yorubas say, *Ẹni a rò pé kò le p'àgọ́, tó kọ́ 'lé aláruru; ẹni a p'ète p'èrò ká d'ọwọ́ ẹ bo lẹ̀ pípele ló tún n pele si* (One that we think cannot make a tent, but builds a magnificent house; one that we plan to bring down but who is increasing more and more). Oh . . . your story will change from this day in the name of Jesus! (Amen).

For the first time since birth, this man mixed with great men and women. Verse 11 says he held on to Peter. The disciples were held in such high honor, esteem, and respect that nobody ever came near them (Acts 5:13). This man became a symbol of Hannah's testimony –

> *[The LORD] raises the poor from the dust*
>   *and lifts the needy from the ash heap;*
> *he seats them with princes*
>   *and has them inherit a throne of honor.* (1 Sam 2:8)

Now, he could begin a new plan for his life. No more begging. He could go into farming and become a celebrated farmer. He could go to school, build a career, develop a vocation, and stop being dependent on others for survival. There was nothing this man could do now that would not attract people. If he became a professional, his testimony would be enough to attract. If he became an evangelist, who would not listen to his story? Most importantly, he had salvation which qualified him for eternity with Jesus. His sins had been forgiven, and he had the hope of eternal life. He had really crossed from the Beautiful Gate into a Beautiful Life!

I speak into your life today; you will cross over in Jesus name!

You will break through every barrier and fulfil your destiny.
This man didn't go from one mountain to another before he got a miracle. Your miracle will locate you. God will remember you and visit you with mercy and favor.
You are no longer an invalid. Jesus heals you today.
You are no longer sitting to admire any beautiful gate.
You are crossing over into to beautiful life.
Rise up from your beggarly position today and become the blessings you are created to be.

* * *

This sermon was preached to a live audience who were predominantly illiterate and the Yoruba chapel of the Nigerian Baptist Theological Seminary, Ogbomoso, was used. This chapel is normally attended by members of the community who are cleaners, laborers, attendants, or other staff who serve as messengers or office clerks. Most of these are either not educated beyond the secondary school level or not formally educated at all. They absolutely fit into the description of primary oral learners or partly residual oral learners.

Seven members of the faculty were invited to passively participate in the worship but were given the evaluation form to make an on-the-spot assessment of the sermon and its effectiveness in communicating to the people. The form gave an opportunity to assess the body language and style of the preacher; the oral vehicles for proclamation and the oral elements and how effective their usage was; the hermeneutics and audience engagement; and how the sermon met the African need.[3]

There was a consensus that the oral elements were well utilized, the audience was well engaged, the body language and style were commendable, the hermeneutics and exegeses were sound, and the sermon met the need of the target audience. The audience was also interviewed three weeks after the sermon to assess how lasting the impact of the sermon had been on them.[4] This interviewing was needed especially knowing that they did not jot anything down while the sermon was being preached. They simply participated in the entire sermonic process with no visible evidence of distraction. The twenty participants interviewed did not struggle to recall the sermon theme, the lessons they went home with, the songs sang, the proverbs used, and the

---

3. See Appendix 5 for the evaluation sheet.
4. See Appendix 6 for the feedback-interview guide.

legend referenced. What most of them loved most about the sermon was the narration of the story of that man at the Beautiful Gate. There was nothing they did not like about the sermon. They thought that an oral method like this is good because it allows for good expression of the Yoruba language and would enhance good listener comprehension. They wished that the preacher (this researcher) would visit their chapel often.

African Oral Expository Sermon

The "African Oral Expository Sermon" is patterned after the segmented narrative sermon. According to Grant Lovejoy, "in the segmented narrative sermon, the preacher tells the biblical story one scene or episode at a time, pausing between segments to offer explanatory comments, give illustrations, make application, and otherwise augment the story."[5] The beauty of this style is the opportunity it gives to skillfully weave in the biblical backgrounds, explanations, illustrations, and applications which are the gems of expository preaching. However, Lovejoy cautions that breaking the story apart can be natural for literate people but makes the story difficult for oral communicators to remember. Therefore he suggests that supplemental material be kept brief and that transitional sentences be well used when resuming each segment of the story.[6]

This "African Oral Expository Sermon" was designed to reach all of the primary, secondary, and residual audiences. As many elements of orality as possible were engaged, and though it is a narrative sermon, effort was made to draw lessons out so that listeners can think of concrete actions to take after hearing the message. The context, problems, and situation of Africa were also considered when developing the sermon.

* * *

Sermon Title:

A Hero on the Battlefield of Integrity

Sermon Text: 2 Samuel 18:1–18

In traditional Africa, our forefathers loved to talk about battles and fight battles. That is why some of us who have praise names (panegyrics) find out that they contain themes that are related to battle, fierce animals, and victory. But battles

---

5. Lovejoy, "Narrative Preaching," 12.
6. Lovejoy, 13.

also produce heroes, and heroes are usually celebrated with special praise poems. For example, Ikoyi is very popular among the Yorubas for war. One of the praise poems for the *Oníkòyí* is this one:

> *Oníkòyí*, the warrior who never received an arrow in his back.
> Child of the water lily, child of the squirrel.
> The bird's foot shall never touch the water.
> The river shall never be at rest.
> *Oníkòyí*, the warrior
> Who frightens death himself. . . .
>
> *Oníkòyí* loves nothing but war:
> When others drink wine, he drinks blood;
> When others plant yams, he is planting heads;
> When others reap fruit, he is reaping dead warriors.

We will be talking about a battle today, but not the kind our forefathers fought in the jungles. We will be sharing a story from the passage read to us and seeing what message God would like to pass across to us.

Absalom woke up one day, and he wanted to take over his father's kingdom. He would not wait for his time because he wanted it now. David his father, too, had lost his moral stamina to lead the people of Israel. The reasons were his adultery with Bathsheba, his murder of Uriah her husband and one of his great fighters, and the other events that followed. David might have been confused in a way: Should he take Absalom's action as a punishment for his own misbehavior, which was exactly as Nathan prophesied it, or should he see Absalom's action as pure rebellion from a spoiled brat? But David must face the reality of the situation. He must either quell this rebellion after making an early decision to flee his throne in Jerusalem, or this rebellion would send him to an untimely grave. Absalom was ready to destroy David his father and his soldiers, and he was ready to take over his throne. He had at least temporarily won over the heart of Israel, took over some of David's key advisers, and slept with his father's concubine publicly as a mark of being serious about what he was doing. What else would he not do? Our people often say *Ọmọ táàkọ́ ni o gbé 'lé táakọ́ tà* (It is a child we refuse to train [build] that will sell the house we built). And that is what Absalom was up to. That's why we sing:

> *Ba mi wò ó láwòyè*
>   (Take good care of him)
> *Kó má se dòkú mọ́ mi lọ́wọ́*
>   (Let him not die in my hands)

> *Ọmọ èyí tí o fi fun mí o*
> (This child you have given unto me)
> *Kó má se dàgbà 'yà láyé o*
> (Should not become a "big for nothing")
> *Kó má se bà mí lórúko jẹ́*
> (Should not destroy my reputation)
> *Ba mi wò ó láwòyè*
> (Take good care of him)

So a battle ensued between Absalom the rebel and his fighters, and David the man after God's heart who greatly disappointed God and got a curse to unsettle him. The son was ready to take on his father, and if he succeeded in getting David, he would gladly remove his head! Let's put the prophecy of Nathan aside a little and ponder on something from the life of this young man. We might want to say that what Absalom did had been predicted just the way we hold to fate and fatalism in many of our societies, but that does not exonerate Absalom from being responsible for his actions and from facing the dire consequences. What really came on Absalom? Why would he go to that length in seeking for power? Why was he so attracted to the throne that he wanted to get it by all means while his father was still alive? He began by standing at the gate and using political gimmicks to promise the Israelites what he could never offer them (2 Sam 15). He continued to steal the people's hearts until he chased his father away from his throne, and right now he is ready to use his own hands to kill the man that birthed him.

When people become desperate for power, they can go to any length. That is the bane of African society today. People want to rule by all means, and they are ready to crush anyone who would stand in their way. They will cajole, engage in diabolic powers, use money to bribe, kidnap, assassinate their rivals and opponents, rig elections, engage in arsons, and just do anything to rule. When they get to leadership positions, you discover they have nothing to offer, and all that attracted them was the paraphernalia of office and the opportunity to enrich themselves with public wealth. The worst of it is when some of them get there and decide not to leave again. That is why in Africa you have a president who is ninety-two years old, and you have another one who promised to rule for a billion years. He was defeated in a poll a few weeks ago after ruling for twenty years, and he is still promising not to leave the seat of power. These are some of the reasons Africa has remained backward in many spheres of life. We must take care of every "Absalomic" tendency in our societies. What do we have that God has not given us? What would we eat in this world that would last forever? [Here the choir comes in with the song.]

Ará mi ẹ se pẹ̀lẹ́ pẹ̀lẹ́ láyé ta wá
  (My people, let's take it easy in this world)
Ará mi ò ẹ se pẹ̀lẹ́ pẹ̀lẹ́ láyé ta wá
  (My people, let's take it easy in this world)
Ilé ayé o kì mà í s'àwá ilọ
  (This world is not a permanent place)
Ilé ayé o kì mà í s'àwá ilọ
  (This world is not a permanent place)
Ará mi ò ẹ se pẹ̀lẹ́ pẹ̀lẹ́ láyé ta wá
  (My people, let's take it easy in this world)

The battle was about to commence. Everyone got his posting, and David was also ready to go with his army. But what was David going to do at the battle front – defend his position as the commander-in-chief of the armed forces of Israel? Or as we see a little later, was he going out to protect his rebellious son from being killed? If that was his goal, then we must ask – what a father! – going to battle to protect a son who wanted you dead? The response of his troops indicates a lot of sincerity and a great love for the king: "But the men said, 'You must not go out; if we are forced to flee, they won't care about us. Even if half of us die, they won't care; but you are worth ten thousand of us. It would be better now for you to give us support from the city'" (2 Sam 18:3). But David's real intention will soon be known as he warned them. Verses 5–6 says, "The king commanded Joab, Abishai and Ittai, 'Be gentle with the young man Absalom for my sake.' And all the troops heard the king giving orders concerning Absalom to each of the commanders."

David's magnanimity to Absalom was the product of a man after God's heart: the real David, notwithstanding the sin that led to this dangerous situation he found himself. It was only God who would love Israel so much that even when they hurt him, he was always showing them love. That was his point in the story of Hosea and Gomer. God is always that Father whose prodigal younger son woke up one day and demanded his portion of inheritance while his father was still alive. The father gave it to him, and the son went to squander it. But when he returned, it was the same father who welcomed him, gave him a kiss, and declared a celebration that his lost son was back. David looks so much like the Father here. How many of us would want to protect Absalom in this case? Won't we stand up straight to him and declare a curse that will follow him and his posterity for the rest of his life?

The battle began without David, and it will not be long until Absalom will run into the deepest trouble of his life. It is in the midst of this that another participant in this battle is introduced to us. The battle was fierce in the woods of Ephraim, and the army that supported Absalom was routed with twenty thousand of them lying dead around the battlefield. In the midst of the battle Absalom himself met the men of David, and he needed to escape on the mule he rode as a king's son. As he did, he went under the thick branches of a great oak tree, and unfortunately there was an asset that became a curse for him – his long hair. Back in 2 Samuel 14:25–26, we have been told that "In all Israel there was not a man so highly praised for his handsome appearance as Absalom. From the top of his head to the sole of his foot there was no blemish in him. Whenever he cut the hair of his head – he used to cut his hair once a year because it became too heavy for him – he would weigh it, and its weight was two hundred shekels by the royal standard." The same beauty (and its components) for which he was praised and with which he warmed the hearts of many in Israel was also his bane. Imagine a man with a beautiful face and an ugly heart. The Balubas would say, "The skin of the leopard is beautiful, but not his heart." Anyway, the same hair that had ever been the symbol of his beauty and glory got him caught up within the tree and got him hung.

Now, I said a third major character in this battle was introduced to us. His name was not mentioned, perhaps because he was not a high-ranking officer in the army. As the battle raged, God just ordered his movement, and he was the first and perhaps the only one to see Absalom hanging on the oak tree by his long hair. Many things would run through this man's mind in seconds – "Should I strike him, or should I leave him?" Maybe he even thought about the name or rewards that would follow if he performed this feat. "But no! I will report this to our commander." Something tied his hands. [The preacher raises the song.]

> Lord you are more precious than silver,
> Lord you are more costly than gold,
> Lord you are more beautiful than diamonds,
> There is nothing I desire compared with you.
>
> I'd rather have Jesus than silver or gold,
> I'd rather be His than have riches untold;
> I'd rather have Jesus than houses or land,
> Yes, I'd rather be led by His nail-pierced hand.
> Than to be the king of a vast domain,
> And be held in sin's dread sway,
> I'd rather have Jesus than anything,
> This world affords today.

This man got an opportunity to "make it fast" as we like to say it. As the first soldier to see Absalom hanging on a tree, all he needed was to run his sword through him, and he would become the "hero" of the day. Not only would he have become a hero on record, he would have become rich overnight. When he reported to Joab the commander, Joab told him in verse 11, "What! You saw him? Why didn't you strike him to the ground right there? Then I would have had to give you ten shekels of silver and a warrior's belt." An attempt to quantify this money in today's currency will not be meaningful because values differ widely. But for Joab to have promised him such an amount, it must have been "mouth-watering." The warrior's belt would have been not just a sign of promotion from the ranks to a commissioned officer but a testimony of great valor and service to the country.

Who does not like to be rich? Who does not love a name? Who does not want to enter a record for quelling one of the greatest rebellions in history, or enter an honor roll or hall of fame? Who does not want to be promoted? But there is a problem, and it is a serious one. This soldier was not ready to kill Absalom and take such honor. Not only was he ready to reject a reward of ten shekels, he was ready to reject a reward of a thousand shekels. What was his reason? He told Joab, "When the king was giving the instruction, 'Protect the young man Absalom for my sake,' I heard it loud and clear. I was not the only one that heard it; we all heard it. The king spoke, and I am required and obliged to obey the command of my king" (verse 13).

At least "It is he who sent one on an errand that one fears; one does not fear who to deliver it to" (*Ẹni bá rán'ni nísẹ́ là á bẹ̀rù, a kì í bẹ̀rù ẹni tá jẹ fún*). Not only that, the soldier said, "I would have put my life in jeopardy – and nothing is hidden from the king. Beyond that, I know who human beings are. I don't trust human beings when it comes to matters like this. They send you on evil errands, and they back out along the way. I know what human beings can do. I know how unreliable they are. *Ẹni a ní kó kíni lẹ́yin, ẹ̀gún ló fi sọ́wọ́, ẹni aní kó fẹ́ni lójú, ata ló fi sẹ́nu, ẹni a tún ní ká fi ọ̀rọ̀ lọ̀, ó jẹ́ aláròkiri ẹ̀dá* (He that one asks to sponge one's back put thorns in the hand, he that one asks to blow off a speck from one's eyes puts pepper in the mouth, and he that one could have told one's tale is a backbiter). If I had done it the way you are now encouraging me, you are the same person who would pretend you knew nothing about the whole case when we get to the presence of the king" (verse 13).

What this man was saying in other words is, "I have a name to protect. I have a face to save. I have a king to obey. I would not use my today to destroy my tomorrow. I chose to be a man of honor." But Joab was not on the same page with a man like this. Blood was swift for him to shed. He had fought so many battles and shed so much blood. He was not the type that separates war times from peacetimes. Blood can be shed anytime. That was why he took the lives of Abner and Amasa. Absalom was too small for a bloodthirsty general like this. The king's command made no meaning to him at this point. He went ahead, and he struck Absalom. He blew the trumpet, and the battle was over.

Now let me ask you. Who won this battle? Who is the hero of this battle? That may not be an easy question to answer. A story is told about the savage Sawi tribes in the jungles of Dutch New Guinea. They placed a high value on treachery and deception. When you deceive people to the point you are able to kill and eat them, you are celebrated. And so when a missionary couple came to stay with them to share the story of how Jesus came to the world, was betrayed, arrested, and crucified, what excited them was the part that Judas played. For them, Judas who betrayed Jesus was their hero, and not Jesus. Judas was a clever deceiver to be admired, and Jesus was a fool to be laughed at. So Judas was their hero!

Absalom is not the hero of this story. He was the badly spoilt son whom no parents would wish to breed. He brought shame to himself and to the kingdom of his father and died a shameful death. David was a confusing role player in this story. He was the cause of it all because he disobeyed God's command and seemed to have problems disciplining his children the way they should be. Yet he must be appreciated for having such a large heart to still love a son who would murder him. Joab was a soldier who felt the duty to protect his nation from a usurper. But his antecedents as one who delights in shedding blood gave him out when he killed Absalom, knowing that he had an opportunity to simply arrest him as a prisoner of war.

My hero is the man without a name! He demonstrated integrity. He heard the king's command and obeyed it. He had no interest in any personal gratification, and he would never sell his conscience for any amount of naira or dollar. He was conscious that he would stand before the king one day and would be accountable for his actions. He understood perfectly the unreliability of humanity and would not trust any man to push him into any regrettable action then desert him to face the consequences alone. He was bold to face up to Joab. Though he was just one of the "men of the rank," he faced Commander Joab to tell him the naked truth, not minding that he could be fired, framed up, jailed, retired, or killed.

We need heroes like this in Africa. We need men and women who will be obedient to God, his word, and the laws of their land. We need men and women whose consciences are alive and who will not sell them for any amount of money, however hard-pressed they are and however savory the offer is – in professional and political offices, schools, churches, and everywhere. We need men and women who are conscious of ultimate accountability so that even when they will not be accountable to any human, they will remember that one day they will stand before the judgment seat of Christ. We need men and women who will not be cajoled or manipulated by peer pressure or the order of the day into taking actions which will bring regret to their lives and shame to the name of Christ. We need men and women who will stand up to the face of anyone who dares to listen and say, "Even if I will have to die, I will not compromise my stand." These are the people who will bring transformation to Africa. These are the men and women who will birth the real revival we have been praying for. These are the heroes that we will celebrate.

Will you be this man or woman? If you will, let us sing this song of commitment to the Lord and his cause together:

> From over hill and plain
>> There comes the signal strain
> Tis loyalty, loyalty, loyalty to Christ;
>> Its music rolls along
> The hills take up the song
>> Of loyalty, loyalty, Yes, loyalty to Christ
> "On to victory! On to Victory!"
>> Cries our great commander: "On!"
> We'll move at His command
>> We'll soon possess the land
> Thro' loyalty, loyalty, Yes, loyalty to Christ[7]

* * *

This sermon was preached to a mixed audience. Among the audience were doctor of ministry students who came for their contact sessions at the Nigerian Baptist Theological Seminary, Ogbomoso, from various parts of Nigeria and various tribes and cultures and represented different denominations, both Baptist and Pentecostal. Other members of the audience were some first-degree students in their early stay in the seminary, coming from secondary school. In between were some master of divinity students and master of theology students, and a few PhD students in different fields of study. So it was a literate community at various levels, but they were all Africans assumed to be an oral community in spite of their education. In all, there were thirty participants.

---

7. Elijah T. Cassel, "Loyalty to Christ," https://hymnary.org/text/from_over_hill_and_plain.

Eight members of the faculty were given the same evaluation sheet used for the "Village Oral Expository Sermon." Six other forms were distributed to six of the DMin students. There was a consensus that the body language, style, oral vehicles for proclamation, oral elements, hermeneutics and exegesis, and audience engagement skills were well utilized to drive the message home and meet the needs of the listeners. It was interesting, however, that one of the DMin students who participated during the evaluation session raised his discomfort about the lack of a usual outline. This is to be expected at his level of education, and this researcher gave him a ready response. If this sermon was preached in the linear-logical deductive outline form, it would look like this: A hero in the battlefield of integrity will demonstrate the following characteristics:

- Faithfulness to godly rules and conscience (vv. 5, 10–13)
- Disregard for personal or corporate gratification (vv. 11–12)
- Consciousness of ultimate accountability (v. 13)
- Awareness of human unreliability (v. 13)
- Boldness to face up to people, whoever they are (v. 13)

One other area that confused evaluators of the sermon was the indication of "celebration" as one of the criteria for assessing audience engagement in an African oral expository sermon. The word "celebration" is not a problem in African-American preaching and parlance, but because of the novelty of coding the nuances of African preaching which was one of the responsibilities of this research, some may not understand its implication. Therefore, the need arose for the researcher to explain that celebration is another word for the climax of the sermon, and not exclusively the point of rejoicing. The confusion actually arose because in the "Village Oral Expository Sermon," there was a climax when the lame man was healed and there was rejoicing. Many saw that as the "celebration." But the story of the man who refused to kill Absalom, there is perhaps nothing to "celebrate" or rejoice about; yet there is a climax. Since this evaluation form may be used for future academic endeavors in African preaching, the criteria of celebration has been slashed with "climax" for easy comprehension.

Discussion Questions

1. Make a personal evaluation of the sermon "From the Beautiful Gate into a Beautiful Life." Comment on its effectiveness as a "Village Oral Expository Sermon" and suggest what you would have done differently with the sermon structure and content.

2. Evaluate the sermon "A Hero on the Battlefield of Integrity." What impression does it make on you and how does it drive home the beauty of using orality in expository preaching?
3. Prepare and attempt to preach your own version of a "Village Oral Expository Sermon" and "African Oral Expository Sermon."

8

Dangers of Contextualization

While this is a book in the category of homiletics, the concept of contextualization has been very pronounced as the medium of making expository preaching relevant and incarnated within an African cultural milieu. From the outset of the book, contextualization was conceptualized as "planting, watering, and nurturing the gospel message within the culture so much that people feel a sense of ownership of it and are ready to run with it without tampering with the biblical roots and essence of the message."[1] Since the context of the book is expository preaching, contextualization is then seen as "making the message first of all biblical, then African, so that it is faithful to the inspired word but incarnated in the culture of Africans."[2] This is the usual stance of many biblical scholars and theologians whenever contextualization is discussed. Kwame Bediako, for example, indicated that from his early Christian conversion experience, he had engaged in the task of seeking clarification for himself on how the "abiding gospel of Jesus Christ relates to the inescapable issues and questions which arise from the Christian cultural existence in the world, and how this relationship is achieved without injury to the integrity of the Gospel."[3]

The fear around contextualiztion is usually one as expressed by Robert J. Schreiter when he raised some questions like, "how thoroughly contextualized does a local church intend to become? Are there limits to contextualization? Can it reach a point where the gospel message is lost or communion between the churches is no longer possible?"[4] The universality of the church, as much

---

1. See page 2 of the Introduction.
2. See page 2 of the Introduction.
3. Kwame Bediako, *Theology and Identity: The Impact of Culture upon Christian Thoughts in the Second Century and Modern Africa* (Oxford, UK: Regnum, 1992), xi.
4. Robert J. Schreiter, *Constructing Local Theologies* (Maryknoll, NY: Orbis, 1986), 145.

as its locality, is usually an age-long pride of the church, but there is the apprehension in some quarters that contextualization might do some harm. Krikor Haleblian asked: "Will the church split apart as we experience the rise of local theologies?"[5] Questions like these have engendered several discussions, especially in the missiological world, which clearly indicates that there may be certain dangers in contextualization that must be nipped in the bud when engaging in it.

Two such dangers are identified by Ed Stetzer as obscurantism and syncretism. Obscurantism makes people think the gospel is synonymous with certain ideas or expressions that are external to it. This happens when, for instance, certain music genres or certain methods of evangelism are held sacrosanct as a means of expressing the Christian faith.[6] The fact that a music genre or evangelistic method evolved from within a culture does not mean it is "scriptural" and must be exported to another culture. Another dimension to this is when theological forms are considered to reflect accurate theological truth for many churches around the world, but are not appropriate for certain local contexts. Such forms may carry "historical or linguistic baggage that overly weigh them down with unintended meaning" which may be difficult to replace in the new context.[7] There must not be an insistence in using such forms.

The other danger of contextualization is that of syncretism. While attempting to contextualize the gospel, it is possible to mix Christianity with something else. There are possibilities of accepting the religious convictions of other cultures "in a way that distorts or denies the Gospel."[8] Syncretism is when Christianity is combined with "unacceptable parts" of other religions, and the gospel becomes compromised, weakened, and ultimately distorted.[9] While there are divergent opinions as to the definition of syncretism and whether it is absolutely a negative term, the challenge is usually that of understanding and

---

5. Haleblian, "Problem of Contextualization," 100.

6. Ed Stetzer, "What Is Contextualization? Presenting the Gospel in Culturally Relevant Ways," accessed 20 Dec 2019, https://www.christianitytoday.com/edstetzer/2014/october/what-is-contextualization.html.

7. Steve Strauss, "Creeds, Confessions, and Global Theologizing: A Case Study in Comparative Christologies," in *Globalizing Theology: Belief and Practice in an Era of World Christianity*, edited by Craig Ott and Harold A. Netland, 140–156 (Grand Rapids, MI: Baker Academic, 2006), 152.

8. Stetzer, "Creeds, Confessions, and Global Theologizing," 152.

9. Curtis A. Peterson, "Dangers and Opportunities in the Contextualization of the Gospel," accessed 7 Jan 2020, http://www.wlsessays.net/handle/123456789/3656.

caution.[10] Writers like Byang Kato had, right from his early days, feared that "the genuine desire to make Christianity truly African has not been matched with the power of discernment not to tamper with the inspired content of the revealed Word of God."[11] This portends danger and the danger always confronts those engaged with contextualization of the gospel in Africa.

Efforts are usually made, therefore, to set limits when contextualizing. Some of those limits include ensuring that the word of God is the foundation or basis of theology, and that the gospel of Jesus Christ remains the center. In this process, the gospel should be applied to particular people and be expressed in the quality of life lived within their specific cultural settings.[12] Someone engaging in contextualization must go with "honest self-evaluation, develop an awareness of the history of the church, and maintain a focus on the Gospel."[13] Before attempting to contextualize the gospel, God's inerrant word must be well understood and correctly proclaimed. The Scripture must establish doctrine and not any tradition or culture. According to Curtis A. Peterson, "We have no other gospel to preach or 'contextualize' except that which is found in the Holy Word."[14] In the words of Nhiwatiwa, "Contextualization must never obscure the message of the gospel. Thus, the focus should not be on the limits of contextualization but on whether Jesus Christ is preached in any context."[15]

What then are the implications of the foregoing for the use of orality in contextualizing expository preaching? First, while orality is prescribed as a medium of communicating the text of the word of God, biblical exposition of that word remains inviolable. Exposition means the literary, grammatical and contextual study, explanation and proclamation of God's Word. It means proper exegesis and hermeneutics has preceded the tasks of pulpit proclamation. Orality is the medium, and biblical proclamation is the message.

Second, those engaged in contextualization should watch out for elements of orality that may be questionable or may compromise the intended message. Oral resources as songs, proverbs, folklore, dance, drama, poetry and

---

10. Schreiter, "Creeds, Confessions, and Global Theologizing." See his extensive discussion of Syncretism and Dual Religious System in chapter 7, pages 144–58.

11. Byang Kato, "The Gospel, Cultural Context and Religious Syncretism," in *Let the Earth Hear His Voice*, ed. J. D. Douglas, 1216–23 (Minneapolis: World Wide Publications, 1975), 1219.

12. Haleblian, "Problem of Contextualization," 100.

13. Stetzer, "Creeds, Confessions, and Global Theologizing."

14. Peterson, "Dangers and Opportunities." The International Mission Board's document on "Principles of Contextualization" is very helpful. http://www.bpnews.net/26854/imb-trustees-define-contextualization.

15. Nhiwatiwa, *Preaching in the African Context*, 22.

storytelling have been discussed in this book. Taking the case of songs for example – it is often argued that there is no spiritual music or even dance. No style came from heaven that was not developed with the creative genius of humans within a particular culture. A song is made up of its lyrics and rhythm. However melodious a song is, its lyrics should be based on Scripture or an exposition of a portion of it. The issue of rhythm is complicated, but some African Christians could be sensitive to the source or effect of certain rhythms. The rhythm may be connected to certain idol worship, or give the person a nostalgia of the kind of traditional worship they were part of before coming to the knowledge of Christ. The rhythm of songs should not be something that will send a wrong signal to the hearers within a certain culture, or block the biblical message which is to be communicated.

The same principle above applies to proverbs, folklore, dance, drama, poetry and storytelling. The word-content should be scriptural, and care must be taken to avoid any iota of syncretism when it comes to costume and the overall message that is passed across by the symbols and insignia engaged in the communication. Not every folklore, proverb, or dance can be brought to the pulpit. However acceptable they may be within a specific culture, they should be filtered through the eyes of Scripture, moral decency and the essence of the gospel of Jesus Christ.

Rochelle L. Cathcart encouraged balance when she wrote, "We must be cautious when listening to culture so that it does not become the agent of contextualization and drive our understanding of the gospel; however, in concert with Christians from around the globe and from all ages, we preachers can become bridge-builders who bring the incarnated Word into connection with contemporary cultures and human realities."[16] Added to this is the admonition of Kurewa that, "Proclaiming the gospel in our cultural context requires that we recognize the fact that we reach people by knowing and understanding their culture. Culture is communication and it cannot be ignored . . . However, we must also recognize that the message to be proclaimed is not culture; it is the gospel, the Christ event."[17] Preaching can surely be done in a contextualized form without compromising the substance of God's infallible word.

---

16. Rochelle L. Cathcart, "Culture Matters: How Three Effective Preachers (Tim Keller, Rob Bell, Father Pfleger) Engage Culture in the Preaching Event," *Trinity Journal* 33NS (2012): 222.

17. Kurewa, *Preaching and Cultural Identity*, 79.

Discussion Questions

1. Discuss further dangers of contextualization you sensed as you studied this chapter. How do they relate to your church and ministry experiences?
2. Identify some of the traces of syncretism you have observed in your ministry environment and discuss what effect these have on the witness of the gospel.
3. As you make the effort to utilize orality elements in preaching, highlight what precautionary measures you would like to take when using songs, drama, proverbs and folklore specifically.

9

Conclusion

In this book an effort has been made to examine the use of orality for contextualizing expository preaching in Africa. The position maintained is that an understanding and utilization of oral elements from African tradition and culture will entrench and enrich expository preaching, making it more meaningful, generating more interest, and impacting more extensively those who listen to sermons. Before reaching certain conclusions, here is a summary.

Two of the major areas of contention when it comes to the concept of expository preaching are form and content. The content of an expository sermon, basically, is the text of God's word with due consideration of its historical, grammatical, and literary intentions. Scripture, subject to proper exegesis and hermeneutical integrity, is non-negotiable in the process and practice of expository preaching. But the form can differ and be varied in response to the genre of the text, the communication needs of the audience, and the creativity of the preacher. The inductive-deductive controversy that has raged over the years is a product of this form-content relationship. The understanding that expository preaching is more of a philosophy of biblical preaching than a homiletical form in competition with other forms will give a leeway for good preachers to choose whether they want to be inductive or deductive, or whether they want to combine the two, all in a bid to remain faithful to the nature of the text and the communication paradigms of listeners.

An attempt was made to locate Africa in the scheme of things when it comes to the task of preaching in general, then specifically expository preaching. Africa has experienced preaching and has produced great preachers from the time of the early church fathers. But besides some of the records the early church fathers left behind, expository preaching has not found footing in the continent's pulpits as it should have. There are, however, semblances of it emanating from adherence to the training some Africans received from some

Western missionaries and evangelical and Protestant theological institutions. Something worthy of note even in the face of the African preference for topical preaching is the evident manifestation of African-ness in preaching that can be gleaned from several quarters of the African church, most especially the African Instituted Churches and the liberation that seemed to greet the pulpit at the advent of Pentecostalism. African preaching demonstrates an inherent celebration, participation, dialogue, expression through myths, songs, stories, drama, and prophetic utterances. These are the characteristics and contents of orality.

Orality, as deduced in this book, is a phenomenon in communication. The indication that Africans are oral people was substantiated with evidence from philosophical and psychological presuppositions, empirical studies, literary statistics, contributions from African diaspora, and Africans' obsession with the power of the spoken word. But orality goes beyond being a tool for communication; for Africans, orality describes and interprets their worldview. It not only helps them to pass their messages across and assimilate them, it is also the means by which they interpret their world and process its wisdom whether the technology of literacy exists or not. When Africans use or listen to a story, proverb, drama, poetry, dance, myth, or folklore, their imaginative world is set alight and their sense of communication is appealed to.

The nature of orality does not relate to Africans alone; it is the character of all oral communities around the world. The book has discussed their various distinctives and highlighted the gems in orality that the gospel preacher can lay hold of to communicate the gospel. This is why the efforts of organizations associated with the orality movement around the world have been lauded in spite of the criticism levelled against them by those who do not see any connection between the gospel and orality. Given that oral communities, including in hard mission fields like the Muslim world, are opening up to the gospel, a nexus is formed between the dire need of the word of God in Africa and the oral asset it possesses that can be exploited. Therefore orality becomes a viable tool for contextualizing the gospel which must be preached in the idiom of a people so as to find a footing and ownership among them.

This book does not deal with the gospel at the level of evangelism or personal witnessing to win souls, even though it has a regard for that; it deals more with pulpit proclamation of the word of God in the form of sermons for gathered congregations. The book establishes that expository preaching is the biblical norm and that it has the capability to deliver the word of God effectively in ways that can transform Africa and change the lot of Africans from present backwardness socially, economically, politically, and even spiritually. Africa's embrace of the gospel and globally acknowledged status of church growth may ultimately be deceptive if measured on the scale of real biblical revival. This work proposes that effective communication of expository preaching will happen when the oral elements of African communication are effectively used to convey the historical, grammatical, and literary context of the Bible and are applied to the day-to-day situations of the people.

For this purpose, two types of narrative sermons akin to the needs of oral audiences are adopted – the narrative plus lessons sermon and the segmented narrative sermon. The choice of narrative sermon which tends more toward the inductive form does not disparage the use of the deductive form, nor does it dismiss genre sensitivity when preaching, even to African audiences. This choice is based on evidence of the needs of oral communities found in the research and an attempt to demonstrate with some sample sermons what the research affirms. Moreover, the two forms of narrative sermons possess a mix of the inductive and deductive movements which was one of the things the book promised at the beginning to be a significant point. The "Village Oral Expository Sermon" and the "African Oral Expository Sermon" were designed for this purpose. As a preamble, similar efforts in contextualized preaching observed in Korean and African-American preaching and Awasi Ofori's "New Ghanaian Sermon" were discussed. The dangers of contextualization were highlighted as obscurantism and syncretism, using the analysis of Ed Stetzer. Limits are therefore set for the task of contextualization and the inviolability of the inspired Word of God upheld.

From the foregoing, therefore, the following conclusions can be reached. The first is that expository preaching remains the biblical method of preaching God's word. This writer agrees with others in thinking that classifying preaching into topical, textual, biographical, and the like has not augured well for the church; and the inclination toward the form defined by topical preaching is not helpful for Africa. Topical preaching has bred much heresy, shallowness in the knowledge of the word of God, and some manipulation in a number of churches around Africa. To make matters worse, this method of preaching has so many enthusiasts that getting them to preach another way will be an onerous task. Faithfulness to the biblical genres, depth, knowledge, and a deep connection with the roots of Christian experience through the study of the historical, grammatical, and literary content and backgrounds of Scripture are greatly needed to strengthen the church in Africa as a leader in what God is doing around the world.

Second it should be concluded that expository preaching does not have to be done in one way. The linear-logical method has been taught in many African seminaries for several decades, but few preachers who are acquainted with it have been faithful in following the method. There is nothing wrong with this method, and it remains one of the best ways to introduce students to the task of preaching by teaching them how to deduce the basic concepts and lessons from the text and apply them to the situations of the audience. However, once the text of God's word is in the right proportion and context is faithfully expounded, illustrated, and applied, expository preaching is being done.

It can also be concluded that since the form of expository preaching engaged in here largely becomes meaningful as a result of proper audience analysis, orality is a vital tool for shaping this preaching form in Africa and deliberately contextualizing it. The era of the gospel and its paraphernalia being "Western" is fast ending, and the quest for indigenization, inculturation, or Africanization calls for pulpit ministry that is indigenous. Orality best serves that quest. African orality is not an escape from authority, unlike the quest for narrative preaching in North America which often is based on the ideals of the New Homiletic. African orality is a product of African nature and communication assets and a wing upon which preaching can ride to the point of fluency and efficacy.

Also, African orality is not a tangent to literacy. Any community that disparages literacy will fall behind in meeting the challenges of a globalized world. Rather, this work has suggested that orality should be a process of filling the rungs of the ladder toward literacy. While people should not be compelled to be literate before they are saved or knowledgeable in the word of God or of things that can make them develop their potential, orality should be a channel of communicating with them that they can rise above whatever limitations are in their background and environment and achieve anything others are achieving anywhere else in the world. Orality can be a means of challenging Africans into literacy.

Finally, it is important to make some recommendations and explore which areas of further research are surfacing from this work. The first major recommendation is to the theological institutions in Africa. The challenge of the dearth of expository preaching in many pulpits may be adduced to a lack of essential skills being taught in the theological institutions. The skills of biblical exposition should be well taught by faculty members who specialize in preaching or homiletics. The idea that any faculty member can teach preaching once they know how to preach, not minding their areas of specialization, has not helped matters. The experience of the Nigerian Baptist Theological Seminary, Ogbomoso, a foremost theological institution in Africa which has just produced its first PhD graduate in Christian preaching after 119 years of existence, challenges all theological institutions to take the specialization of preaching seriously and adequately staff it.

Another need in the theological institutions is related to the curriculum of preaching. While curriculum writing and review is a tedious task, African theological institutions have no choice but to begin to inculcate such elements as would indigenize their teaching, learning, and practice of preaching. With orality projected in this book as a viable tool for the contextualizing process, it is recommended that the subject or orality itself be taught either as a course or as part of the preaching syllabus. However, this teaching should keep in mind that biblical exposition is the norm and orality simply a tool.

The viability of establishing an oral Bible school for those who minister to the multitudes of people in rural areas is something that needs to be explored. Efforts have been made by organizations like the Global Missions Board of the Nigerian Baptist Convention, but these efforts have been limited to teaching "storying" to missionary participants in their conferences. A substantive school where preaching and orality are taught will be of great benefit to people who are not literate and are still far from the facilities of literacy.

It is also recommended that a stronger, concerted effort be made to develop and showcase to the world the concept of African Christian preaching. Much work has been done on African Christian theology, African Christian philosophy, African Christian ethics, and other fields of study emanating from the African Christian experience. African Christian preaching is still waiting to be explored with such vigor. The field of orality is a viable partner to an effort of this nature.

The second set of recommendations goes to preachers who labor in the pulpits in the nooks and crannies of Africa. First is the need to develop a new paradigm of preaching that will move the status quo from any other thing to expository preaching. This may call for attending refresher courses in expository preaching, reading new books on expository preaching, and practically learning from those who engage in expository preaching. Second, acknowledging the oral nature of African audiences is vital to successful communication of the word of God in Africa. Preachers should do more to study and learn African proverbs, folklore, myths, idioms, and sayings present in their culture or the culture of those to whom they are ministering, and they should know how to utilize them in their sermons. Preachers need to register in their subconscious that even if only once in a while, expository preaching should be done using songs, poetry, drama, and other oral means of expression in Africa.

Third is the recommendation to meet the needs of the vast majority of Africans in the rural areas. Experiences during this research have revealed how bored these innocent listeners can be when a preacher sweats through a sermon by outlining it or quoting profuse scriptural passages to people who do not have Bibles or have one but cannot read it. Some of these listeners sleep or just stare in the face of the preacher, longing for the monologue to be over. How excited they are when another preacher spends a few minutes telling them a story from the Bible, livening it up with their own idioms and oral resources.

Audience analysis is definitely a continuous process for African preachers. When they need to communicate in a variety of communities like university campuses or their environs, theological institutions, business executive gatherings, artisan graduation ceremonies, trade union prayer meetings, market women associations, churches in the countryside or churches in the highbrow cities, they must know what elements of orality to engage and what best ways to structure their sermons to reach the heart of the listeners. In all, the leadership of the Holy Spirit in giving the right message to the right people at the right time should never be trivialized.

Further research is needed on the best ways to communicate Bible backgrounds to primary oral communities in Africa who definitely have issues with Hebrew and Greek words and who have a hard time comprehending facts related to Bible geography, archaeology, dates, and the like. The questions are to what extent will they need this information, and what level of knowledge and growth will they attain spiritually? These questions need to be reflected on in the expository sermons served to them, especially when they are presented in narrative form.

Most critical to further research is the need to address the relative backwardness of Africa technologically. If orality does not mean illogicality, then we need to know what in oral societies can propel them to discover the world around them and use their God-given natural resources and genius to improve their lives and communities technologically. If Africans cannot attain the level of breakthrough that will affect their economies and self-sustenance, then embracing Christianity may not ultimately produce the meaning it ought to, and the virtues of orality may continually be a subject of debate among literate-preference communities.

Appendix 1

Drama Sketch: An African Homiletical Drama

This appendix is the script of the drama presentation discussed in chapter 5, which was modified and re-scripted for the research for this work. It was staged on 25 January 2017 for twenty minutes in the Chapel of Nigerian Baptist Theological Seminary, Ogbomoso, with about two hundred people participating from both within and outside the seminary.

Title: As It Was in the Days of Noah

Setting: In a typical African market, people began to gather one after the other and display their wares, while others patronize. Coming from different directions, **Mama Gbotemi** and **Mama Deolu** suddenly met.

Mama Gbotemi: Mama Deolu!

Mama Deolu: Ah Mama Gbotemi! [They hug each other and exchange pleasantries.]

Mama Gbotemi: So what have you come to buy in the market?

Mama Deolu: Hum, we are preparing for the wedding of my daughter. You know she is getting married to the son of Chief Laosebikan, and in fact everything is almost set. I just wanted to see Iya Laje for the cord lace we are going to use for the engagement.

Mama Gbotemi: This is great! It's as if our direction is the same. I also wanted to pick a cloth for the family thanksgiving for my late mother's remembrance. You know she died ten years ago, and we need to turn her side . . . *àbí báwo ni*?

Mama Deolu: That's true *o jàre*. Even though the economic recession is biting hard, God has promised that he will supply all our needs according to his riches in glory. So, let's go and see what stuffs are available at Iya Laje's shop.

Mama Gbotemi: But wait o. Have you heard about Noah's rain?

Mama Deolu: [She laughs] Rain? Rain *kó*, rain *ni*. Have you ever heard about anything called rain before? Please forget about this man called Noah. Maybe old age is worrying him.

Mama Gbotemi: I have also thought about it o. How could somebody become so stupid in his thinking that for all these years, he has no message than to say rain is coming . . . rain is coming? Did you see the big ark he is building?

Mama Deolu: Who has not seen it? Even news media keep reporting it. The man is out of his mind. I wish his wife or children could advise him. Unfortunately, they are all together in the business. Please let's go and see Iya Laje and celebrate God's goodness *o jàre*!

[They both laugh and jeer as they move ahead. The stage freezes, and a voice comes from the background.]

Narrator: Luke 17:26–27 says, "Just as it was in the days of Noah, so also will it be in the days of the Son of Man. People were eating, drinking, marrying and being given in marriage up to the day Noah entered the ark. Then the flood came and destroyed them all." [Those on the stage begin to exit and the voice continues.] "But will Christ really come? That was the big question in the days of Noah too. Will the rain really come?"

[**Professor** begins to approach the stage carrying different volumes of books. The **Journalist** catches up with him.]

Journalist: Excuse me sir! Excuse me Prof! [**Professor** slows down to look at him.] Have you heard about Noah's rain?

Professor: Ah ah ah! Rain? Aa ah ah! Noah is out of his mind! Something must be wrong with his medulla oblongata. I have been a professor for how many decades now? I have been to the topmost universities in the world – Harvard, Princeton, Oxford, Yale, mention it. I have degrees in geography, geology, climatology, and meteorology. When you see this grey hair on my head, it is not just age; it is research and publications. Does Noah know what it takes for rain to fall? Before there can be rainfall, there must be evaporation.

It is evaporation that leads to condensation. After condensation you have saturation. It is saturation that finally leads to precipitation which we call rain. All those conditions are not present in the atmosphere today. Since time has been, what simply happens is that mist comes from under the ground to water the earth, and the Holy Book itself affirms that. Where did Noah come about a rain from heaven that will destroy the earth? If such rain comes, be assured it is only Noah and his family that it will destroy. Period!

[**Professor** takes his volumes and goes away, followed by the **Journalist**.]

Narrator: In other words, there won't be rain. As people doubted the coming of the rain in the days of Noah and made no preparations for it, so do people doubt the coming of the Son of Man in our days. But all the signs he mentioned in Matthew 24 are being fulfilled right before our eyes: False prophets and false prophecy, wars and rumors of wars, famines, earthquakes, and persecutions of the saints. Wickedness has increased greatly, and the love of many is waxing cold on a daily basis. But wait a moment . . .

[After a pause, there is a long blast of trumpet. The market women in the first scene began to jump to the stage with amazement that the rapture has taken place and they have been left behind. This includes **Mama Gbotemi** and **Mama Deolu**. The **Professor** also comes in dropping all his volumes on the floor. The **Narrator** begins to come up to the stage, and the stage freezes again.]

Narrator: Luke 17:26–37 has been read to us. It has also been acted. What else would we say? You have watched and heard it all. When the rapture takes place, where will you be? The problem in the days of Noah was unbelief. They never thought any rain could fall and that Noah was only fooling himself. These may not be our problems as minsters in training. I doubt if you would be here if you did not believe in the second coming of Christ. Our problem is that of priority and preparation. What is your priority? In the days of Noah and of Lot at Sodom, they were eating and drinking, marrying and being given in marriage, buying and selling, planting and building. Now, is anything wrong with these activities? No. But when they become our priority above the gospel and the kingdom business committed into our hands, we miss it. When we are so committed to these mundane things that we refuse to prepare for the coming of the Lord, then we miss the point. On that day, [he turns to the frozen actors and sings]

Narrator: Man and wife asleep on the bed,
 She heard a noise she turned her head he's gone

All Actors: I wish we'd all been ready

Narrator: Two men walking on the street
 One disappears and one's left standing still

All Actors: I wish we'd all been ready

Chorus: There's no time to change your mind
 The Son is gone and you've been left behind
 There's no time to change your mind
 The Son is gone and you've been left behind.

Narrator: Many would love to be caught up that day, but they will be tied down by the weight of their priorities. Like Lot's wife who looked back at the destruction of Sodom, they were not focused on the one thing that is most important, God's kingdom – their relationship with God, their love for him, and their walk with him. I challenge you to think deeply, reorder your priorities, and get prepared for the coming of the Lord. It won't be long before Jesus will come again. As a sign of commitment, we will sing this song together, after which we will pray over whatever decisions we individually need to make before God.

[All Actors and the congregation sing]
 Ràn mí lọ́wọ́, kí nmá se sọ ìlépa mi nù
 (Help me {Lord}, not to lose my focus)
 Kí nmá se sọ, ibi tí mo nlọ nù
 (So as not to miss my destination)
 Ràn mí lọ́wọ́, kí nmá se sọ ìlépa mi nù
 (Help me {Lord}, not to lose my focus)
 Kí nmá se sọ, ibi tí mo nlọ nù
 (So as not to miss my destination)

[Prayer is said, and all walk off the stage.]

THE END

Appendix 2

Assessment of an African Homiletical Drama

Name of Assessor: _____

Sex _____

Age _____

1. Title of the Drama _____
2. Bible Text: _____
3. Do you think the drama explained the passage/text?
   _____
   How? _____
   _____
4. Did you get a clearer meaning of the passage/text?
   _____
5. How did the drama bridge the world of the Bible and the contemporary world? _____
   _____
6. Do you think this is a good way to minister to an African audience? _____
   Why? _____
   _____
7. What are the practical lessons/messages that you are taking home from the drama? _____
   _____
   _____
8. Is this presentation enough as the sermon for the day, or does someone still need to come and preach a full length sermon?
   _____
   Why? _____

9. How often should this type of drama presentation be done in the church? Tick your answer.

    a. Every Sunday   [   ]
    b. Once in a while   [   ]
    c. As often as possible   [   ]
    d. Never   [   ]

Other Comments _____
_____
_____
_____
_____

Appendix 3

Kò sí ohun tí Ọlọ́run kò le se
(There Is Nothing Impossible for God)

A Yoruba Poetry (*Ewì*) based on Acts 3:1–10
by Matthew Adebare Ayanyemi

Ìbà ni n ó maa fòní jú
(I design today for worship)
Ìbà Olódùmarè
(I worship the Lord)
Adániwáyé
(My creator)
Ọba tó mọ'ni kó tó dá'ni
(Who knows me before he created me)
Ká bi Ọ òsí
(No one can query him)
Alágbára tó m'ohun gbogbo nínú ohun gbogbo
(The powerful one who knows all things)
O mọ̀`nà t`ẹ́da `ó rìn kó tó ní láárí
(He knows man's bearing to success)
T`ólórí burúkú `ó fi já gbangba
(For an unfortunate person to become successful)

Ta ni nínú wa n`bí layé ti sú?
(Who among us here is fed up of their situation?)
Ta ni nínú wa lo ti sọ̀`rèti nù?
(Who has lost hope?)
Ta ló ti rò pé kò s`ọ̀nà àbáyo mọ́?
(Who has concluded that there is no way out?)
Ta ló ti rò pé ipa òun ti pin?
(Who has thought his hope is ended?)
Àbí, iwọ ti rò pé kò se é se fún ọ mọ́?

(Or have you thought that it is not possible for you again?)
Bí arọ tí wọ́n gbé jù sójúnà Témpìlì.
(Like the lame dropped at the Temple's gate.)
Onílé apá ọ̀tún n wá Olúwa wá
(Worshippers troop into the temple from the right side)
Onílé apá òsi ò gbẹ̀yìn
(Worshippers also troop into the temple from the left)
Arọ kúkú wá
(The lame also came)
Owó lò n wá wá l`ọ́jọ́ gbogbo
(But, he is after begging for alms)

Ọjọ́ l`ọjọ́ nlá ọ̀hún
(Until that great day)
T`Olúwa fi`gbàlà bẹ̀ ẹ́ wò l`airòtẹ́lẹ̀
(That the Lord visited him with salvation)
`lolórí burúkú bá d`olórí ire
(And an ill-luck person became fortunate)
Arọ se bẹ́ẹ̀; ó dìde rìn
(The lame stood and walked)
Ibi t`ó f ojú sí ọ̀nà ò kúkú bá `bẹ̀ lọ
(He was blessed beyond his expectation)
B`ádániwáyé ti sisẹ́ Rẹ̀ `ò kúkú yé `èyàn.
(How the Creator does his work is beyond human imagination.)

Ò n bẹ níbí`lónìí;
(You are here today)
O rò pe tì e ti tán,
(You think all hope is lost)
Adániwáyé ní n sọ fún ọ;
(The creator asks me to inform you)
Pé, orí burúkú ti tán fún ọ.
(That your ill-luck has ended)
B`órí burúkú ti tán fárọ lójú`nà témpìlì tó jókoo sí,
(As ill-luck vanished from the lame sitting at the Temple's gate)
Peterù òun Johánú `o kuku gbìmọ̀,
(Peter and John had no intention)
Pe arọ làwọ́n fẹ́ lọ wòsàn,

(to heal the lame)
Ohun tí wọ̀n `ò ní,
(It is what they don't have)
N larọ n tọrọ lọ́wọ́ wọn,
(That the lame were requesting from them)
Sùgbọ́n, ohun ti wọ́n ní, n ni wọ́n fọ̀ l`édè
(But they uttered what they possessed)
Ó j`ohun t`árọ n fẹ́,
(It is beyond his expectation)
O kọjá ohun to n tọrọ lọ́wọ́ wọn,
(It is beyond his request)

Jọ̀wọ́, mo bẹ̀ ọ́ àwé;
(Please, I beseech you brother/sister)
J`Ólúwa Ó fi ọ́ se`hun t`Ó fẹ́ fi ó se.
(Let God's purpose be fulfilled in your life)
Àní, mo fẹ́ kó o gbàgbó pé;
(And, I want you to believe that)
Olúwa Ó sè`yanu kan kanka,
(God will do a very marvellous thing)
Tí yóò jọ ọ́ l`ójú,
(That will surprise you)
Tí yóò ya ayé l`ẹ̀nu,
(And people will marvel)
Àní, ẹni tí `ò mọ̀ ọ́,
(And, those who don't know you)
Yoò ya wá bá ọ gbégbá opé,
(Will surface to glorify God with you)

Appendix 4

The New Ghanaian Sermon

The God Who Is Close By
Akwasi O. Ofori

Scriptural Texts: Psalms 35:22; 50:21; and 83:1

Many Ghanaians often cry out, "Onyameee! Onyameee! Help us and guide us through life's struggles because we cannot go it alone." This common cry of our people is true of our human experience. As humans we are always struggling in our existence, often in search of the one who will be constantly available to answer our calls of desperation. Could this be God, assumed by the Psalmist as an ever-present help in times of need? Is God a being we can entirely entrust with our future and our fortunes?

Sometimes when things seem to go astray, we may feel that God is far away and beyond our reach. Yet our ancestors saw God to be very close to humans, one who directly took part in their daily affairs. Perhaps what we experience is more similar to the time when this close relationship was severed due to the action of an old woman who would continuously hit God with the tip of her pestle while pounding her fufu. The story tells how God withdrew higher and higher into the heavens to escape her pestle to the point of playing only a nominal role in the affairs of humans. In much the same way, do we not sometimes feel that God is inaccessible and unavailable, particularly when we need him most? Certainly the writer of the Psalms or at least his readers may have felt the same way. Where was God when their enemies seemed to have overwhelmed them? Where was God when the wicked seemed to have escaped punishment? Why were they rewarded with riches and happiness? Where was God when the godly suffered and faced the scorn of society? Silent perhaps! But is silence the same as absence?

I imagine myself pounding my knuckles at the door of a friend who lives close by, wondering: *Is he home or not?* Only silence answers my knock. Has he gone outside? Has he kept quiet until he can peek out the window to see who it is? Finding no answer to my knocking, I persist. Giving up is not an option. I need to see him and to reconnect with him. Then I stop knocking, and I stand for what seems like eternity. The silence is broken by a faint sound from within. Then it becomes louder, somebody is stretching. Maybe my friend is awakening from sleep. Then the sound ceases, and then there is absolute silent, but for a moment. Momentarily there is the sound of keys turning, and hesitatingly the door swings open. Kofi is standing there still half asleep.

Kofi did not open the door because he was sleeping. Can we say the same thing about the silence of God? Let's take a closer look at the three scriptural texts above; there we may find help. In the twenty-second verse of the thirty-fifth Psalm, a man in deep trouble cries out to God: "LORD, you have seen this [my affliction]; do not be silent. Do not be far from me, Lord." His pleadings are for God to exalt him above his enemies who may want to seize every opportunity to attack him.

Similarly, Psalm 83:1 is a lament by a person who obviously is not concerned about his personal safety, but that of Israel as a nation. His pleas are for God not to keep silent but to act on behalf of his nation. Here God is urged to intervene for his people against their enemies; it is a call to action.

Surely lament in the sense of crying out is so much a part of our culture. We cry out about our wants and desire to get closer to loved ones. We cry out because we want a need fulfilled or a problem removed. We cry out weeping for unfulfilled dreams and aspirations. We cry out because of injustice. We cry out for practically any aspect of life for which we fall short of achieving goals.

How surprised we are by Psalm 50:21. Here God is speaking, yet there is the same subject: the perceived silence of God. In this Psalm, the psalmist had God enumerate his deeds and capabilities and the shortcomings of his people. According to the psalmists, God makes it clear that he has been silent for a reason. He is waiting for the appropriate time to bring his recompense. The common thread in all three scriptural verses is the silence of God. At the same time, all three affirm God's active involvement in the affairs of humans.

How should we respond to this? As Ghanaians we know the saying, "God is nowhere, but God is in everything, and therefore humans can be God to themselves." Does this imply that because of God's perceived silent he is absent, unavailable, and so we can be gods to ourselves?

Musical interlude from congregation:
>If there is a God and he cares for his people
>>why do we have all the problems?
>
>Problems of disease
>Problems of poverty
>Problems of accidents
>If there is God does he care?
>If there is a God and he cares for his people
>>why do we have all the problems?
>
>Oh God, why the silence? Oh God, why the silence?

Preacher continues:
God, why the silence? Is your perceived silence simply a difference in timing? Are we humans impatient in our approach to issues? Are you God restraining people or nations asking them to repent of their shortcomings? In the Bible there is the story of Jonah, a man who was entrusted with a mission to the city of Nineveh to warn the inhabitants of imminent destruction as a result of the atrocities they had committed against other nations including Israel. These people had not been punished for a long time. Was God asleep or absent as they continued daily with their cruelties? After sometime God surprisingly decided to punish them, but not before he gave them the chance to repent. Was God sleeping? Even absent? No! Oh no! We presumed God was silent because God didn't respond in terms of our time frame. But God works on his own timing and not that of humans. In his silence he gave the Ninevites time to repent, and they did. Other Bible passages try to clarify situations like this in 2 Peter 3:8–9: "But do not forget this one thing, dear friends: With the Lord a day is like a thousand years, and a thousand years are like a day. The Lord is not slow in keeping his promise, as some understand slowness. Instead he is patient with you, not wanting anyone to perish, but everyone to come to repentance."

In your life are there times when you feel that God is far away or even silent, that God doesn't care? Usually such thoughts occur but are not limited to times of need; times when the poor and vulnerable see suffering; times when we feel that our life is threatened; times when we face the danger of losing all we have worked for; times when we are bereft at the loss of a love one. The other day I overheard some neighbors talking about our friend Kofi Appiah and how he left the shores of Ghana to go to the United States in search of greener pastures. He spent his time there doing different jobs – housekeeping, care giving as well as other odd jobs in hopes of escaping poverty on his return. From his meager earnings, he saved a substantial amount of money which he remitted to relatives to invest in a housing project. Just when he thought he could finally resettle in Ghana, the house catches fire and his life's work is destroyed. Is God silent or absent in his life?

Or think of Yaw Manu and his wife whose son was drowned in a well full of water. It was a beautiful afternoon; the sun was up, the birds were singing. It was an afternoon for families to gather and enjoy a family meal. Manu's wife had prepared a sumptuous fufu meal. Kwaku their son, who was playing outside, was called to come and eat. Playing outside, his hands were dirty and needed a thorough wash. He could have fetched water from a bucket that was sitting right beside them, but he decided to go to the household well to draw out some water. His parents were talking and eating and didn't realize how much time had passed. When they realized how long it had been, his mother got up to look for him. Alarmed she raised her voice for help. After a frantic search, they found Kwaku's lifeless body floating in the well.

Do you remember the cocoa farmer who suffered during the great bushfire that occurred in 1983? This farmer spent all his time working on his farm. He observed all the cultural practices necessary including the clearing of weeds, the application of insecticides, and cutting down of extra branches all in hopes of ensuring a bumper harvest. He would wake up every morning to bask in a future full of success and prosperity. Suddenly the rains stops, the dry conditions begin, and bushfires break out. His hopes of a windfall are obliterated. If there is a God who is active in the affairs of humans, why would God allow such a calamity? Does God care? What are we to make of it all?

A man has a dream where he is walking through some marshy field. In his dream he sees two sets of footprints. At places the two sets of footprints become one set; these are spots where it is marshiest. Puzzled he presses for answers. In a revelation, God appears to him. "Why are there sometimes two set of footprints, and at other times only one?" the man asks.

"Why?" replies God. "Because one set of footprint is mine, and the other is yours."

The dreamer even more puzzled asks, "Why then do the prints become single at spots where it is marshiest?"

"Then you were too weak to walk, so I carried you on my shoulders," God replies.

Musical interlude from congregation:
> He is the everlasting rock. God is not asleep.
> He is the everlasting rock. God is not asleep.
> He is not asleep.
> He is not asleep.

Preacher continues:
God is not asleep! God is not asleep! Though we may perceive God to be silent, he is definitely not absent nor indifferent to events happening in the world. Maybe he chooses to be silent to test our faith. Maybe it is to protest our sinful attitudes. Maybe it is to bring about a grand victory and an enduring glory; or maybe like the dream, in our times of need he is simply present prodding us on or even carrying us on his shoulders to ease our suffering. Such knowledge is too high for us.

Question from the congregation:
But we can't deny our experience. Where is God? We need more help. If we do not sense him in our lives, what should we do?

Preacher:
Perhaps we need to persist in prayer (Luke 18:1–8). Perhaps we need to cry out for repentance (Ps 50:22). Perhaps we may simply need to be patient while waiting particularly for God's timing (Isa 49:8a). Perhaps God is silent because he wants us, his children who are believers, to remain obedient and to latch on to greater victory and glory as eventually good shall prevail over evil. Perhaps if we draw closer to God through habitual prayers and study of his word, we will feel his ever-closer presence always in times of difficulty and in times of ease. Perhaps we think he is far away because we have stayed apart from him ourselves or are inconsistent in appropriating his goodness.

God does exist. When we think of all that happens around us, it is inconceivable to view our existence without God. Given the grandeur of what is around us can we really imagine God to be absent?

The reality is that it is not always easy to believe that God exists. Like the cocoa farmer who lost his farm through the destructive bush fire or the friend whose house was burnt down, or the parents whose son was drowned in a well, God did not seem present at that moment. Apparently at their moment of need, he is silent. The other side would be if he is present, how could he let this happen? Doesn't he care? Let us look at the example of Job. He lost all and cries out to God that he is unjust and absent. Then God responds from the whirlwind challenging Job's limited knowledge. So you see God may not necessarily be silent or absent. In another sphere, God's silence could be for one among us who is an errant child of God to repent from wayward ways. Maybe in the case of the unbeliever, God may be silent allowing them time to repent from their sinful ways. But whatever our life situation, God is always with us. Through thick and thin, God is with us. As Francis Tawiah, manager of the pharmaceutical company GR Pharma says, "With God you will always stand still in the cloud of any hustle and bustle."

Though sometimes overwhelmed by life's difficulties, we may doubt God's existence. But are we not forgetting something? We wake up not knowing where the next meal will come from, but somehow at the end of the day we get our fill. We get into dire straits not knowing how we will get out of that corner, but suddenly somebody is present and ready to come to our aid. We may be down and out, but suddenly an utterance from someone becomes the omen we needed to spur us on and to negotiate the difficult terrain. Sometimes we lose all hope of making it through the next hurdle, but suddenly an answer surfaces in the horizon. Could these things be God speaking to us, meeting our needs, urging us to go on when we can barely stand on our feet? When all hopes are deflated, don't we feel God's presence in the fresh new breeze of the dawn of a new day? Of course we do! Thanks be to God. Amen.

Appendix 5

African Oral Expository Sermon Evaluation Sheet

Name of Preacher _____

Evaluation by _____

Title of Sermon _____

Bible Texts _____

The Man
Body Language

        Gestures _____

        Appearance, Posture, and Mannerisms _____

        Eye Contact and Facial Expressions _____

        Vocal Production and Variation _____

Style

        Clarity _____

        Force _____

The Method
Oral Vehicle(s) for Proclamation

        Story/Narrative   (   )

        Song   (   )

        Drama   (   )

        Poetry   (   )

        Others   (   )

Oral Element(s) in Sermon

    Proverb (　　)

    Song (　　)

    Folktale (Myth, Legend) (　　)

    Story/Narrative (　　)

    Poetry (　　)

    Other (　　)

Effectiveness _____

The Message

Hermeneutics/Exegesis _____

Audience Engagement

    Dialogue _____

    Participation _____

    Celebration/Climax _____

Meeting the "African Need" _____

Appendix 6

Feedback-Interview Guide for a Village Oral Expository Sermon

Name _____

Sex _____

Age [20–25] [26–35] [36–45] [46–55] [56 and above]

Level of Education:

Primary School/Secondary School/Others _____

1. Can you still remember the Bible text of the sermon you heard?
   _____
   _____

2. Did you notice that the preacher did not give points in the sermon? Did you take home any lessons? What lessons did you take home that day? _____
   _____
   _____

3. Can you remember any songs the preacher sang?
   _____
   _____

4. Can you remember any proverbs the preacher used?
   _____
   _____

5. Can you remember any myths or legends the preacher used?
   _____
   _____
   _____

How did those things help you to understand the sermon?
_____
_____

6. In what ways was your life affected? _____
_____
_____

7. What did you like most about the sermon? _____
_____
_____

8. What did you not like? _____
_____
_____

9. Do you think using an oral form like this to preach is a good method? _____
Why? or why not? _____

10. Based on this sermon, do you have any advice for pastors who preach especially to people in the villages and those who are not well educated? _____
_____
_____

11. Any other comments _____
_____
_____

Bibliography

Abalogu, Uchegbulam N., Garba Ashiwaju, Regina Amadi-Tshiwala, eds. *Oral Poetry in Nigeria*. Lagos: Emaconprint, 1981.

Abioje, Pius O. "Magic and Science in Yorubaland: Towards Africa's Technological Development." In *Science and Religion in the Service of Humanity*, 181–96. Ilorin: Local Societies Initiatives and NASTREN, 2006.

Adamolekun, Taiye. "Main Trends in the Church Growth in Nigeria." *European Scientific Journal* 8, no. 23 (October): 1–14.

Adams, Daniel J. "Korean Preaching from a Western Perspective." *Journal of Korean American Ministries and Theology* 2 (Spring 2009): 43–52.

Adelegan, Femi. *Nigeria's Leading Lights of the Gospel Revolutionaries in Worldwide Christianity*. Bloomington, IN: WestBrow, 2013.

Adeney, Miriam. "What Is Enough? Oral Bible Teaching in Three Dimensions." In *Beyond Literate Western Contexts: Contextualizing Theological Education in Oral Contexts*, edited by Samuel E. Chiang and Grant Lovejoy, 93–101. Hong Kong: International Orality Network, 2013.

"African Poetry: Oral Traditions." eNotes. Accessed 13 December 2016, updated 26 October 2020. https://www.enotes.com/topics/african-poetry/in-depth.

Agilenko, Steve. "A Re-assessment of the Relevance of African Culture to the Church in London with Particular Reference to Predominantly African Churches." Accessed 15 July 2015. https://cutt.ly/blkHlVo.

Ajayi, S. Ademola. *Baptist Work in Nigeria 1850–2005: A Comprehensive History*. Bodija, Ibadan: Book Wright, 2010.

Ajibade, Ezekiel Adewale. "The African Preacher and the Demands of Postmodernism." Edited by E. E. Nihinlola. *Ogbomoso Journal of Theology (OJOT)* 20, no. 1 (2015): 12–26.

———. *Common Pulpit Errors and Solutions*. Ibadan: Baptist Press Nigeria, 2016.

———. "The Potency of Words in African Philosophy: Its Relevance to Contemporary Christians." In *Theological Educators: Academic Papers in Honour of Rev Prof O. G. Adetunji and Rev. Dr. F. K. Babalola of the Nigerian Baptist Theological Seminary, Ogbomoso*, edited by Peter Ropo Awoniyi and G. O. Olaniyan, 334–47. Ogbomoso: NBTS Publishing Unit, 2016.

———. *Treasure Mine: Living Gems from Searching the Scriptures*. New Bussa: Hope for a Generation International, 2012.

Akinmade, C. Arinola. "The Decline of Proverbs as a Creative Oral Expression: A Case Study of Proverb Usage among the Ondo in the South Western Part of Nigeria." *AFRREV LALIGENS: An International Journal of Language, Literature and Gender Studies, Bahir Dar, Ethiopia* 1, no. 2 (April–July 2012): 27–148.

Akinwowo, Akinsola. "The Place of Mojola Agbebi in the African Nationalist Movements: 1890–1917." *Phylon* 26, no. 2 (2nd Qtr. 1965): 122–39.

Akinyemi, Akintunde. "African Oral Tradition Then and Now: A Culture in Transition." *Centrepoint Humanities Edition* 14, no. 1 (n.d.): 27–51.

Akomeah, Dennis, "Build Your ASE." 27 May 2005. http://www.arcane-archive.org/religion/african/ase-power-over-nature-1.php.

Alabi, Adetayo. "On Seeing Africa for the First Time: Orality, Memory, and the Diaspora in Isidore Okpewho's *Call Me by My Rightful Name*." *Research in African Literatures* 40, no. 1 (Spring 2009): 145–55.

Alabi, Job Adegboyega. "Memorial Service and Its Lessons." Accessed 12 December 2016. http://copea-inc.blogspot.com/2012/08/memorial-service-and-its-lessons-texts.html.

Allen, Bob. "Because He Lives – an Easter play based on a true story." The Scripture Story Teller. 3 February 2016. http://scripturestoryteller.blogspot.com.ng/2016/02/because-he-lives-easter-play-based-on.html.

Allen, David L. "Introduction." In *Text-Driven Preaching: God's Word at the Heart of Every Sermon*, edited by David L. Allen, Daniel L. Akin, and Ned L. Matthews. Nashville: B&H Academic, 2010.

———. "Preaching and Postmodernism: An Evangelical Comes to the Dance." *Southern Baptist Journal of Theology* 5, no. 2 (Summer 2001): 63–80.

———. "Preparing a Text-Driven Sermon." In *Text-Driven Preaching: God's Word at the Heart of Every Sermon*, edited by Daniel Atkin, David L. Allen. and Ned L. Matthews, 101–34. Nashville: B&H Academic, 2010.

———. "A Tale of Two Roads: Homiletics and Biblical Authority." *Journal of the Evangelical Theological Society* 43, no. 3 (Sep 2000): 490–522.

Allen, Robert A. "The Expository Sermon – Cultural or Biblical?" *Journal of Ministry and Theology* 2, no. 2 (Fall 1998): 213–28.

Allen, Ronald J. "African Christianity: A Soft Report." *Homiletic* 16, no. 1 (1991): 5–9.

———, ed. *Patterns of Preaching: A Sermon Sampler*. St. Louis: Chalice, 1998.

Aribisala, Femi. "The Rise and Fall of Sunday." FemiAribisala.com. 8 August 2012. http://www.femiaribisala.com/the-rise-and-fall-of-sunday-adelaja/.

Arthurs, Jeffrey D. *Preaching with Variety: How to Re-create the Dynamics of Biblical Genre*. Grand Rapids: Kregel, 2007.

Ashimolowo, Matthew. *What Is Wrong with Being Black?: Celebrating Our Heritage, Confronting Our Challenges*. Shippensburg: Destiny Image, 2007.

Awolesi, David. "Jesus Hunters Ode Jesu Oruko ati Oriki Olodumare." YouTube. 11 August 2011. https://www.youtube.com/watch?v=Q1hLGLrLOrk.

Ayegboyin, Deji Isaac, and S. Ademola Ishola. *African Indigenous Churches: An Historical Perspective*. Bukuru: Africa Christian Textbooks, 2013.

Bada, S. O. *Owe Yoruba ati Isedale Won*. Ibadan: University of Ibadan Press, 1985.

Barnes, Cedric, and Tim Carmichael. "Editorial, Introduction Language, Power and Society: Orality and Literacy in the Horn of Africa." *Journal of African Cultural Studies* 18, no. 1 (June 2006): 1–8.

Bartle, Neville. "A Model for Contextualizing Theology for Melanesia." *The Mediator* 3, no. 1 (2001): 83–110.

Bascom, William. *African Folktales in the New World*. Bloomington: Indiana University Press, 1992.

———. "Folklore, Verbal Art, and Culture." *The Journal of American Folklore* 86, no. 342 (Oct–Dec 1973): 374–81.

Bauer, Bruce L. "Christian Worship and Cultural Diversity: A Missiological Perspective." *Journal of Adventist Mission Studies* 5, no. 2 (2009): 34–40.

Bediako, Kwame. *Theology and Identity: The Impact of Culture upon Christian Thoughts in the Second Century and Modern Africa*. Oxford, UK: Regnum, 1992.

Bevans, Stephen B. *Models of Contextual Theology*. Maryknoll, NY: Orbis, 2004.

Bland, Dave L. "Deductive." In *The New Interpreter's Handbook of Preaching*, edited by Paul Scott Wilson, 375–77. Nashville: Abingdon, 2008.

Bright, Jake. "Meet 'Nollywood': The Second Largest Movie Industry in the World." *Fortune*. 24 June 2015. https://www.fortune.com/2015/06/24/Nollywood-movie-industry/.

Brilioth, Yngve. *A Brief History of Christian Preaching*. Translated by Karl E. Mattson. Philadelphia: Fortress, 1965.

Broadus, John A. *On the Preparation and Delivery of Sermons*. New York: A. C. Armstrong and Son, 1870.

Bromiley, Geoffrey W. "*Peitho*." In *Theological Dictionary of the New Testament Abridged in One Volume*, edited by Gerhard Kittel and Gerhard Friedrich. Grand Rapids: Eerdmans, 1992.

Brothers, Michael A. "Inductive." In *The New Interpreter's Handbook of Preaching*. Edited by Paul Scott Wilson, 390–92. Nashville: Abingdon, 2008.

Bryan, Steve. "Review of *How Africa Shaped the Christian Mind: Rediscovering the African Seedbed of Western Christianity* by Thomas C. Oden." *Africa Journal of Evangelical Theology* 27, no. 1 (2008): 77–81.

Butrus, Daniel. *Legacy of Wisdom: Stories and Proverbs from Africa*. Bukuru, Jos: Africa Christian Textbooks, 2007.

Buttrick, David. *A Captive Voice: The Liberation of Preaching*. Louisville, KY: Westminster John Knox, 1994.

Cahill, Dennis M. *The Shape of Preaching: Theory and Practice in Sermon Design*. Grand Rapids: Baker Books, 2007.

Campbell, Charles L. "Inductive Preaching." In *Concise Encyclopedia of Preaching*, edited by William H. Willimon and Richard Lischer, 270–72. Louisville, KY: Westminster John Knox, 1995.

Carman. "Lazarus Come Forth." Christian Lyrics Online.com. Accessed 11 January 2017. https://genius.com/Carman-lazarus-come-forth-lyrics.

———. "Lazarus Come Forth (Unofficial Music Video) by Carman." YouTube. 17 March 2015. https://www.youtube.com/watch?v=XvAqvr8_TP8.

Cathcart, Rochelle L. "Culture Matters: How Three Effective Preachers (Tim Keller, Rob Bell, Father Pfleger) Engage Culture in the Preaching Event." *Trinity Journal* 33NS (2012): 209–22.

Chan, Sam. "Storytelling Seeking Understanding." In *Beyond Literate Western Contexts: Continuing Conversations in Orality and Theological Education*, edited by Samuel E. Chiang and Grant Lovejoy, 81–86. Hong Kong: International Orality Network, 2014.

Chapel, Bryan. *Christ-Centered Preaching: Redeeming the Expository Sermon*. Grand Rapids: Baker Academic, 2005.

"Christianity in Africa." Wikipedia. Accessed 14 October 2016 and 14 January 2016. https://en.wikipedia.org/wiki/Christianity_in_Africa.

Craddock, Fred B. *As One without Authority*. 1983, reprint St. Louis: Chalice, 2011.

Cztery Strony Bajek. "The Deamon, the Woman and the Bird – African fairy tale from Senegal." YouTube. 11 April 2013. https://youtu.be/TeNw0hOh0hk?list=PLQyef0XSS867fk9AhrtxT00BD_HkHEJc.

Daniel, Kasomo. "An Assessment of the Connectedness of Mainstream and Independent Churches in Africa." *International Journal of Applied Sociology* 2, no. 2 (2012): 1–9.

Dargan, Edwin Charles. *The Art of Preaching in the Light of Its History*. New York: Doran, 1992.

Davidson, Basil. *The Black Man's Burden: Africa and the Curse of the Nation-State*. New York: Times Books, 1992.

Dinkins, Larry. "My Bumpy Road to Orality." Accessed 17 October 2016. http://online.fliphtml5.com/kwow/jtcm/#p=1.

Dlanga, Khaya. "'I Am an African': Thabo Mbeki's Speech. Possibly the Greatest African Speech Ever." *Afrika* 1, no. 1. Accessed 11 December 2016. http://afrikatanulmanyok.hu/userfiles/File/beszedek/Thabo%20Mbeki_Iam%20an%20African.pdf.

Doll, Margaret. "Literacy and Orality Working Together: The Intersection of Heart and Mind." *Orality Journal* 4, no. 1 (2015): 63–76.

Duduit, Michael. "Doctrine That Flies: Using Story to Communicate Truth." In *Our Sufficiency Is of God: Essays on Preaching in Honor of Gardner C. Taylor*, edited by James Earl Massey, Robert Smith Jr., and Timothy George, 62–81. Macon, GA: Mecer University Press, 2010.

Edwards, O. C., Jr. "History of Preaching." In *Concise Encyclopedia of Preaching*, edited by William H. Willimon and Richard Lischer, 184–227. Louisville, KY: Westminster John Knox, 1995.

Encarta Dictionaries. Microsoft Encarta 2009.

Enyinnaya, John. "Pentecostal Hermeneutics and Preaching: An Appraisal." *Ogbomoso Journal of Theology* 13, no. 1 (2008): 145–53.

———. "A Theological Approach to Political Transformation in Africa." *Ogbomoso Journal of Theology* 11 (2006): 77–92.

Eslinger, Richard L. *The Web of Preaching: New Options in Homiletic Method.* Nashville: Abingdon, 2002.
Ezenweke, Elizabeth Onyedinma, and Loius Kanayo Nwadialor. "Understanding Human Relations in African Traditional Religious Context in the Face of Globalization: Nigerian Perspectives." *American International Journal of Contemporary Research* 3, no. 2 (2013): 61–70.
Fagunwa, D. O. *In the Forest of Olodumare.* Translated by Wole Soyinka. Ibadan: Nelson, 2010.
Falade, Adeoye Dennis. "Oral Tradition in Africa: Poetry as a Means of Preserving Cultural Heritage and Engendering Social Change among the Yoruba." Academia. September 2013. https://www.academia.edu/7728284/ORAL_TRADITION_IN_AFRICA_POETRY_AS_A_MEANS_OF_PRESERVING_CULTURAL_HERITAGE_AND_ENGENDERING_SOCIAL_CHANGE_AMONG_THE_YORUBA.
Falaye, Tiwatola Abidemi. "The Relevance of African Independent Churches to the Yoruba of South Western Part of Nigeria." *Journal of Philosophy, Culture and Religion* 13 (2015): 10–16.
Falk, Peter. *The Growth of the Church in Africa.* Bukuru: African Christian Textbooks, 1997.
Fant, Clyde E., and William M. Pinson Jr., eds. *20 Centuries of Great Preaching: An Encyclopedia of Preaching.* 13 vols. Waco: Word, 1971.
Fiorio, Elisa. "Orality and Cultural Identity." *Museum International* 58, no. 1–2 (2006): 68–75.
Francis, Keith A., and William Gibson. *The Oxford Handbook of the British Sermon 1689-1901.* Oxford: Oxford University Press, 2012.
Fukada, Robert Mikio, and Tsuneaki Kato. "Homiletics and Preaching in Asia." In *Concise Encyclopedia of Preaching,* edited by William H. Willimon and Richard Lischer, 231–34, Louisville, KY: Westminster John Knox, 1995.
Fuller, Lois. *A Missionary Handbook on African Traditional Religion.* Bukuru: African Christian Textbooks, 2001.
Galindo, Israel. *The Craft of Christian Teaching.* Ibadan: Scripture Union Nigerian Press & Books, 1998.
Gibson, Scott M. "Critique of the New Homiletic: Examining the Link between the New Homiletic and the New Hermeneutic." In *The Art and Craft of Biblical Preaching: A Comprehensive Resource for Today's Communicators,* edited by Haddon Robinson and Craig Brian Larson, 476–81. Grand Rapids: Christianity Today International, 2005.
———. "Point Form." In *The New Interpreter's Handbook of Preaching,* edited by Paul Scott Wilson, 401–4. Nashville: Abingdon, 2008.
Greer, Ivor Calvin. *Orality and Christian Discipleship: Developing a 'Living' Word.* MA Dissertation, Bangor University, 2011.
Gregory, Joel C. "Expository." In *The New Interpreter's Handbook of Preaching,* edited by Paul Scott Wilson, 381–83. Nashville: Abingdon, 2008.

Greidanus, Sidney. "Moralism." In *The New Interpreters Handbook of Preaching*, edited by Paul Scott Wilson, 127–28. Nashville: Abingdon, 2008.

———. *The Modern Preacher and the Ancient Text: Interpreting and Preaching Biblical Literature*. Grand Rapids: Eerdmans, 2003.

Haleblian, Krikor. "The Problem of Contextualization." *Missiology: An International Review* 11, no. 1 (January 1983): 96–111.

Hassan, Rashidat. "African Tales (ijapa ologbon ewe)." YouTube. 27 May 2013. https://www.youtube.com/watch?v=yrNQuuDwyE0.

Hayford, Jack. "Foreword." In *We Are the Church: The Untold Story of God's Global Awakening*, edited by Leonard Sweet and James O. Davis, xi–xii. Orlando, FL: Billion Soul Publishing, 2014.

Hayward, Douglas. "Measuring Contextualization in Church and Missions." *International Journal of Frontier Missions* 12, no. 3 (Jul.–Sept. 1995): 135–38.

Hiebert, Paul G. *Transforming Worldviews: An Anthropological Understanding of How People Change*. Grand Rapids, MI: Baker, 2008.

Hill, Harriet. "Conversations about Orality." *Missiology: An International Review* 38, no. 2 (April 2010): 215–17.

Hoezee, Scott. *Actuality: Real Life Stories for Sermons That Matter*. Nashville: Abingdon, 2014.

"Hubert Ogunde: Nigerian Playwright, Actor, and Musician." *Encyclopedia Britannica*. Accessed 18 November 2016. https://www.britannica.com/biography/Hubert-Ogunde.

Ibeun, M. O., and M. Mdaihli. *Media of Comunication among Fishermen around Kainji Lake Basin*. New Bussa: Nigerian-German Fisheries Promotion Project, 1994.

Ishola, S. Ademola. "Contextualized Missiological Approach to the Yoruba Religio-Cultural Milieu." PhD diss., Southwestern Baptist Theological Seminary, 1992.

Jagerson, Jennifer. "The *Simply the Story* Method: Next Steps in Oral Strategies." In *Beyond Literate Western Contexts: Honor and Shame and Assessment of Orality Preference*, edited by Samuel E. Chiang and Grant Lovejoy, 109–16. Hong Kong: International Orality Network, 2015.

Jeong, Seungyoun. "Korean Preaching, Han, and Narrative (American University Studies. Series VII. Theology and Religion." Asian American Theological Forum. 31 October 2014. https://aatfweb.org/2014/10/31/korean-preaching-han-and-narrative-american-university-studies-series-vii-theology-and-religion/.

Johnson, Graham Macpherson. *Preaching to a Postmodern: A Guide to Reaching Twenty-First Century Listeners*. Grand Rapids: Baker Books, 2006.

Johnson, John William. "Orality, Literacy, and Somali Oral Poetry." *Journal of African Cultural Studies* 18, no. 1 (June 2006): 119–36.

Kadangs, Beatrice. "A Case Study of Women and Widows as It Relates to Orality and How It Works with Them." In *Beyond Literate Western Contexts: Honor and Shame and Assessment of Orality Preference*, edited by Samuel E. Chiang and Grant Lovejoy, 135–40. Hong Kong, International Orality Network, 2015.

Kanyinsola, Dabi Ayanlola. "Oriki: The Yoruba-Praise-Poetry." Accessed 22 December 2016. https://www.youtube.com/watch?v=1_dHR0sCbMg.

Karnga, Abba. *Bassa Proverbs for Preaching and Teaching*. Accra: Asempa, 1996.

Kato, Byang. "The Gospel, Cultural Context and Religious Syncretism." In *Let the Earth Hear His Voice*, edited by J. D. Douglas, 1216–23. Minneapolis: World Wide Publications, 1975.

Keith, James A. "The Concept of Expository Preaching as Represented by Alexander Maclaren, George Campbell Morgan, and David Martyn Lloyd Jones." PhD diss., Southwestern Baptist Theological Seminary, 2003.

Keller, Timothy. *Preaching: Communicating Faith in an Age of Skepticism*. New York: Viking, 2015.

Kemp, Stephen. "Leadership Development of Oral Learners: A Case Study of Operation Agape Using BILD Resources." In *Beyond Literate Western Contexts: Honor and Shame and Assessment of Orality Preference*, edited by Samuel E. Chiang and Grant Lovejoy, 141–47. Hong Kong: International Orality Network, 2015.

"KICC, Ashimolowo's Church under Alleged Fraud Investigation." *Vanguard* 16 February 2017, accessed 22 February 2021. https://www.vanguardngr.com/2017/02/kicc-ashimolowos-church-alleged-fraud-investigation/.

Killingray, David. "Passing on the Gospel: Indigenous Mission in Africa." *Transformation* 28, no. 2 (April 2011): 93–102.

Kim, Unyong. "Book Review: Korean Preaching: An Interpretation." Accessed 23 February 2021. https://doi.org/10.1177/002096430005200227.

Knappert, Jan. *African Mythology: An Encyclopedia of Myth and Legend*. London: Diamond, 1995.

Knighton, Ben. "Orality in the Service of Karamojong Autonomy: Polity and Performance." *Journal of African Cultural Studies* 18, no. 1 (June 2006): 137–52.

Koschorke, Klaus, Frieder Ludwig, and Mariano Delgado, eds. *A History of Christianity in Asia, Africa and Latin America, 1450–1990: A Documentary Source Book*. Grand Rapids: Eerdmans, 2007.

Krabill, James R. "Important Lessons from Indigenous Movements and Locally Initiated Churches in the Global South." In *Beyond Literate Western Contexts: Contextualizing Theological Education in Oral Contexts*, edited by Samuel E. Chiang and Grant Lovejoy, 113–20. Hong Kong: International Orality Network, 2013.

Kudadjie, Joshua N. "Using Ga and Dangme Proverbs for Preaching and Teaching." *WAJIBU* 14, no. 1 (1999): 12–18.

Kunhiyop, Samuel Waje. *African Christian Ethics*. Bukuru: Africa Christian Textbooks, 2008.

———. *African Christian Theology*. Nairobi: WordAlive, 2012.

Kurewa, John Wesley Zwomunondiita. *Preaching and Cultural Identity: Proclaiming the Gospel in Africa*. Nashville: Abingdon, 2000.

Kwiyani, Harvey C. *Sent Forth: African Missionary Work in the West*. Maryknoll, NY: Orbis, 2014.

Lane, Belden C. "The Oral Tradition and Its Implications for Contemporary Preaching." n.d.: 17–25.
Larsen, David L. *The Anatomy of Preaching: Identifying Issues in Preaching Today.* Ibadan: Christ and We, 2000.
———. *The Company of Preachers: A History of Biblical Preaching from Old Testament to the Modern Era.* Grand Rapids: Kregel, 1998.
LaRue, Cleophus J. "African American Preaching Perspectives." In *The New Interpreter's Handbook of Preaching*, edited by Paul Scott Wilson, 293–97. Nashville: Abingdon, 2008.
Lee, Jung Young. *Korean Preaching: An Interpretation.* Nashville: Abingdon, 1997.
Lim, David. "Expository Preaching and Generation X: Honoring 2 Timothy 4:5." In *Preaching to Postmodern-Minded Listeners.* Oradea, Bihor: Emmanuel University Press, 2007.
Lischer, Richard. "The Limits of Story." *Interpretation* 38, no. 1 (January 1984): 26–38.
Litchfield, Hugh. "Outlining the Sermon." In *Handbook of Contemporary Preaching*, edited by Michael Duduit, 162–74. Nashville: Broadman & Holman, 1992.
"Literacy and Non-Formal Education." Accessed 7 October 2016. https://unesdoc.unesco.org/ark:/48223/pf0000222125.
Long, Thomas G. *Preaching and the Literary Forms of the Bible.* Minneapolis: Fortress Press, 1988.
———. *The Witness of Preaching.* Louisville, KY: Westminster John Knox, 2005.
Loscalzo, Craig A. "Rhetoric." In *Concise Encyclopedia of Preaching*, edited by William H. Willimon and Richard Lischer, 409–16. Louisville, KY: Westminster John Knox, 1995.
Lovejoy, Grant. "'But I Did Such a Good Exposition': Literate Preachers Confront Orality." IMB. Accessed 6 October 2016. https://journal.ehomiletics.org/index.php/jehs/article/view/9/4.
———. "The Extent of Orality: 2012 Update." *Orality Journal* 1, no. 1 (2012): 11–39.
———. "Shaping Sermons by the Literary Form of the Text." In *Biblical Hermeneutics*, edited by Bruce Corley, Steve Lemke, and Grant Lovejoy, 398–417. Nashville: Broadman & Holman, 1996.
———. "That All May Hear." Lausanne Content Library. Lausanne Movement. 3 June 2010. https://www.lausanne.org/content/that-all-may-hear-2.
Lowry, Eugene. *The Sermon: Dancing the Edge of Mystery.* Nashville: Abingdon, 1997.
Madinger, Charles. "Coming to Terms with Orality: A Holistic Model." *Missiology: An International Review* 38, no. 2 (April 2010): 201–13.
———. "Will Our Message 'Stick?': Assessing a Dominant Preference for Orality for Education and Training." In *Beyond Literate Western Contexts: Honor and Shame and Assessment of Orality Preference*, edited by Samuel E. Chiang and Grant Lovejoy, 125–34. Hong Kong: International Orality Network, 2015.
Malaba, Mbongeni. "Review Article: African Oral Poetry." *English in Africa* 15, no. 2 (October 1988): 101–11.

Martey, Emmanuel. "Prophetic Movements in the Congo: The Life and Work of Simon Kimbangu and How His Followers Saw Him." *Journal of African Instituted Church Theology* 2, no. 1 (2006): 1–16.

Matthewson, Steven D. "What Makes Textual Preaching Unique." In *The Art and Craft of Biblical Preaching: A Comprehensive Resource for Today's Communicators*, edited by Haddon Robinson and Craig Brian Larson, 412–17. Grand Rapids: Christianity Today International, 2005.

McClellan, Dave. "Preaching by Ear." Accessed 10 October 2016. E-Book. https://www.scribd.com/read/389144615/Preaching-by-Ear-Speaking-God-s-Truth-from-the-Inside-out.

McClure, John S. "Expository Preaching." In *Concise Encyclopedia of Preaching*, edited by William H. Willimon and Richard Lischer, 130–32. Louisville, KY: Westminster John Knox, 1995.

McDill, Wayne. *The 12 Essential Skills for Great Preaching*. Nashville: B&H, 1994.

Meredith, Martin. *The State of Africa: A History of Fifty Years of Independence*. London: Free Press, 2006.

Milco, Michael. "Exegeting Your Congregation." In *Moody Handbook on Preaching*, edited by John Kossler, 351–60. Chicago: Moody, 2008.

Mitchell, Henry H. "African-American Preaching." In *Concise Encyclopedia of Preaching*, 2–9. Louisville, KY: Westminster John Knox, 1995.

———. "Celebration." In *The New Intepreter's Handbook of Preaching*, edited by Paul Scott Wilson, 297–98. Nashville: Abingdon, 2008.

Monson, Ingrid, ed. *African Diaspora: A Musical Perspective*. New York: Routledge, 2003.

Moon, W. Jay. "African Proverbs: Stepping Stones within Oral Cultures." IMB. Accessed 10 October 2016. https://orality.imb.org/resources/?id=57.

———. "I Love to Learn but I Don't Like to Read: The Rise of Secondary Oral Learning." *Orality Journal* 2, no. 2 (2013): 55–65.

———. "Teaching Oral Learners in Institutional Settings." In *Beyond Literate Western Contexts: Contextualizing Theological Education in Oral Contexts*, edited by Samuel E. Chiang and Grant Lovejoy, 143–52. Hong Kong: International Orality Network, 2013.

Motty, Bauta D. "Contextualizing Theological Education in Africa: A Case of ECWA Theological Seminary, Jos, Nigeria (JETS)." In *Beyond Literate Western Models: Contextualizing Theological Education in Oral Contexts*, edited by Samuel E. Chiang and Grant Lovejoy, 153–62. Hong Kong: International Orality Network, 2013.

Nhiwatiwa, Eben Kanukayi. *Preaching in the African Context: Why We Preach*. Nashville: Discipleship Resources International, 2012.

Nihinlola, Emiola. *The Task of Bible Interpretation*. Ogbomoso: Nigerian Baptist Theological Seminary, 2014.

———. *Theology under the Mango Tree: A Handbook of African Christian Theology*. Alausa-Ikeja, Lagos: Fine Print & Manufacturing, 2013.

Nihinlola, Emiola, and Mojisola Olaniyan, eds. *Discovering the Other Side: Challenges of Other Religions*. Ibadan: Flourish Books, 2008.

Nzira, Viola. *Social Care with African Families in the UK*. Abingdon: Routledge, 2011.

O'Donnell, Katherine. "Umuhimu wa Biblia: An Investigation into How Tanzanian Christians Perceive and Engage with God's Word." MA dissertation, Redcliffe College, 2013. Scripture Engagement. http://www.scripture-engagement.org/content/umuhimu-wa-biblia.

O'Donovan, Wilbur. *Biblical Christianity in African Perspective*. Carlisle, UK: Paternoster, 1996.

Odekunle, Raphael. *Yoruba Proverbs*. Ibadan: Daystar, 1985.

Oden, Thomas C. *How Africa Shaped the Christian Mind: Rediscovering the African Seedbed of Western Christianity*. Downers Grove, IL: InterVarsity, 2007.

Ofori, Akwasi O. *Recovering Storytelling for Ghanaian Preaching: An Adaptation of the New Homiletic for an African Culture*. Bloomington, IN: WestBow, 2015.

Ogone, James Odhiambo. "Remediating Orality: The Cultural Domestication of Video Technology in Kenya." *Critical Arts* 29, no. 4 (2015): 479–95.

Oh, Church Hyunchul Henry. *Preaching as Interaction between Church and Culture: With Specific Reference to the Korean*. PhD Thesis, University of Pretoria, 2004.

Oikelome, Segun. "Amona Tete Mabo.flv." YouTube. 28 June 2011. https://www.youtube.com/watch?v=Q8mQ_iSXwJs.

Ojo, Olagoke. *Ijapa Tiroko*. Ikeja, Lagos: Longman Nigeria, 2005.

Okpewho, Isidore, ed. *The Oral Performance in Africa*. Ibadan: Spectrum, 1998.

Old, Hughes Oliphant. *The Reading and Preaching of the Scriptures in the Worship of the Christian Church*. Vols. 1–7. Grand Rapids: Eerdmans, 1997–2004.

Oleka, Sam. "The Authority of the Bible in the African Context." In *Issues in African Christian Theology*. Nairobi: East African Educational, 1998.

Olford, David L., ed. *A Passion for Preaching: Reflections on the Art of Preaching; Essays in Honor of Stephen F. Olford*. Nashville: Thomas Nelson, 1989.

Olford, Stephen. *Heart Cry for Revival*. Ross-shire, Scotland: Christian Focus, 2005.

Olford, Stephen, and E. A. Johnston. *Olford on Scroggie: Stephen Olford's Notes on the Sermon Outlines of Graham Scroggie*. Port Colborne: Gospel Folio, 2008.

Olford, Stephen, and David Olford. *Anointed Expository Preaching*. Nashville: B&H Academic, 1998.

Ololade, Yinka. *Drama as Catalyst in Christian Worship and Evangelism*. Ibadan: Ola-Oluseye, 2013.

Ong, Walter J. *Orality and Literacy: The Technologizing of the Word*. London; New York: Routledge, 1983.

Opoku, Kofi Asare, *West African Traditional Religion*. Accra: FEP International, 1978.

"Orality: The Newest Heresy of the NAR." Discernment Group. 4 May 2006. https://www.crossroad.to/articles2/006/discernment/orality.htm.

Oriloye, S. A. "Contents and Features of Yoruba Incantatory Poetry." *Journal of Communication and Culture* 1, no. 1/2: 32–44, accessed 26 February 2021.

file:///C:/Users/Ezekiel%20Ajibade/Downloads/284245958-Yoruba-Incantatory-Chants.pdf.

Oroniran, D. F. *The Baptist Heritage: A Nigerian Perspective*. Ibadan: Titles, 2013.

Oruka, H. Odera. *Sage Philosophy: Indigenous Thinkers and Modern Debate on African Philosophy*. Leiden: Brill, 1990.

Osho, Sulaiman A. "The Uniqueness of African Means of Communication in the Contemporary World." Seminar on Cultural Diplomacy in Africa (CDA), Institute for Cultural Diplomacy (ICD), Kurfurstendamm, Berlin, Germany, 11 July 2011.

Oyemomi, Emmanuel O. *Essentials of Christian Preaching: With Sample Sermons for African Theological Institutions*. Lagos: Praise Publications Ventures, 2013.

Packer, J. I. "Why Preach." In *The Preacher and Preaching: Reviving the Art*, edited by Samuel T. Lorgan Jr., 1–29. Phillipsburg, NJ: P&R, 1986.

Page, Jesse. *The Black Bishop, Samuel Adjai Crowther*. New York: Revell, 1908. http://www.archive.org/stream/blackbishopsamue00page#page/n19/mode/2up.

Paggit, Doug. *Preaching Re-Imagined*. Grand Rapids: Zondervan, 2005.

Palmer, Gus. "Power of the Spoken Word." *American Indian Quarterly* 38, no. 4 (Fall 2014): 512–23.

Park, Sangyil. *Korean Preaching, Han, and Narrative*. New York: Peter Lang, 2008.

Peek, Philip M. "The Power of Word in African Verbal Art." *The Journal of American Folklore*, no. 94 (Jan.–March 1981): 21–27.

Peeters, Marguerite A. "Postmodernity and Africa: In the Balance." *Faith Magazine*, (April 2008), accessed 22 February 2021. https://www.faith.org.uk/article/march-april-2008-postmodernity-and-africa-in-the-balancepgs.

"Peitho." In *Vine's Complete Expository Dictionary of New Testament Words*, edited by William White, W. E. Vine, and Merill F. Unger. Nashville: Thomas Nelson, 1996.

Peterson, Curtis A. "Dangers and Opportunities in the Contextualization of the Gospel." Accessed 7 Jan 2020. http://www.wlsessays.net/handle/123456789/3656.

Pew Research Center. "Global Christianity – A Report on the Size and Distribution of the World's Christian Population." Pew Research Center: Religion and Public Life. 19 December 2011. https://www.pewforum.org/2011/12/19/global-christianity-exec/.

Phillips, John. *The Life and Legacy of Stephen Olford*. Memphis, TN: Olford Ministries, 2006.

Piper, John. "What Are Your Thoughts on Drama and Movie Clips in Church Services?" desiringGod. 15 July 2009. http://www.desiringgod.org/interviews/what-are-your-thoughts-on-drama-and-movie-clips-in-church-services.

Pitts, Walter. "West African Poetics in the Black Preaching Style." *American Speech* 64, no. 2 (Summer 1989): 137–49.

Plant, Deborah G. "The Folk Preacher and Folk Sermon Form in Zora Neale Hurston's *Dust Tracks on a Road*." *Folklore Forum* 21, no. 1 (1988): 3–19.

Plantinga, Cornelius. *Reading for Preaching: The Preacher in Conversation with Storytellers, Biographers, Poets, and Journalists*. Grand Rapids: Eerdmans, 2013.

Prior, Randall. "Orality: The Not-So-Silent Issue in Mission Theology." *International Bulletin of Missionary Research* 35, no. 3 (July 2011): 143–47.

Quicke, Michael J. *360-Degree Preaching*. Grand Rapids: Baker Academic, 2003.

Quinn, Frederick. *African Saints: Saints, Martyrs and Holy People from the Continent of Africa*. New York: Crossroad, 2002.

Reid, Richard. "War and Remembrance: Orality, Literacy and Conflict in the Horn." *Journal of African Cultural Studies* 18, no. 1 (2006): 89–103.

Richard, Ramesh. *Preparing Expository Sermons: A Seven-Step Method for Biblical Preaching*. Grand Rapids: Baker Books, 2001.

Robinson, Haddon W. *Biblical Preaching: The Development and Delivery of Expository Messages*. Wheaton, IL: Oasis, 2012.

———. "My Theory of Homiletics." In *The Art and Craft of Biblical Preaching: A Comprehensive Resource for Today's Communicators*, edited by Haddon Robinson and Craig Brian Larson, 58–59. Grand Rapids: Christianity Today International, 2005.

Ross, Michael F. *Preaching for Revitalization*. Ross-Shire, Scotland: Christian Focus, 2006.

Rottman, John M. "Literary Forms." In *The New Interpreter's Handbook of Preaching*, edited by Paul Scott Wilson. Nashville: Abingdon, 2008.

Runyon, Daniel C. "God's Communication Challenge: Oral Preference and the Tribal Bible." In *Beyond Literate Western Contexts: Honor and Shame and Assessment of Orality Preference*, edited by Samuel E. Chiang and Grant Lovejoy, 95–100. Hong Kong: International Orality Network, 2015.

Rydelnik, Michael. "Preaching Historical Narrative." In *The Moody Handbook of Preaching*, 127–41. Chicago: Moody, 2008.

Sachs, Jonah. *Winning the Story Wars: Why Those Who Tell (and Live) the Best Stories Will Rule the Future*. Boston: Harvard Business Review Press, 2012.

Sample, Tex. *Ministry in an Oral Culture: Living with Will Rogers, Uncle Remus, and Minnie Pearl*. Louisville, KY: Westminster John Knox, 1994.

Saxon, Wolfgan. "Walter J. Ong, 90, Jesuit, Teacher and Scholar of Language." *The New York Times*. 25 August 2003. http://www.nytimes.com/2003/08/25/us/walter-j-ong-90-jesuit-teacher-and-scholar-of-language.html.

Scharf, Greg R. *Let the Earth Hear His Voice: Strategies for Overcoming Bottlenecks in Preaching God's Word*. Phillipsburg, NJ: P&R, 2015.

Schreiter, Robert J. *Constructing Local Theologies*. Maryknoll, NY: Orbis, 1986.

Shields, Bruce E. "Preaching and Culture." *Homiletic* 22, no. 2 (Winter 1997): 1–9.

Shorter, Aylward. "History of Preaching." In *Concise Encyclopedia of Preaching*, edited by William H. Willimon and Richard Lischer, 184–227. Louisville, KY: Westminster John Knox, 1995.

———. "Homiletic and Preaching in Africa." In *Concise Encyclopedia of Preaching*, edited by William H. Willimon and Richard Lischer, 229–31. Louisville, KY: Westminster John Knox, 1995.

Simala, Kenneth Inyani, "Orality, Modernity and African Development: Myth as Dialogue of Civilization." Abstract, *CODESRIA* (December 2011): 1–2.

Simmons, Martha, and Frank A. Thomas, eds. *Preaching with Sacred Fire: An Anthology of African American Sermons, 1750 to the Present*. New York: W. W. Norton, 2010.

Singerman, Jeff. "Orality Observations among Francophone West African Adults: Storying to Orality." In *Beyond Literate Western Models: Contextualizing Theological Education in Oral Contexts*, edited by Samuel E. Chiang and Grant Lovejoy, 121–27. Hong Kong: International Orality Network, 2013.

Smith, Robert, Jr. "Call and Response." In *The New Interpreter's Handbook of Preaching*, edited by Paul Scott Wilson, 297. Nashville: Abingdon, 2008.

―――. *Doctrine That Dances: Bringing Doctrinal Preaching and Teaching to Life*. Nashville: B&H Academic, 2008.

So, Damon. "How Should a Theological Institution Prepare Students/Leaders Who Will Go Out into the Fields to Train Local People (Storytellers) to Tell Bible Stories Effectively?" In *Beyond Literate Western Models: Contextualizing Theological Education in Oral Contexts*, edited by Samuel E. Chiang and Grant Lovejoy, 29–38. Hong Kong: International Orality Network, 2013.

Sogolo, Godwin W. "Logic and Rationality." In *The African Philosophy Reader*, edited by P. H. Coetzee and A. P. J. Roux, 217–33. London: Routledge, 1998.

Spiro, Melford E. *Children of the Kibbutz*. Cambridge: Harvard University Press, 1958.

Stedman, Ray. "The Primacy of Preaching." In *A Passion for Preaching: Reflections on the Art of Preaching, Essays in Honor of Stephen F. Olford*, edited by David L. Olford, 61–67. Nashville: Thomas Nelson, 1989.

Steffen, Tom. "My Reluctant Journey into Orality." Address to the 4th Conference on Reaching Oral Communicators. Anaheim, California, 13 July 2005.

―――. "Tracking the Orality Movement: Some Implications for 21st Century Missions." *Lausanne Global Analysis* 3, no. 2 (March 2014). https://www.lausanne.org/content/lga/ 2014-03/tracking-the-orality-movement-some-implications-for-21st-century-missions.

Stetzer, Ed. "What Is Contextualization?: Presenting the Gospel in Culturally Relevant Ways." Accessed 20 Dec 2019, https://www.christianitytoday.com/edstetzer/2014/october/what-is-contextualization.html.

Stitzinger, James F. "The History of Expository Preaching." *Masters Seminary Journal TMSJ* 3, no. 1 (Spring 1992): 6–32.

Stott, John R. W. *Between Two Worlds: The Art of Preaching in the Twentieth Century*. Grand Rapids: Eerdmans, 1982.

―――. *Between Two Worlds: The Challenge of Preaching Today*. Grand Rapids: Eerdmans, 1994.

Strauss, Steve. "Creeds, Confessions, and Global Theologizing: A Case Study in Comparative Christologies." In *Globalizing Theology: Belief and Practice in an Era of World Christianity*, edited by Craig Ott and Harold A. Netland, 140–56. Grand Rapids, MI: Baker Academic, 2006.

Stringer, Stephen, ed. *S-T4T: Storying and Church Formation Training for Trainers.* WigTake Resources, 2010.

Strydhorst, Albert. "Emerging World Christianity." *Calvin Theological Seminary Forum* (Winter 2015): 3–5.

Sundkler, Bengt, and Christopher Steed. *A History of the Church in Africa.* Cambridge: Cambridge University Press, 2000.

Sunukjian, Donald R. "The Biblical Topical Sermons." In *The Art and Craft of Biblical Preaching: A Comprehensive Resource for Today's Communicators*, edited by Haddon Robinson and Craig Brian Larson, 421–23. Grand Rapids: Christianity Today International, 2005.

———. *Invitation to Biblical Preaching: Proclaiming Truth with Clarity and Relevance.* Grand Rapids: Kregel, 2007.

———. "Preaching Inductively and Deductively: How to Employ Each Style for Maximum Results." *Preaching Today.* n.d. http://www.preachingtoday.com/skills/themes/structure/200007.10.html.

Sweet, Leonard. *Giving Blood: A Fresh Paradigm for Preaching.* Grand Rapids: Zondervan, 2014.

Tanye, Gerald K. *The Church-as-Family and Ethnocentrism in Sub-Saharan Africa.* Berlin: LIT Verlag, 2010.

ThabisoAflame. "Africa God's General series: Nicholas Bhengu – The African Apostle." ThabisoAflame Blog. 6 November 2010. https://thabisoaflame.wordpress.com/2010/11/06/africas-gods-general-series-nicholas-bhenguthe-african-apostle/.

Thompson, LaNette W. "Helping Adults Learn: Lessons from Andragogy and the Challenge of Context." In *Beyond Literate Western Models: Contextualizing Theological Education in Oral Context*, edited by Samuel E. Chiang and Grant Lovejoy, 105–12. Hong Kong: International Orality Network, 2013.

Thompson, William D., and Gordon C. Bennett. *Dialogue Preaching: The Shared Sermon.* Valley Forge, PA: Judson, 1969.

Traore, Bakary. *The Black African Theatre and Its Social Functions.* Ibadan: Ibadan University Press, 1972.

UNESCO. *Adult and Youth Literacy: National Regional and Global Trends, 1885–2015.* Montreal: UNESCO Institute for Statistics, 2013.

van Poelje, Rob. "Consultancy Training in Communication Strategy Development and Materials Production." Mission Report. New Bussa: Nigerian-German (GTZ) Kainji Lake Fisheries Promotion Project, 1996.

Vine, W. E., Merrill F. Unger, and William White Jr. "Persuade." In *Vine's Complete Expository Dictionary of Old and New Testament Words.* Nashville, TN: Thomas Nelson, 1996.

Warren, Timothy S. "Can Topical Preaching Also Be Expository?" In *The Art and Craft of Biblical Preaching: A Comprehensive Resource for Today's Communicators*, edited by Haddon Robinson and Craig Brian Larson, 418–20. Grand Rapids: Christianity Today International, 2005.

———. "Topical Preaching on Bible Characters." In *The Art and Craft of Biblical Preaching: A Comprehensive Resource for Today's Communicators*, edited by Haddon Robinson and Craig Brian Larson, 424–26. Grand Rapids: Christianity Today International, 2005.

———. "Topical Preaching on Contemporary Issues." In *The Art and Craft of Biblical Preaching: A Comprehensive Resource for Today's Communicators*, edited by Haddon Robinson and Craig Brian Larson, 427–30. Grand Rapids: Christianity Today International, 2005.

———. "Topical Preaching on Theological Themes." In *The Art and Craft of Biblical Preaching: A Comprehensive Resource for Today's Communicators*, edited by Haddon Robinson and Craig Brian Larson, 431–33. Grand Rapids: Christianity Today International, 2005.

Waugh, Geoff. "Astounding Church Growth." *Renewal Journal*. 28 February 2016. https://renewaljournal.wordpress.com/2016/02/28/astounding-church-growth-bygeoff-waugh/.

Wedland, Ernst. *Sewero! Christian Drama and the Drama of Christianity in Africa*. Zomba: Kachere Series, 2005.

"West African Folktales Full Audiobook Unabridged." YouTube, 16 July 2014. https://www.youtube.com/watch?v=3g9AkRgDGWY.

Wiher, Hannes. "Worldview and Oral Preference Learners and Leaders." In *Beyond Literate Western Contexts: Continuing Conversations in Orality and Theological Education*, edited by Samuel E. Chiang and Grant Lovejoy, 109–25. Hong Kong: International Orality Network, 2014.

"Will Europe's Third-Largest Church Punish Pastor for Multiple Affairs?" Accessed 22 February 2021. christianitytoday.com/news/2016/may/will-embassy-of-god-punish-sunday-adelaja-multiple-affairs.html.

Willhite, Keith. "Audience Relevance in Expository Preaching." *Bibliotheca Sacra* 149, no. 595 (July 1992): 356–374.

Williams E. S. "Beware of the Orality Movement." Bible League Trust. n.d. https://www.bibleleaguetrust.org/beware-of-the-orality-movement/.

Wilson, Paul Scott. *The Practice of Preaching*. Nashville: Abingdon, 1995.

———. *Preaching and Homiletical Theory*. St. Louis: Chalice, 2004.

Worrall, Kelli. "Drama and the Sermon." In *The Moody Handbook of Preaching*, edited by John Koessler, 293–307. Chicago: Moody, 2008.

Wumi, Curious. "A Yoruba Poem – Ise Logun Ise (Work is the antidote for poverty)." Curious Wumi. 9 April 2012. http://wumikay.blogspot.com.ng/2012/04/yoruba-poem-ise-logun-ise-work-is.html.

www.ingramcontent.com/pod-product-compliance
Lightning Source LLC
Chambersburg PA
CBHW071430150426
43191CB00008B/1096

Preaching is a critical task of evangelism in the global church. Since the work of theological education is to serve, support, and empower the church, biblical preaching occupies a pride of place in ministerial formation and equipping. This publication that contextualizes expository preaching in the African context is innovative and exciting. The principles and techniques for effective biblical proclamation through orality, as espoused by Dr. Ezekiel Ajibade, deserve to be considered and applied to advance the Great Commission, to grow the church, and to expand the kingdom of God. I heartily recommend and commend this book for the enrichment of contemporary homiletical scholarship and practice worldwide.

Rev. Prof. Emiola Nihinlola, PhD
President, The Nigerian Baptist Theological Seminary, Ogbomoso
Chair, Association for Christian Theological Education in Africa (ACTEA)

I am highly pleased to recommend this work by Dr. Ajibade on expository preaching in the African context. I had the privilege of serving as one of the supervisors for Dr. Ajibade's research. This ground-breaking volume addresses the importance of the contextualization of biblical exposition in more than 1,000 languages on the African continent. Dr. Ajibade's goal is to blend the orality of African culture with a text-driven approach to expository preaching. The approach championed here is not bound by either a deductive or inductive methodology, but is one where the boundaries are permeable in such a way that preaching is adapted to African culture, and yet, stays true to the text of Scripture. Every preacher preaching in an African context will benefit from this excellent work. Indeed, there is much to be learned here for any preacher in any context!

David L. Allen, PhD
Distinguished Professor of Preaching, George W. Truett Chair of Ministry
Southwestern Baptist Theological Seminary, Fort Worth, Texas, USA

One of the most recent efforts of the International Orality Network is to explore ways in which orality can take root in theological education for the purpose of sustainability. Here is a resourceful book moving in this direction. This volume explores one of the critical subjects of theological education, which is preaching in its expository form. Bringing orality as a tool for its contextualization is a unique contribution that will not only provide a means of effective sermonic communication from African pulpits but will also serve as a model in contextualizing all possible facets of theological education, making them more relevant, sustainable and invaluable to the effort of winning the world for Christ. I therefore endorse this book and recommend it for pastors, theological educators, and all who love the preaching of God's word in such a manner that results in salvation and transformation.

Zephaniah Victor Madziakapita, PhD
Regional Director for Africa, International Orality Network

This is a very important and needed contribution to the field of homiletics. This well-researched study embraces both the apostolic mandate for the faithful proclamation of biblical truth and the need for such truth to be communicated clearly and relevantly. Dr. Ezekiel Ajibade's work is driven by a love for faithful expository preaching and also the desire to see such preaching meaningfully and appropriately engage the cultural context he addresses. Dr. Ajibade has not presented theory for casual discussion; rather, as one with pastoral, preaching, and lecturing experience, he is putting his well-informed passion on display for our benefit. This book is not only very important as it pertains to the ministry of the Scriptures in Nigeria and West Africa, it presents a discussion of homiletical issues that are also faced in numerous cultural contexts. For those involved in Great Commission work, and those who seek to preach the word outside of their own four walls, there is much to learn from this volume. This is a book written by a serious practitioner for those who are serious about cultural engagement with a commitment to "rightly dividing the word of truth" (2 Tim 2:15).

David Olford, PhD
President, Olford Ministries International, Inc., USA

Preaching in any context is extremely essential if one wants the audience to understand what God has prepared the preacher to deliver. This book is a product of dedicated efforts of the author to stress the importance and necessity for preachers to engage in the exposition of God's word. While orality is one emphasis of this book, the use of aspects of it, such as songs, drama, proverbs, folk-tales, and story-telling should be means by which the word of God penetrates into the lives of the audience or recipients. This book is a tool for students in theological institutions, researchers, and emerging church leaders to make preaching a delight. I am so excited to recommend this book to pastors ministering among students and to the general audience – it is deep in research and thorough in its practical approach.

Ademola Ishola, PhD
Former General Secretary, Nigerian Baptist Convention

Proponents of expository preaching emphasize interpreting Scripture correctly and proclaiming the meaning of a text clearly and faithfully. On this, the proponents agree. But do expository sermons have to take a particular form? Dr. Ezekiel Ajibade contends convincingly that they do not. Instead, he argues, a sermon's form should be attuned to the hearers in their cultural context. In Africa, as in most parts of the world, oral cultures are influential in shaping people's identity, values, and preferred forms of learning and communication. This book is a thorough treatment of that neglected topic in relationship to preaching. *Expository Preaching in Africa* is a well-researched, well-argued, and practical exploration of the nature of expository preaching and how to contextualize preaching for an African (and thus oral) context.

Grant Lovejoy, PhD
Director of Orality Strategies,
International Mission Board, Southern Baptist Convention, USA

Contextualization has been a major theological pursuit in Africa. This concern is borne out of the necessity to integrate Christianity into African life and culture. Beginning with the premise that preaching is more meaningful and effective when it is rooted in the context of the audience, Dr. Ezekiel Ajibade explores African orality as a resource for developing expository preaching that will be biblical and relevant to the African audience. This task cannot be over-emphasized, bearing in mind that any preaching that is not biblical and fails to employ the cultural elements of the audience will not engender spiritual transformation. Being a product of extensive academic research, this book is a ground-breaking undertaking in homiletical study and praxis which will stimulate future research. I hereby endorse the book and commend it to seminarians and preachers who are seeking for authentic Christian preaching in Africa.

Very Rev. Sunday Ola. Onadipe, DMin
Bishop, Methodist Church Nigeria, Diocese of Badagry
Former Rector, Methodist Theological Institute, Sagamu, Ogun State, Nigeria